HISTORY AND

MEMORY IN THE

TWO SOUTHS

History and Memory in the Two Souths

Recent Southern and Spanish American Fiction

DEBORAH N. COHN

VANDERBILT UNIVERSITY PRESS

NASHVILLE AND LONDON

Copyright © 1999 by Vanderbilt University Press
Nashville, Tennessee 37235
All Rights Reserved under International and Pan-American Copyright Conventions

First Edition 1999
99 00 01 02 03 5 4 3 2 1

This publication is made from paper that meets the minimum
requirements of ANSI/NISO Z39.48-1992 (R 1997)—Permanence of Paper for
Printed Library Materials. ⊚

Library of Congress Cataloging-in-Publication Data

Cohn, Deborah N., 1967–
  History and memory in the two souths : recent Southern and
Spanish American fiction / Deborah N. Cohn.
  p. cm.
  Includes bibliographical references (p.) and index.
  Contents: Introduction: the U.S. South and Spanish America: neighboring
spaces and the search for meaning in difficult pasts—The case of the fabricated
facts: invented information and the problems of reconstructing the past in
Absalom, Absalom! and the real life of Alejandro Mayta—To see or not to see:
invisibility, clairvoyance, and re-visions of history in Invisible man and The
house of the spirits—Paradise lost and regained: the old order and memory in
the Miranda stories and Pedro Páramo—Conclusion: race and place in
indentity and history—Notes—Works cited—Index.
  ISBN 0-8265-1332-8 (alk. paper)
  ISBN 0-8265-1337-9 (pbk. : alk paper)
  1. American fiction—Southern States—History and criticism. 2. Historical
fiction, American—Southern States—History and criticism. 3. Literature and
history—Southern States—History—20th century. 4. Spanish American
fiction—20th century—History and criticism. 5. Literature and history—Latin
America—History—20th century. 6. Historical fiction, Spanish American—
History and criticism. 7. Literature, Comparative—American and Spanish
American. 8. Literature, Comparative—Spanish American and American.
9. Autobiographical memory in literature. 10. Southern States—In literature.
11. Latin America—In literature. 12. Memory in literature. I. Title.
  PS261 .C54 1999
  813'.5409975—DC21   98-58119
                                                                CIP

Manufactured in the United States of America

for Tam, Les, and Peter

CONTENTS

ACKNOWLEDGMENTS

I offer my heartfelt thanks to the faculty members who have encouraged me over the years: Beth Bauer, Charles Faulhaber, Gwen Kirkpatrick, Geoffrey Ribbans, Arnold Weinstein, and the entire faculty of the Department of Hispanic Studies at Brown University, who generously gave of their time, energy, and encouragement. Most of all, I am eternally indebted to Stephanie Merrim, to whom this book owes its existence.

I am grateful to the friends who have given advice and companionship throughout this project: David Boruchoff, Carrie Chorba, Erika Haber, Patrick McMorrow, Jean O'Bryan, Gus Puleo, Jamie Samons, and Lisa Sherman; to my parents, Irene and Paul Cohn, for taking me to Central America and, more recently, to behold the heights of Macchu Picchu; to Leslie Cohn, for her friendship and surrogate home; to Peter Sauer, for his love, support, and photography skills; and, it goes without saying, to my sister, Tam Cohn.

Many thanks go to the staff of Vanderbilt University Press for their tireless work in turning this project into a book. I am also grateful to Earl Fitz and Michael Kreyling, whose comments on an earlier version of this manuscript greatly helped me to focus my project.

Financial support came from the Mellon Foundation, which generously assisted me throughout my graduate career, and from a Council Grant for Research in the Humanities from Columbia University.

Finally, I am grateful for permissions granted by the editors of *The Comparatist, Comparative Literature Studies, Hispanófila,* and *Revista Hispánica Moderna* for substantive use of previously published articles: earlier versions of chapters 1 and 3 appeared in *Comparative Literature Studies* 34, no. 2 (1997) and 33, no. 4 (1996), respectively; an earlier version of chapter 2 appeared in *The Comparatist* 21 (May 1997); an earlier version of chapter 4 appeared in *Hispanófila* 124, while several additional segments appeared in *Revista Hispánica Moderna* 49, no. 2 (December 1996).

I am also grateful to the publishers and copyright holders for permission to quote from the following sources. Even though I believe that the quotations cited here are covered by the conventions of fair use, I have preferred to seek, and have been granted, permission for their appearance here.

Jacques Stephen Aléxis, "Du réalisme merveilleux des Haïtiens," *Présence Africaine* 8–10 (1956): 247–71; "Of the Marvellous Realism of the Haitians," in *The Post-Colonial Studies Reader* (Routledge, 1995).

Isabel Allende, "La magia de las palabras," *Revista Iberoamericana* 51, nos. 132–33 (1985): 447–52.

Roger Bartra, "El edén subvertido," in *La jaula de la melancolía: Identidad y metamorfosis del mexicano* (Editorial Grijalbo, 1987).

Jorge Luis Borges, "The Aleph," in *A Personal Anthology* (Grove, 1967).

Donald Davidson, "A Mirror for Artists," in *I'll Take My Stand* (Louisana State University Press, 1962).

Ralph Ellison, "Brave Words for a Startling Occasion," in *Shadow and Act* (Random House, 1964).

William Faulkner, *Absalom, Absalom!* (Random House, 1972); *Go Down, Moses* (Random House, 1973); and *The Unvanquished* (Random House, 1966).

Katherine Anne Porter, "Why I Write About Mexico," in *The Collected Essays and Occasional Writings of Katherine Anne Porter* (Houghton Mifflin, 1970).

Katherine Anne Porter, 8 April 1951 letter to William Goyen, in the Papers of Katherine Anne Porter, Special Collections, University of Maryland Libraries.

CHAPTER ONE

The U.S. South and Spanish America

Neighboring Spaces and the
Search for Meaning in Difficult Pasts

W hen asked why the American South had produced so many good writers, novelist Walker Percy used to answer, simply, "Because we lost." Defeat in the Civil War left the South haunted by the sins of its past and plagued by a sense of frustration and failure. Gone was the Old South, retrospectively idealized as an aristocratic civilization where traditional values held sway. In its place was an impoverished society ravaged by war and radically challenged by the aftermath of emancipation; there to stay as well were Reconstruction policies which resulted in the South's perception of itself not just as defeated but as conquered, and of the North as a conquering nation. In the years that followed, through Reconstruction, the rise of the New South, and the socioeconomic difficulties of the early twentieth century, southerners struggled with a need to justify the South's actions, to understand its defeat, to reconcile its past with their present and future, and to assess their position in relation to the rest of the nation. William Faulkner, of course, stands out as perhaps the most accomplished southern author to have addressed the burden of his history. And from the moment that his works became available in Spanish in the early 1930s, Faulkner and the South that he depicted captured the imagination of Spanish American writers. The latter interpreted the South's experiences, its Civil War and resulting sense of regional difference and marginalization, its exclusion from the economic and military successes of the rest of the nation, as well as its problems of underdevelopment in the early decades of this century as analogous to their own nations' struggles to break the yoke of colonialism and dependency, and to break out of the "backward" position to which they had been relegated. Carlos Fuentes, who has often acknowledged his debt to Faulkner, once told an American audience that Sinclair Lewis "is yours, and as such, interesting and important to us. William Faulkner is both yours and ours, and as such, essential to us. For in him we see what has always lived with us and rarely with you: the haunting face of defeat" ("Central and Eccentric Writing," 119): that is, Faulkner and his South exercised such a strong hold over the Spanish Americans because, to paraphrase Percy, we lost, too.

This study examines how this sense of commonalities of experience has undergirded Spanish American authors' attraction to Faulkner and has led them to see in the South's past a counterpart to their own. Southern scholar Frederick Hoffman once wrote that the "values of place in literature come from its being . . . associated with neighboring spaces that share a history, some communicable tradition and idiom, in terms of which a personality can be identified" (60). Thus I will further consider the South and Spanish America to be "neighboring spaces" with similar "personalities" deriving from shared histories. To this end, this study establishes parallels in regional history and social organization, analyzes recurrent themes and preoccupations in light of these shared experiences, and explores how these are further manifested in the attribution of comparable values to place and past in literature. These points of contact, in turn, allow me to draw parallels between authors' treatment of the relationship between the past and the present, as well as their use of unconventional and counterrealist discourses to achieve this goal, and to delineate what Lois Parkinson Zamora has called "a shared comprehension of America and a shared mode of narrating its history" (*Writing the Apocalypse*, 34). In order to set the stage for the comparative textual analyses of the following chapters, this initial chapter is dedicated primarily to identifying several key contextual issues. Foremost among these are assessing the state of criticism on inter-American literary relations and examining the role played by Faulkner and Euro-American modernism in the development of modern Spanish American fiction. I will also review Spanish American authors' recognition of parallels in their historical experiences and those of the South. Subsequent chapters pair and compare texts by authors from each region: Faulkner's *Absalom, Absalom!* and Mario Vargas Llosa's *The Real Life of Alejandro Mayta*; Ralph Ellison's *Invisible Man* and Isabel Allende's *The House of the Spirits*; Katherine Anne Porter's Miranda stories and Juan Rulfo's *Pedro Páramo*.[1] I focus on correspondences in the works' revisions, retellings and rewritings of regional history, and on the similar perceptions of the past that underlie them; the study further takes into account the relationship between the consciousness of regional history and the approaches taken to narrate it. Additionally, I examine how many of the works also strive toward new modes of collective self-representation and toward the characterization of a group's identity through the unwriting and rewriting of history from the perspective afforded by the knowledge of one's own difference.

As a result of historical pressures, tasks of self-definition and redefinition have been particularly urgent in the South and Spanish America. C. Vann Woodward's thesis that (contrary to the belief of many southerners) the South's history was not unique but, rather, representative of that of many nations—and of the Third World in particular—provides

the backdrop for my identification of parallels in the literary representations of history in the southern U.S. and Spanish America , as well as
for my assessment of the reasons motivating the appeal of Faulkner and
the South to Spanish American authors. The renowned southern historian averred that, in contrast to the U.S. as a whole, with its myths of
innocence, prosperity, and success, "The South had undergone an experience that it could share with no other part of America—though it is
shared by nearly all the peoples of Europe and Asia—the experience of
military defeat, occupation, and reconstruction" (190). When "America" is replaced by "the United States" in order to reflect the referent more
accurately, Woodward's statement acknowledges that the experience
of conquest and subordination is, of course, shared not just with Europe
and Asia, but also with another part of America: Latin America. Authors
from this region have been acutely aware of this aspect of the South's
history, and, in particular, of its parallels with their own experiences; in
fact, in an unintended echo of Woodward, Fuentes himself declared in
an analysis of Faulkner's works that only the South "had shared an experience that was so common outside of the United States" (*Casa*, 65).

On what grounds, one might ask, can one justify, first, labeling
each of these broad spaces a "region" with a single, dominant personality and, second, comparing these constructs on the basis of shared experiences? Might this approach not risk overlooking or simplifying the
differences that exist within each region? It would be difficult to ignore
either the magnitude or the sheer number of differences that separate
the South and Spanish America.[2] Politically, the former was a confeder-
ation of states that chose to unite within and, eventually, against the
nation of which they were a part; the individual states considered themselves to be part of a larger entity that shared certain practices and beliefs,
asserted itself as a unit against the central government to defend them,
and collectively suffered the same punishment and ostracism by the rest
of the nation. Spanish America, in contrast, comprises a number of separate nations—each with its own cultures and history, each building on

pre-Columbian civilizations, each achieving independence from Spain by a different date and in a distinct manner, and each experiencing its own difficulties establishing and preserving a viable form of government and autonomy in the face of neocolonialism. Consequently, for the most part these nations lacked consciousness of any overriding construct such as "Spanish America" until the mid-twentieth century; also, as the late Chilean author José Donoso has claimed, authors reproduced this atomism by writing as regionalists, "cataloging the flora and fauna, the tribes and the proverbs which were unmistakably ours . . . all that which specifically makes us different—which separates us—from other areas and other countries of the continent" (15). Even when one takes into account the differences between the Upper South and the Deep South (for instance, how formerly French Louisiana is distinct from the rest of the South in cultural background and historical moment of entry into the union)[3]—differences that much literary criticism tends to overlook in its treatment of the South as a monolithic entity—the region is still far more socially homogeneous than the cultural spectrum represented in the Spanish American nations: each with its own forms of cultural expression, its own history of contact with colonial culture, and its own peculiar result of mixing European, African, and indigenous populations.

Despite these differences, however, the South and Spanish America can nevertheless be said to share a history—of dispossession, of socioeconomic hardship, of political and cultural conflict, and of the export of resources to support the development of a "North." From the self-assertion of secession to loss in the Civil War, from Reconstruction through modernization, the difficulties attendant upon the South's status as a defeated territory and the upheaval that accompanied industrialization are troubles with which Spanish America is quite well-acquainted. Defeat in the Civil War destroyed the South's social and economic foundations. Despite rapid industrial growth in the last two decades of the nineteenth century, its economy resembled that of lesser-developed countries: an agriculture dominated by the monocultural system;

displacement of local companies by imported goods; production oriented toward the demands (and dependent on the fluctuations) of an external market, a reactive system affording the region little control over national policy; and low wages and absentee ownership (Ayers, 21–22; also 81–103). These circumstances resulted in a semi-colonial economic dependency on the North and had a direct negative impact on the region's long-term development: in the 1920s the South's standard of living had dropped to the lowest in the nation, its illiteracy rate the highest; by 1938, it had become, in President Roosevelt's words, the nation's "number one economic problem—the nation's problem, not merely the South's." Likewise in the Spanish American nations, struggles with underdevelopment, imposed forms of governance, and the continual threat and reality of political intervention have gained in intensity rather than lessening since the achievement of nationhood by 1830 in most of the region. Subordination to foreign governments and, increasingly, to transnational corporations, has compromised their autonomy and constrained the policy decisions that they take. Economies oriented to the export of prime products have left them, too, dependent on the world market for their income and for the goods that they need to import. Also, the impact of industrialization on the agrarian South in the first half of this century aggravated or produced conditions resembling those increasingly characteristic of Spanish American nations: poverty, malnourishment, illiteracy, and low standards of living. Further parallels between the South and parts of Spanish America may be attributed to the role of the plantation and its various Spanish American manifestations (e.g., the *hacienda* and the *latifundio*; in the case of Brazil, the *Casa Grande*) as a fundamental paradigm structuring social organization and relations, as well as leaving a legacy of strict social hierarchization and a deeply rooted aversion to miscegenation.[4]

That subject matter and themes in literature from both regions overlap and coincide is hardly surprising, nor that Spanish American authors draw upon concerns similar to those addressed by Faulkner, whom they view as metonymical of southern writing and a filter for the reality that it depicts. However, other than in the case of Faulkner, whose legacy I discuss in a later section of this chapter, the goal of this study is not to establish the influence of the southern writers.[5] Rather, my approach corresponds to what Gustavo Pérez Firmat, in the introduction to *Do the Americas Have a Common Literature?*, has labeled an "appositional" framework for inter-American literary studies (3): I rechannel the question of influence away from direct textual contacts in order to examine convergences, similar features and strategies that have developed as responses to analogous sociopolitical and historical circumstances. These convergences may be seen in the fact that writers from both regions trace a rocky transition from an agrarian social system, as well as the changing sense of community that this process entails, and show how memories of the old ways continue to haunt the present. Their works also reflect the disorder attendant upon rapid and widespread urbanization; the breakdown and/or entrenchment of patriarchal systems at the level of the family and the collectivity; problems of prejudice and violence; exploitation and injustice; the themes of racial tensions, miscegenation, and incest. Often, these issues are dramatized in family sagas. Many texts also speak to difficulties of neocolonialism and dependency: they depict wars and intervention by external powers that threaten their financial stability and self-governance.

After a brief overview of the status of inter-American literary criticism, I will set the stage for the textual comparisons of the following chapters by describing the literary periods during which the works in this study were written. Subsequently, I will explore the stylistic and thematic influences of Euro-American modernism on Spanish American authors, correlating this with their efforts to rechannel the nature and course of Spanish American literature. Finally, I will examine Faulkner's appeal as a modernist and as a southern writer whose combination of content and form suggested to the Spanish Americans possible means of exploring and re-presenting their own realities.

Despite the many social and historical parallels between the regions, and despite many homages to Faulkner by Spanish American authors, no critical studies have focused exclusively on the fiction of the southern U.S. and that of Spanish America. Thus, my perspective represents an approach that is radically different from those taken by most inter-American comparative studies as well as by most studies of Faulkner's legacy, which broadly frame their topic as the influence of an American writer, without taking into account the southerner's regional orientation. In a statement representative of this approach, Mark Frisch posits that Faulkner's influence "derives from the New World experience: from a need by these authors for self-definition and a search for a redefinition of reality and its representation" (115). He further suggests that the study of Faulkner's impact sheds light on general correspondences between North and South American literatures. While I agree with the broad terms of Frisch's argument, I believe that Faulkner's legacy speaks much more directly to parallels in the pasts of the U.S. South and Spanish America, as well as in the literature that has arisen to address them. More satisfactory answers to some of the questions posed by comparatists might be found if they were to focus more narrowly on the common experiences of Spanish America and the South, rather than comparing Spanish America and the U.S. as New World former colonies and uncharted territory; that is, they might more fruitfully explore Faulkner's influence as the legacy of a southern, not simply an American, writer. The goal of this study is to explore some of these parallels and to open up a new branch of inter-American literary criticism.

A number of important works in the broader field merit recognition because they provided the framework within which I began my own research. Current inter-American comparative studies generally fall into one of two categories: analyses of Faulkner's influence on individual Spanish American writers and those which take a much more general approach, examining issues and themes common to U.S. and Spanish

American literature. James Irby's prescient early work, "La influencia de William Faulkner en cuatro narradores hispano-americanos," is generally the first reference cited in studies of Faulkner's legacy. In 1956, Irby identified a constellation of ideological, social, and literary concerns shared by the "Lost Generation" of authors in the U.S. after the first World War (including Faulkner, John Dos Passos, and Ernest Hemingway), and four Spanish American authors writing a generation later: Lino Novás Calvo (whose 1934 translation of *Sanctuary* initiated the translation of Faulkner's work into Spanish), Juan Carlos Onetti, José Revueltas, and Juan Rulfo. These common issues and attitudes included fatalism; the collapse of traditional value systems and the concomitant nostalgia for a lost past; and the search for new beliefs to replace those that had been invalidated. Irby further correlated the authors' sense of loss, bitterness, and defeat with a rejection of traditional literary realism and the adoption of stylistic techniques associated with Euro-American modernism, including the rejection of chronological order, recourse to multiple perspectives to convey a fragmented picture of reality and to problematize truth, and the subjectivization of narrative. Irby contended that Spanish American writers assimilated the new style of writing from Faulkner more than from any other modernist or writer of his "generation." Irby attributed this fascination with Faulkner to his use of a specific, regional setting—the writer's own little "postage stamp of native soil" (Interview by Stein, 255)—to play out upheavals and express a sense of disillusionment and moral bankruptcy that resonated strongly with Spanish American authors. And yet, despite these significant insights, few studies since Irby's have followed up on these suggestions as to why Faulkner has been so important to Spanish American authors.

Lois Parkinson Zamora offers an exception to this rule with her acknowledgment and neat summation of

> the parallel histories of Hispanic America and the Deep South: colonization and exploitation of the land; feudal systems of land tenure with their

accompanying aristocracies and enslaved or indentured peoples of color; the burden of defeat by invading armies from the North (Yankees/yanquis); belated and abrupt modernization that masked (and sometimes exacerbated) long histories of political and racial and economic inequity . . . [as well as] intersections of Southern Protestant and Hispanic Catholic attitudes. ("The Animate Earth," 63)

Otherwise, discussions of Faulkner's place in modern Spanish American fiction since Irby have tended either to foreground his influence on a single author or to sketch general textual and thematic coincidences with the works of several authors;[6] some offer occasional but limited and peripheral discussions of similarities between their respective homelands.[7] Much attention has been given to Faulkner's influence on Fuentes, Onetti, Rulfo, and Vargas Llosa, but his relationship to Gabriel García Márquez has been by far the favorite subject of critical studies in this field.[8] Numerous similarities have been pointed out in the biographies and works of the two authors: both were raised in traditional rural communities that longed nostalgically for periods of grandeur long since brought down by war and economic ruin; both create and explore recurrent fictional microcosms whose foundings represent the violation of an undeveloped, primeval paradise; both, of course, have won the Nobel Prize for literature. Some of these similarities are, in turn, reflected in parallels between the histories and social organization of Yoknapatawpha County and Macondo.

In an infrequently referenced study, *El espejo hablado: Un estudio de "Cien años de soledad,"* Suzanne Jill Levine draws one of the best and most extensive comparisons of the southerner and García Márquez that I have seen. Her analysis speaks to many of the affinities already noted and is worth quoting at length:

In part, the most enduring similarities between both authors reflect the similarities between Faulkner's decadent South and rural South America.

The southern states and Colombia alike were ruined by civil war and later victimized by exploitation from the North: in Colombia and other parts of Latin America, the creators of the banana empire were responsible for the exploitation; in the U.S. South, it was northern industry and the speculators ... the "carpetbaggers." ... Both Macondo and Jefferson are imaginary microcosms of the authors' respective feudal societies, structured around a central tribe or family: García Márquez's Buendías correspond to Faulkner's Sutpens or Sartorises. ... These families are, at the same time, the creators and destroyers of their respective communities. The Buendías and the Sutpens are dominated by a head-of-the-family who is a genuine feudal lord: Colonel Buendía or Thomas Sutpen ... the entire community is at their beck and call, as in the olden days, in exchange for the lord's protection. This continuity of traditions and superstitions demonstrates the medieval character of these communities. (87–88)

In "Faulkner y García Márquez: Una aproximación," Octavio Corvalán invokes the South's troubled and violent past, its racial conflicts, semi-feudal agrarianism, resistance to change (e.g., capitalism and industrialization) imposed and enforced from outside, and the resulting nostalgia for a dead past, now seen as paradisiacal. The enumeration of these attributes leads up to his assertion that "the U.S. South—the 'Deep South' of Mississippi, Alabama, Georgia—exhibits social and cultural characteristics that are not much different from those of our South American world" (80). Finally, Harley Oberhelman has written several strong essays establishing important points of contact between the two authors. In "García Márquez and the American South," he, too, ascribes the strength of Faulkner's presence in the Colombian's writings to similarities between the depicted regions. However, he declines to explore the parallel any further and downplays its significance by explaining the legacy in terms of general stylistic and thematic similarities.

Despite the intervening years and scholarship, James Irby's work has remained so strong a presence in the field of Faulkner's Spanish

American legacy that Tanya Fayen devotes the first chapter of her recent *In Search of the Latin American Faulkner* (1995) to a consideration of the strengths and shortcomings of Irby's thesis, and to defining her own position in relation to his work. Fayen foregrounds what she perceives to be the limitations of Irby's approach, claiming that his framework presumes the superiority of the influencing text and authors and the necessarily derivative nature of the works by the authors receiving the influence. In contrast, she purports to espouse an explicitly Spanish American cultural orientation, from which she traces the "cycle of reception" of Faulkner's work in Spanish American letters (primarily through literary criticism, focusing in particular on articles appearing in *Sur*) from the 1930s to the 1980s. She documents the rise of interest in Faulkner, correlating it with the gradual weakening of the hegemony of literary models and norms still imposed by Spain, and with a concomitant increasing receptiveness to foreign innovations. I agree wholeheartedly with this part of her analysis and will develop a related argument in the following pages. However, I question her rejection of Irby's assumption of a correlation "between extra-literary reality and fictional reality" in Faulkner and his Spanish American readers (7). Fayen argues that the mimetic relationship between world and literary representation, which she defines as the tenet that "World defines Form" (2), should preclude the influence of literature arising from a specific set of circumstances on work reflecting a different reality (8–9). In contrast, I would claim that it is precisely the Spanish American authors' perception of parallels in their extra-literary experiences and those of Faulkner—what Irby describes as "the fundamental similarities in vital experiences that link Spanish America's 'lost generation' to that which followed the first World War" (167)—that gave the southerner such a strong foothold in Spanish American fiction.

Otherwise, several studies that more generally compare literature written in the Americas have often been framed by hemispheric provenance. Some of these studies offer valuable insights, which are peripheral to their main emphasis but which both anticipate and inform my own argument. In *Rediscovering the Americas: Inter-American Literature in a Comparative Context*, Earl Fitz claims that the American quest for identity is carried out through the expression of a "sense of place." However, while he notes that this "place" is more frequently a geographic region rather than the abstract political construct of a nation, he does not explore his theory through a comparison of literature from the southern U.S. and Spanish America. The essays in *Reinventing the Americas: Comparative Studies of the Literature of the United States and Spanish America* also pursue continuities in the literatures and critical writings of the Americas and in fields such as cultural and women's studies. In their general introduction, Bell Gale Chevigny and Gari Laguardia examine the problems of self-definition that have faced the U.S. and the Spanish American nations after severing ties with their respective colonizing powers. They note that North and South America met with different degrees of success in establishing their independence, which, in turn, was reflected in their economic and political successes on an international stage. The U.S. South's development, though, is much closer to that of Spanish America, for both lagged behind their northern neighbors for many years, and the resulting position on the outskirts of modernity is a frequently addressed theme in both regions' literatures. In *Writing the Apocalypse: Historical Vision in Contemporary U.S. and Latin American Fiction*, Lois Parkinson Zamora observes that the fiction of both regions reflects a late and sudden entrance of progress into traditional societies and conveys the sense of having reached a turning point (122–23). She also notes that southern authors until the end of the modernist period, and Spanish American writers until the present, emphasize literature's importance to the construction of a national or regional identity (179). José David Saldívar's *The Dialectics of Our America* identifies commonalities in marginalized literary traditions of the Americas (Chicano, African American, and Spanish American). Saldívar draws a parallel between the two regions when he claims, echoing southern critic Lewis Simpson, that "the writing of fiction in Our America has retained its autonomy, like U.S. Southern literature, by making its subject the very loss of its subject" (Saldívar, 23, paraphrasing Simpson, 156). Similarly, Mary Louise Pratt's "Margin Release: Canadian and Latin American Literature in the Context of Dependency" identifies connections between the literatures of Latin America and Canada and their experiences as dependent and neo- or post-colonial societies on the basis of the centrality of dependency and colonialism to the consciousness and identities of the regions (247). These parallels, of course, are analogous to those that I have found in the literature of the South and Spanish America.

Interestingly, some studies do compare works from these two regions but without taking into account the authors' geographical origins. For example, Ellison's *Invisible Man* and García Márquez's *One Hundred Years of Solitude* have been studied as examples of burgeoning marginalized literary traditions (African American and Spanish American; see Michael Cooke's "Ellison and García Márquez"). Others, such as Lisa Davis's "An Invitation to Understanding among Poor Women of the Americas," make important observations that could be developed further by recognizing similarities between the regions. Davis's comparison of Alice Walker's *The Color Purple* and Elena Poniatowska's *Hasta no verte, Jesús mío* (Here's to You, Jesus) turns on depictions of the lives of oppressed, impoverished women. Racial and cultural differences between the protagonists notwithstanding, Davis posits a commonality of oppression, experience, and, ultimately, vision that transcends geographic borders, concluding that "there are similarities in character and theme and development between the two novels: the parallels between their stories are revealing about the experiences of poor women north and south" (228). I would suggest that the parallels speak even more directly to analogous experiences of poor women *South* and south.

With this in mind, I return for a moment to Irby's study. Irby further elaborates on how a common core of experience underlay the appeal of Faulkner's works, subject matter, and style to Spanish American authors:

> In transforming their experiences into a consciousness of reality, and giving both body and details to this consciousness in a literary format, these authors discovered in Faulkner a wealth of extremely powerful and effective techniques for constructing a similar experience and consciousness. Upon taking an initial stand towards a segment of reality, these writers often assume a 'Faulknerian' attitude and vision; deeds, events, and scenes seem to allude to a hidden, sinister reality that is pregnant with violence and possessed by a strange and magic attraction to an indirect and partial focus. (167)

Irby sells his thesis short when he concludes that Faulkner's influence was primarily stylistic, that "Faulkner's themes and ideas seem to have had little influence" (167). These are, as he himself notes, implicated and imbricated in the southerner's style and help to explain the power of his legacy.

The central premise of this study argues that "the fundamental similarities in vital experiences" identified by Irby have by no means been limited to Spanish America's "lost generation." Faulkner's influence, in conjunction with that of other modern writers, represents a turning point in Spanish American literature. Although Irby's study was written immediately after the 1955 publication of Rulfo's *Pedro Páramo*, and before the Cuban Revolution of 1959, many of the paradigms that it delineated remained germane throughout the literary "Boom" that followed. The set of concerns that he identifies as shared by Faulkner and earlier Spanish American authors has continued to be of vital importance as the literary context has become more revisionist of the past. Following a discussion of these literary transformations, as well as a brief sketch of the Southern Renaissance, the dominant movement of the years when Faulkner and the other authors in this study wrote, I propose to examine how Irby's insights have held true, especially for some of the Boom's most prominent authors, who were just beginning to make names for themselves when Irby wrote his thesis.

[The arts] have been produced in societies which were for the most part stable, religious, and agrarian; where the goodness of life was measured by a scale of values having little to do with the material values of industrialism; where men were never too far removed from nature to forget that the chief subject of art, in the final sense, is nature. . . . In America, the South, past and present, furnishes a living example of an agrarian society, the preservation of which is worth the most heroic effort that men can give in a time of crisis.

—Donald Davidson, "A Mirror for Artists"

Let us remember the saying that "the people who have no more legends are condemned to perish of cold," and let us objectively recognize the fact that modern life with its stern rates of production, with its concentration of great masses of men into industrial armies . . . with its inadequate leisure, and its context of mechanized life, hampers and slows down the production of legends and a living folk lore. By way of contrast, the under-developed populations of the world who have still quite recently had to live in contact with Nature, have for centuries been compelled particularly to sharpen their eyes. . . . The peoples among whom industrial life is the most highly developed, have, for their part, used their senses to a lesser extent during the last few centuries, since material civilization has saved them a great deal of effort.

—Jacques Aléxis, "Of the Marvellous Realism of the Haitians"

The southern literature discussed in this study spans the 1920s through the 1950s, while the Spanish American works follow the rise of the "new narrative" and the Boom and were written between 1955 and the 1980s. A brief summary of the dominant literary currents of these years will lay the foundation for my discussion, in the following section, of how authors from both regions during these periods drew upon the techniques of international literary modernism to depict their histories. My goal in using periodic terms such as the *Southern Renaissance* and the *Boom* is not to be deterministic or reductionistic, or to posit all-encompassing unities in southern and Spanish American writing. Rather, I use them as starting points from which to identify and explicate recurrent themes in light of sociopolitical circumstances.

The 1920s to the 1940s were years of rapid change in the South, as well as a period of intense self-scrutiny and efforts at regional self-definition. The South, living with the moral burden left by that "peculiar institution"—that is, slavery—and in the shadow of defeat, found itself in a double-edged relationship with the national ideal: it was subsumed within the broader (id)entity but at the same time felt alienated from the master narratives of progress and success that the U.S. as a whole projected to the world; it was condemned by the larger political corpus for its tarnished history, and it rejected identification with the larger corpus because of its own differential construction of self. Allen Tate's is the orthodox definition of the renaissance in southern fiction that took place during these years: "With the war of 1914 to 1918, the South reentered the world but gave a backward glance as it slipped over the border: that backward glance gave us the Southern renascence, a literature conscious of the past in the present" (292). Tate himself, Faulkner, Porter, Robert Penn Warren, Eudora Welty, Thomas Wolfe, and many others contributed to this surge of literary activity. Many of their texts are situated in or, alternatively, trace the demise of agrarian, plantation-based communities—that is, of what the Fugitive-Agrarians, twelve prominent southern writers and intellectuals based in

Vanderbilt University during the 1920s and 1930s, deemed the "Southern way of life" in their 1930 manifesto, *I'll Take My Stand*, the basis of the regional identity which was to withstand the encroachment of "the American or prevailing way" (*I'll Take My Stand*, xix).

Since the late nineteenth century, definitions of southern identity had centered around the plantation. Following the Civil War, the image of the agrarian lifestyle was resurrected and retrospectively recast as the symbol of what the battles had been fought for, and of what had been lost. Some writers of the Southern Renaissance followed along these lines, offering nostalgic images of a time of plenty, nobility, and honor, of a society that valued leisure and in which aesthetic and religious considerations prevailed over economic pursuits—in direct contrast, of course, to their present (Davenport, 85). Other authors, meanwhile, offered critical reassessments of the flaws of the Old Order, drawing attention to the racism and injustice that had been its legacy. Yet others, such as Caroline Gordon, Porter, and Welty took both stands, holding onto the past even as they questioned its values and legacies (Gray, 151). Despite conflicting attitudes toward the way of life depicted, the works display an undeniable coincidence in themes and subject. And while treatment of these issues is, of course, by no means limited to this period, the thematic cluster lies at the heart of what was perceived and promoted as a literary movement.[9] As Richard Gray observes, the very interest in and reinterpretations of the South's history and traditions supplied the writers "with a certain common ground marked out for them by their region." He continues by saying that "the contemporary situation and the interest in a shared history, were in fact linked, since it was precisely the disorienting experience of social change in the present that eventually drove the writers of the southern 'renaissance' to an investigation of their past" (3). In short, the works of the Southern Renaissance reflect an intense preoccupation with the South's history and the sense of a disjunction between the region's traditionalism and the questionable value(s) of modern industrial society.

Although Ralph Ellison's literary career took off after the end of the Southern Renaissance (designated by many critics as 1946, the year of publication of Warren's *All the King's Men*), I include him in this study precisely because his essays and fiction alike respond to a set of concerns similar to that which informed the writers of the renaissance; additionally, they reflect the profound impact of modernist aesthetics. Ellison is traditionally studied as an African American writer, and relatively little emphasis is placed on his southern affiliations, including his Oklahoma roots and his years at the Tuskegee Institute in Alabama. He himself used to stress his southwestern origins, claiming that growing up on the frontier of a periphery, in a culture still in the process of defining itself, had given him a greater sense of his potential than would have been possible in the rigidly segregated South. His insistence on this distinction was partly motivated (and thus, perhaps, over-emphasized) by a desire to distance himself from Richard Wright, a literary "relative" from the South to whom critics compared him but whom Ellison did not care to claim as his "ancestor," that is, as a chosen model or source of influence. Moreover, Ellison's southern sojourn was crucial to his attitude in later years, as here he did encounter prejudice and segregation that forced him to define himself in relation to a hostile world. "Thus was I forced to evaluate my own self-worth," he wrote, "and the narrow freedom in which it existed, against the power of those who would destroy me. In time I was to leave the South, although it has never left me, and the interests which I discovered there became my life" (*Shadow & Act,* 122). He joins other black writers, from the South and North alike, in drawing upon southern history for his subject matter, a move that acknowledges the region as a formative part of individual and collective black identity (T. Davis, 7).

Tate's identification of historical consciousness and of the transition between orders and value systems as the hallmark of a literary movement also parallels the concerns of the Spanish American texts in this study. Since Independence, Spanish America and its literature have been deeply engaged in the task of establishing cultural, regional, and national identities that are distinct from the molds and modes imposed by Spain, and in the search for endogenous means of expression. Where southerners upheld the plantation as an idyll emblematizing their (now fallen) way of life, Spanish America's experiences have repeatedly been expressed in images situated in a paradigm presupposing an earlier paradise. Originally celebrated as a New World for its innocence, social and political utopianism has, time and again, failed to bear fruit. The evils associated with Europe—the immorality, corruption, tyranny, and unequal distribution of privilege—quickly arose in the colonies and became even more pronounced as the newly independent republics struggled to overturn colonial systems of government and assert their own. The lament of the fall of such worlds has been a constant in the literature of this century, coupled with a desire to recover and revive them; redemption has frequently been sought in an idealized, primitivist vision of the pre-Columbian past, in which nature was still perceived to be inviolate, and in social institutions devoted to maintaining the integrity and well-being of the communities. In 1919, Ramón López Velarde wrote of the "subverted Eden" that greeted the prodigal son returning home after the Mexican Revolution. The war that was intended to break up the entrenched regime of Porfirio Díaz—which had initiated an intensive campaign of modernization whose benefits extended to the privileged classes alone and which had left the bulk of the population behind in a weakened feudal agrarian society—instead left the land and population decimated and the previous power structures relatively intact. For Velarde's compatriot Octavio Paz, the Conquest represented a Fall into European history and civilization that sundered Mexico from the All, "from that eternity in which all times were one" (208). In his view, though, the blow to European hegemony brought about by the Second World War and the concomitant decentering of European identity ought to permit a reassertion of, if not the primal culture, then the power of those who had been marginalized. Alejo Carpentier, in turn, sought in his work to recuperate that "world of . . . vegetation dating back to the origins of the earth" (83).

In the 1940s and afterwards, the period that is the subject of this study, one begins to observe what Donoso called the "internationalization" of Spanish American literature and culture, in tandem with, finally, the development of a sense of regional (or continental) consciousness akin to that of the southerners (9–10). As Zamora notes, this period gave rise to "an unprecedented literary conversation," in which writers read and responded to one another's works, "emphasiz[ing] the communal nature of their literary project . . . self-consciously engaging, and in some sense also creating, a reality shared by the many countries and cultures of their region" (*Writing the Apocalypse,* 20–21). During these years, authors such as Fuentes and García Márquez openly declared that they wrote as Latin Americans, rather than, in Donoso's words, writing for their "parishes" (11). And in 1959, the Cuban Revolution introduced a new spark into the region's political and artistic climates. Hope for change, for a better future, was high, and commitment to shaping and promoting a collective identity through literature and politics soared. The 1960s and 1970s witnessed a dramatic increase in literary production, a much broader distribution of new works to a non–Spanish American (and non–Spanish speaking) readership, and a renovation of technique and style—the so-called Boom in which Spanish American literature entered and became a full participant in the international "mainstream." Like the Southern Renaissance, the Boom represents a cultural response to a given set of political and socioeconomic circumstances: on the one hand, novels of this period are marketed through channels created by the modernization of Spanish America following the Second World War; on the other, they depict the social chaos, the rapid change and upheaval that was a concomitant of this process and of the related struggles of neocolonialism and dependency (Beverley and Zimmerman, 18–19). As in the fiction of the Southern Renaissance, Boom fiction reexamines the past, assesses local (and international) forces competing for economic and political control, as well as their impact on social dynamics, and speculates on the region's future. And, like the Agrarians, the author-intellectuals of the Boom (including Julio Cortázar, Donoso, Fuentes, García Márquez, and Vargas Llosa) also comprised a literary movement with ties to a cultural project, the redefinition and reconstitution of Spanish American reality.[10] Since the experimental novels of the 1940s, these issues have remained both vital and compelling and are at the heart of the historical fiction that rewrites and thereby reappropriates the region's past and is such a prominent category in modern Spanish American fiction.

I arrive, now, at the ineffable center of my story. And here begins my despair as a writer. All language is an alphabet of symbols whose use presupposes a past shared by all the other interlocutors. How, then, transmit to others the infinite Aleph, which my fearful mind scarcely encompasses? . . . [T]he central problem is unsolvable: the enumeration, even if only partial, of an infinite complex. In that gigantic instant I saw millions of delightful and atrocious acts; none astonished me more than the fact that all of them together occupied the same point, without superposition and without transparency. What my eyes saw was simultaneous: what I shall transcribe is successive, because language is successive.

—Jorge Luis Borges, "The Aleph"

In addition to addressing similar sets of immediate concerns, the literature of the Southern Renaissance and Spanish America's "new narrative" also trace their stylistic and thematic roots to a common source: the Euro-American modernist tradition. Times of historical tension—of transition and revolution, turning points marked by a sense of the disappearance of an established form of society and its "givens"—

are often implicated in the emergence of literary movements. As we have seen, Tate correlates the origins of the Southern Renaissance with a crisis point in history and with the resulting perception of discontinuities between past and present. Such ruptures were also encoded in literary modernism, which was in part a response to the inability of modern civilization's deities of reason, order, and logic to explain events in a war in which, in Winston Churchill's words, "all the horrors of all the ages were brought together." Authors in Europe and the U.S. explored the flux of experience with techniques that called into question realism's presumptions of a fixed reality that might be apprehended, comprehended, and transcribed. In Virginia Woolf's words, the modern writers were "attempt[ing] to come closer to life, and to preserve more sincerely and exactly what interests and moves them, even if to do so they must discard most of the conventions which are commonly observed by the novelist" (2034). They drew upon psychoanalysis's explorations of the unconscious, and used stream of consciousness to render the relationship between reality and perception, the individual's filtering of experience; their texts proceed through the association of ideas and emotions, moving between thought and action. Authors experimented with perspective and challenged traditional representations of time. Linearity, causality, and chronological order are rejected and, instead, one finds events evoked, revived, and relived at memory's whim, as well as unmarked transitions between past, present, and future. As in life, connections and causal relations in a work may be tenuous or left unclarified. As James Joyce's *Ulysses* and Woolf's own *Mrs. Dalloway* demonstrate, the coexistence of multiple levels of consciousness in a character's mind, in memory, transcends and obviates the formal unity of time marked out by one calendar day. The past cannot simply be left behind, for previous experience and the memories thereof continue to bear on an individual's actions and reactions. Heightened awareness of the difficulty of expressing the simultaneity of experience through language, successive by nature, further eroded confidence in realism's presumed mimetic capabilities.

As Daniel Singal points out, during the late 1920s and 1930s, the Agrarians reconciled their own modernism (which had placed some of the writers in the literary vanguard even as it led them to eliminate all references to the South from their work) with a developing southernism by apotheosizing their heritage, elevating it to the status of myth and ideal (198–202). Thus they promoted the image of the plantation as a bastion of the South, of civilized values characterized by order, stability, and immunity to the ravages of time, and as a space that set the region apart from the North's materialism and commercialism. In Spanish America, the upheaval that plagued Europe and the U.S. following World War I, as well as the attendant sense of alienation, spiritual emptiness, and the loss of a shared moral foundation, became visible during the 1940s and 1950s. In 1941, Juan Carlos Onetti wrote that his novel, *No Man's Land*, depicted

> a group of people who, while they might seem exotic in Buenos Aires, are, in truth, representative of a generation; a generation that, in my opinion, replicates twenty years afterwards that of Europe following the War. The old moral values were abandoned by it and as of yet none have appeared that might be able to take their place. The situation is such that in the most important country in South America, in young America, the figure of the morally indifferent man, the man without faith or interest in his destiny, is emerging. (quoted in Irby, 42)

The time lapse separating the two "generations," as well as the delayed incorporation of modern techniques in the Spanish American narrative, ties in with the matter of translation and the differential rates at which socioeconomic and political changes swept the regions.[11] These were the circumstances within which the new mode of prose writing gained currency, edging out the regionalist *novela de la tierra* (novel of the land) which in the 1920s and 1930s had characterized Spanish American reality in a predominantly realist, mimetic mode.

Surprisingly, however, the role of Euro-American modernism in the development of Spanish American literature is only generally alluded to in most critical discussions. Although many Spanish American authors have admitted to seizing upon the innovations of modern writing, for the most part these are not frequently linked, as they were in Irby's study, to international literary currents. Instead, techniques and themes associated with modernism are often identified in a decontextualized manner. Donald Shaw, for example, describes the Boom in terms strongly reminiscent of Euro-American modernism: in comparison with earlier, regionalist novels, he describes the movement as reflecting a "shift from observed reality to created reality, from mimesis to myth, from confidence in to questioning of our ability to understand ourselves or the world around us [with a] tendency towards the *novela totalizadora* [totalizing novel], its questioning of the human condition, its experimentalism" ("Towards a Description," 93). Elsewhere, he makes the following assessment of the problematization of reality and the concomitant skewing and eschewing of linear time, which also brings modernist aesthetics to mind:

> Because reality includes time; and if we are no longer sure of our ability to understand the reality that is outside of us (that is, if it exists), nor our internal, psychological reality, why privilege time? Thus, logically, in the narratives of Borges, Rulfo, Fuentes, García Márquez, and others, time ceases to be linear and chronological and becomes part of our enigmatic surroundings. (*Nueva narrativa,* 83)

Boom authors' tributes to Faulkner, Joyce, Franz Kafka, Marcel Proust, Woolf, and others, though, merit attention. They identify sources and models, and also draw attention to the symbiotic relationship between form and content, style and subject, that held such a strong appeal. García Márquez, for example, openly declared his affinity for Faulkner and Woolf in the early years of his career. Additionally, in 1950, he lamented the lack of a Colombian novel influenced by Faulkner, Joyce, or Woolf and predicted that their techniques had set the course that Colombian literature would eventually follow ("Los problemas," 269).

Spanish American authors saw in modernist stylistics a medium that was not only suited to the description of a universally problematic reality but that could also be used to overcome what they perceived to be the inability of traditional realist discourse to capture and represent Spanish American reality. In particular, the exploration of alternatives to linear time dovetailed with the Spanish American authors' efforts to express their preoccupation with troubled pasts, the unresolved conflicts and hatreds that overshadow and impinge upon the present. Numerous efforts at regional and national self-definition have in fact been grounded in these new conceptualizations of time. Carpentier's characterization of Spanish America's marvelous reality, for example, hinged upon his identification of the coexistence of multiple temporal moments as one of the region's defining qualities: "I saw the possibility of establishing certain synchronisms, American, recurrent, [above time,] relating this to that, yesterday to today" (84). In contrast, Paz believed this atemporal or supertemporal stratum to have been eradicated. For him, the Conquest signaled Mexico's expulsion from a continuous present outside of measured time, from a time "when time was not succession and transition, but the perpetual source of a fixed present in which all times, past and future, were contained." "When man was exiled from that eternity in which all times were one," he continues, "he entered chronometric time and became a prisoner of the clock" (208). That is, he fell into the convulsions of the European civilization of which linear time is a metonymy. In addition to being the handmaiden of realism, then, linear time also represents for Paz the mark and sign of Spanish America's colonial status.

For both southern and Spanish American authors, memory, the point at which notions of time and individual perspective intersect, came to be a particularly powerful correlative to explorations of historical consciousness. After all, memory by definition transports past experiences to the present. For many authors, it functions as a microcosm: characters' struggles are interwoven with and played out on the broader stage of regions marked by their pasts' traumas. As we shall see, in the works in this study, memory often concentrates the past into a single moment, a dead end which obstructs progress and from which there is no passage into the future for character or region. In this respect, Faulkner's depiction of his characters' immersion in and obsessive reliving of the South's history was an especially potent model for the Spanish Americans. In *Light in August*, Gail Hightower spends his life reenacting his grandfather's ignominious death in the Civil War: "for fifty years I have not even been clay: I have been a single instant of darkness in which a horse galloped and a gun crashed . . . my dead grandfather on the instant of his death" (540). For Gavin Stevens of *Requiem for a Nun*, "The past is never dead, it's not even past" (285). For the Canadian Shreve McCannon in *Absalom, Absalom!* the past is "something my people haven't got," whereas it is his southern roommate's "entailed birthright," part and parcel of a culture that is "always reminding us to never forget" (361). Works such as Rulfo's *Pedro Páramo*, Fuentes's *The Death of Artemio Cruz*, and García Márquez's *Leaf Storm* and even his *One Hundred Years of Solitude* revolve around similar beings, individual and collective, for whom time stops or is suspended. For the characters in these novels, the past is that door through which the Quentin Compson of *Absalom, Absalom!* simply cannot "pass."

It is García Márquez—who, of course, spear-headed efforts to break the path for Colombian literature with the publication of *Leaf Storm* in 1955—who perhaps best illustrates how Faulkner's understanding of time was assimilated contemporaneously with formal elements. Faulkner's desire to condense "everything into one sentence—not only the present but the whole past on which it depends and which keeps overtaking the present" (quoted in Cowley, *The Faulkner-Cowley File*, 115), which resulted in his incredibly long and often baroque sentences—is literalized in the very first sentence of *One Hundred Years of Solitude*, which encompasses past, present, and future in a single breath: "Many years later, as he faced the firing squad, Colonel Aureliano Buendía was to remember that distant afternoon when his father took him to discover ice" (11). This condensation of time is duplicated structurally in Melquíades's manuscript, which "had not put events in the order of man's conventional time, but had concentrated a century of daily episodes in such a way that they coexisted in one instant" (382) and which somehow (apocalyptically) "reconciles" the simultaneity of experience and the successiveness of language that the narrator of Borges's "The Aleph" cannot. The temporal confusion, conflations, and manipulations of both authors are complemented by the use of pronouns without clarification of their referents and by the ambiguous repetition of characters' names: Quentin Compson, for example, is one of the narrators of *The Sound and the Fury* and *Absalom, Absalom!* but is also the name of his sister Caddy's daughter, while many generations of and variations on José Arcadio and Aureliano march through the pages of *One Hundred Years of Solitude*. The reader is constantly challenged to ascertain not just *who* is being referred to or *what* has happened and to *whom* but also *when* the actions are taking place. And once an event can no longer be pinpointed as having happened at a specific moment, and having ended, the possibility arises that it is ongoing and that its ramifications, too, are overtaking the present. As the Quentin of *Absalom, Absalom!* thinks, "Maybe nothing ever happens once and is finished. Maybe happen is never once but like ripples maybe on water after the pebble sinks, the ripples moving on, spreading" (261).

Modern writing's undermining of linear time as a structuring principle has a counterpart in the use of images of puzzles and labyrinths that are on the brink of resolving into an intelligible whole (but that rarely do) and that serve as metaphors for the contingency of the self, knowledge, history, and order—temporal, narrative, and experiential. Thus does Faulkner's Charles Bon try to understand the lawyer's plans for his life: "almost touching the answer, aware of the jigsaw puzzle picture integers of it waiting, almost lurking, just beyond his reach, inextricable, jumbled, and unrecognizable yet on the point of falling into a pattern which would reveal to him at once, like a flash of light, the meaning of his whole life" (*Absalom,* 1972, 313). Similarly, in Warren's *All the King's Men*, the protagonist writes that

> as I experienced that day, there was at first an impression of the logic of the events, caught flickeringly at moments, but as they massed to the conclusion I was able to grasp, at the time, only the slightest hints as to the pattern that was taking shape. This lack of logic, the sense of people and events driven by impulses which I was not able to define, gave the whole occasion the sense of a dreamlike unreality. It was only after the conclusion . . . that the sense of reality returned, longer after, in fact, when I had been able to gather the pieces of the puzzle up and put them together to see the pattern. This is not remarkable, for, as we know, reality is not a function of the event as event, but of the relationship of that event to past, and future, events. (383)

Ellison's invisible man likewise impresses upon his readers that "the mind that has conceived a plan of living must never lose sight of the chaos against which that pattern was conceived" (502). And we see this in Borges's "Aleph" but also in "The Garden of Forking Paths," where the labyrinth whose mystery the narrator seeks to unravel belongs not to the third dimension but to the fourth: the labyrinth is an infinite book, made of words rather than walls, and is built not in space but around a riddle whose answer is a form of non-linear time.

For southern and Spanish American writers addressing the presence of the past and the burden of history that overshadows them, then, time is both form and substance. The innovations of modernism allowed the expression of thematic concerns through style, grammar, and structure. The movement's impact is evident in prodigious sentences that span and conflate many moments, as well as in a polyphonic style that describes the same event from different perspectives, returning to the same moment time and again, and therefore impeding the progress of the narrative. Also, the patterns and puzzles that represent temporary orderings of raw experience double as analogues to memory, which itself houses images from multiple moments in time side by side, and which is ever-searching to make sense of them.

As we shall see in subsequent chapters, each of the authors in this study, southern and Spanish American, perceived the modernist movement and the material that they were describing to be consubstantial. They heeded Woolf's charge to discard realist conventions, and they seized upon the stylistics and underlying problematics of modernism to "come closer to life," in this case to a collective experience of life considered to be different from conventional ideas of reality. The marvelous, baroque, fantastic, and grotesque are cornerstones of the aesthetics that have been enhanced by the adoption and adaptation of experimental techniques. They represent narrative correlatives to ongoing efforts to establish regional, national, and continental identities, apposite modes for transmitting the otherly realities with which they are perceived to be coextensive. For these reasons, Wendy Faris has described magic realism as having "enabled a broader transculturation process to take place, a process within which postcolonial Latin American literature established its identity" ("Scheherazade's Children," 165). And Theo D'haen has likewise correlated the decentered position of magic realist authors with their decentering intentions, that is, with their goals of challenging dominant views of and visions for reality. To this end, he describes the mode as "*correcting* so-called existing reality [in order to] right the wrongs this 'reality' depends upon." He further characterizes it as

> a way of access to the main body of 'Western' literature for authors not sharing in, or not writing from the perspective of, the privileged centers of this

literature for reasons of language, class, race or gender [or as] a means for writers coming from the privileged centers of literature to dissociate themselves from their own discourses of power, and to speak on behalf of the ex-centric and un-privileged. (195)

The amplified conception of experience that nonrealist discourses convey is well suited to the renegotiation of what dominant powers and discourses have labeled reality, or have legitimated by recognizing as "history." Fuentes has, in fact, on numerous occasions directly correlated tragic historical experience with the artistic originality of southern fiction. He pinpoints Faulkner's work as a challenge to the national ideal, the defiant outgrowth of the South's experience of failure in a country whose self-image is predicated on success, and identifies the same principle at work in Spanish American literature. He writes, "I feel I have been deeply influenced by William Faulkner" and continues,

> I think Faulkner, of the American writers, is the closest to us because he is the only novelist of defeat, in a country that basically has been a nation of optimism and success. Furthermore, he is the only baroque writer in the U.S. Once, Alejo Carpentier told me . . . that we Latin Americans are baroque because *el barroco* is a way of seeking truth. When there are established truths, accepted by all, one can be classical. When there is no stable truth, we have to be baroque.[12] (quoted in Sommers, *After the Storm,* 197n.8)

And, of course, Carpentier himself posited *lo real maravilloso* (the marvelous real) as a literary analogue to the "ex-centric" experience and prodigious reality of Spanish America, "a world . . . [where] events tend to develop their own style, their own unique trajectories" (83). Thus in the same way that the experiences of defeat, failure, and alienation are parallels in the histories of the South and Spanish America, so, too, are the styles that have been cultivated to communicate them.

In the spirit of Harold Bloom's "anxiety of influence," the refutation of realism in Spanish America was further implicated in the assertion of an emic mode of expression over and above those left in place by the former colonizing power. Thus, authors have denounced not just realism but, specifically and repeatedly, *Spanish* realism, as an inherited discourse that they felt only permitted them to depict a reality that they did not consider to be compatible with their own.[13] Donoso, Jorge Edwards, García Márquez, and Rulfo, among others, have leveled this charge against this and other modes of Spanish literature that held sway in Spanish American fiction in the late nineteenth and early twentieth centuries, and against the Spanish American writers whom they felt had not sufficiently distanced themselves from their models. Rulfo once remarked that the literary models most popular during his school years represented the "worst of Spanish literature": "Pereda, the Generation of '98 . . . I knew that was the backwardness of Spanish American literature: the fact that we were absorbing a literature that was foreign to our character and disposition" (quoted in Harss and Dohmann, 272). Chilean novelist Edwards rejects the efforts of even the later and more innovative Spanish writers (including, ironically, several of the Generation of 1898, whose self-exploration and questioning of national identity following Spain's final collapse as a colonial power was not wholly dissimilar from that of the Spanish Americans) as being, it would seem, insufficiently "baroque" to express his reality:

> After the great writers of the seventeenth-century, there was no prose writing of [Faulkner's] particular poetical force in the Spanish language. There were writers like Gabriel Miró, Azorín, Ramón del Valle Inclán, that tried to be poetical through elegance. . . . The problem was that the writing of Ramón del Valle Inclán sounded anachronistic to us, strange to our own world, a sort of cardboard prose.[14] (64)

Donoso has noted that, "with their legacy of vassalage to the Spanish Academy of the Language and to outmoded attitudes toward literature and life" (13), the classic Spanish American *modernista* and regionalist novels "seemed alien to us and very distant from our sensibility and our times, located at an immense distance from the brand-new esthetics, defined as much by the problems of the modern world as by our indiscriminate reading of these new writers who were dazzling us with their sparks" (12).[15] In contrast, he claims that he and his contemporaries found in Faulkner, Joyce, Kafka, and Jean-Paul Sartre, among others, models who "seemed to us more 'ours,' much more 'our own,'" and without whom "the Boom would be impossible to define" (14).

In Faulkner in particular—Faulkner who was both modernist and southerner—the Spanish Americans at once found a model, a discursive mode, and a writer whom they could, at long last, call their own. His strong hold on them both catalyzed and reinforced the profound transformations of modernism, for, as Irby suggested, authors were drawn to the new stylistics through Faulkner's application of its technical innovations and thematics to a subject that resembled their own. It is no coincidence that Borges—who was active in fomenting *ultraísmo,* the avant-garde poetic movement in Argentina in the 1920s, and who was a pioneer of Spanish America's new fiction—was also among the early translators of Faulkner (*Wild Palms* in 1940). García Márquez invokes Faulkner as an example of modernism's fruitful concordance of style and subject, and similarly comments on the appropriateness of the symbiosis to his own project:

> The 'Faulknerian' method is very effective for describing Latin American reality. Unconsciously, that was what we discovered in Faulkner. That is, we saw this reality and wanted to narrate it, and we knew that the method of the Europeans didn't work, nor did the traditional Spanish method; and suddenly we found the Faulknerian method extremely apt for describing this reality.[16] (*La novela,* 52–53)

Similarly, Luis Harss and Barbara Dohmann quote him as saying that "[t]he chaotic materials that went into Faulknerian art . . . were much like the raw stuff of life in Colombia" (322). Thus, while modernism, like realism, was a discourse whose origins lay outside of Spanish America, and which was also learned from foreign models, it represented a choice: it was seized on precisely because its flexibility allowed for further experimentation and was suited to a different way of understanding and experiencing reality.

Debts to Faulkner are frequently acknowledged within the context of analogous historical experiences, for his works are, as we have seen, regarded as encapsulating not just the South's past, but the Spanish Americans' own as well. Implicitly and explicitly, he has been both filter and touchstone for Spanish American authors' understanding of the South. Exploring these authors' homages to Faulkner yields significant insight into why the Nobel laureate who gave other southern authors pause both in their choice of regional subject matter and their approach to writing about it—even Flannery O'Connor declared that "the presence alone of Faulkner in our midst makes a great difference in what the writer can and cannot permit himself to do. Nobody wants his mule and wagon stalled on the same track the Dixie Limited is roaring down" (45)—instead provided many Spanish American writers with both fuel and inspiration.

Several authors and author-critics have deliberately drawn upon images associated with the South's heyday and decline to describe periods of "boom and bust" in the pasts of their own nations. For Edwards, the Golden Age of prosperity corresponds to Chile's mining-related growth in the late 1800s, which culminated in the civil war of 1891. His description of the war's aftermath is couched in terms reminiscent of the South's physical circumstances and backward-glancing attitude alike. He writes how within the buildings "that had represented the nitrate splendor of the nineties, a sort of créole 'belle époque' . . . there were impoverished families, and in the rear dormitories, sometimes hiding from the outside world, old people that remembered and told stories about that lost splendor and about the terrible civil strife." Moreover, he claims that his generation grew up "between memories of a brilliant and glorious past, in contrast with a decayed present, a present whose main quality was stagnation, frustration, poverty, underdevelopment" (69).

In 1961, in an homage to Faulkner, García Márquez journeyed through the South by bus. Here, he has said, "I found evidence—on those hot, dusty roads, with the same vegetation, trees, and great houses—of the similarity between our two worlds" (quoted in Guibert, 327). He attributes the resemblances to the fact that

> I was born in Aracataca, the banana growing country where the United Fruit Company was established. It was in this region, where the Fruit Company was building towns and hospitals and draining some zones, that I grew up and received my first impressions. Then, many years later, I read Faulkner and found that his whole world—the world of the southern United States which he writes about—was very like my world, that it was created by the same people. . . . What I found in him was affinities between our experiences, which were not as different as might appear at first sight. (quoted in Guibert, 327)

García Márquez once again specifically invokes the South—*Faulkner's* South, that is—when discussing the destruction and financial ruin left in Macondo (Aracataca fictionalized) by the United Fruit Company following the first World War:

> Macondo is the past, and, well, since I had to give this past streets and houses, temperature and people, I gave it the image of this hot, dusty, finished, ruined town, with wood houses with zinc roofs, which look very similar to those in the southern U.S.; a town which looks very similar to Faulkner's towns, because it was constructed by the United Fruit Company. (*La novela,* 54)

In an article on García Márquez, Vargas Llosa describes the aftermath of the Colombian "banana fever" in terms which, like Edwards's, evoke the South's sentimental cult of the Lost Cause:

> When García Márquez was born, almost none of this was left: paradise and hell alike belonged to the past, the present reality was a limbo made of misery, heat, and routine. However, this extinct reality was still alive in the memory and imagination of the people . . . and it was their best weapon for fighting the abandon and emptiness of the present reality. For want of anything better, Aracataca—like so many American towns—lived off of memories, myths, solitude, and nostalgia. ("García Márquez," 128)

The southerner's depictions of war, defeat, and defeatism also strike home. Fuentes once wrote that "we feel that Faulkner's work is very close to us, to Latin Americans: only Faulkner . . . in a closed world of optimism and success, offers us an image that is common to both the United States and Latin America: the image of defeat, of separation, of doubt: of tragedy" (*Casa*, 66).[17] Edwards similarly concludes that Faulkner's appeal was "so strong in other Spanish-speaking countries [because] this panorama of civil wars and of a certain past splendor, the legend of the past, took very different forms, and I must insist on the differences in each national case, but it existed in all of Latin America" (69–70).

In 1960, southern writer Caroline Gordon declared that

> after the Civil War there was a school of literature foisted on us by Northern publishers. They demanded moonlight and magnolias and a lot of people furnished it to them and that idea stuck in people's heads ever since. If a Southerner writes a novel now, whoever is reviewing for the *New York Times* will make a point of saying it isn't moonlight and magnolias. It's all nonsense. We are a conquered nation and abominably treated and we paid

the greatest tribute perhaps ever paid by any conquered nation. Our history was miswritten and our children were taught lies and therefore the Northerners could not bear the image of us as we were and therefore the Northern publishers would publish only novels full of white columns and magnolias.[18] (Porter, O'Connor et al., 13)

Gordon's anger at the fact that both her history and literature were being written by the winners, in conjunction with the similar reactions of other southern and Spanish American authors, underlies this study's questioning of historical discourse's truth-value and its exploration of challenges to the power relations dictating historiography. The following chapters take a variety of approaches to detailing how, in texts from both regions, the act of rewriting the official historical record is a means of reclaiming the past and achieving a different future.

Chapter 2 focuses on the search for historical truth and explores how it comprises the plot of Faulkner's *Absalom, Absalom!* and Vargas Llosa's *The Real Life of Alejandro Mayta*. The characters in these novels—each person representing a distinct point of view—attempt unsuccessfully to reconstruct the events leading up to a historical "fact"—the fall of Thomas Sutpen's dynastic design and a failed socialist uprising in the Peruvian highlands, respectively. Both novels thus problematize history's claim to represent the past objectively and deny the possibility of arriving at a version of events that is not always already mediated. Also, in both cases, the version of the story that ultimately provides the most satisfactory explanation of the events in question is an imaginative reconstruction, attesting to the fact that the need to address and redress the ramifications of past actions takes precedence over the more academic issue of establishing an empirically verifiable version of history.

In Chapter 3, I discuss how Ralph Ellison and Isabel Allende avail themselves of the doubly marginalized perspectives of groups in peripheral regions that have been further disenfranchised by race and gender. *Invisible Man* addresses the problem of racism in the U.S., while *The*

House of the Spirits exposes the abuses committed by Chile's patriarchal social system, the violence of the Pinochet dictatorship to which it gave rise, and women's efforts to resist both. The narrators' awareness of how a center's descriptions and prescriptions of reality fail to apply to their own experiences enables them to provide correctives to official views of history. Both authors, then, would seem to echo the query of one southern historian who asks, "Who is better able to state the social ideal in unqualified terms than those who have experienced the bankruptcy of old social realities in their own lives?" (Davenport, 136). Thus I examine how these subversive voices have deliberately positioned themselves, in the invisible man's oft-repeated words, "outside of history," in order "to tell you what your eyes were looking through" (*Invisible Man,* 503).

Chapter 4 turns from written history to explore the alternative modes of preserving the past depicted by Katherine Anne Porter and Juan Rulfo within the context of parallels between antebellum southern plantation society and its fate after the Civil War, on the one hand, and, on the other, Mexico's *hacienda*-centered social system and its fate after the Mexican Revolution. In particular, I focus on the communal structures (family in Porter's stories and town in *Pedro Páramo*) threatened with disintegration by the changing of orders. I discuss why, despite the authors' depiction of shared memory as a vehicle for transmitting a group's history, their assessments of the role of shared memory in the configuration of the new order diverge. Whereas the renunciation of class memory and the flight from family in the Miranda stories is construed as a necessary step in the southern woman's path to self-determination, in *Pedro Páramo* the collective amnesia induced by the dislocations of *caciquismo*, as well as the distortion of familial bonds, marks the dissolution of communal relations and ultimately brings about Comala's subordination. In either case, though, memory's power to console proves ephemeral, as it perpetuates what has been lost, what perhaps never existed.

The themes that I discuss in each chapter are not limited to the individual works being compared precisely because they arise out of and reflect similar historical and social circumstances. Consequently, different but equally valid pairings of the same texts are conceivable. Many studies of Faulkner's influence on Rulfo have, of course, been written. One could even compare *Absalom, Absalom!* and *The House of the Spirits* on the basis of their explorations of competing visions of history, as well as their treatment of common themes—unrecognized offspring, the vengeance sought for dispossession, the relationship of the patriarchy, the plantation (or *latifundio*), and the social order—within the context of a family saga. And, of course, there are numerous significant parallels in the notions of "southern" womanhood depicted (and debunked) by Katherine Anne Porter and Isabel Allende, as can be seen in the female characters who try to break away from the rigid and unchanging roles authorized for women, as well as from the authoritarian, patriarchal figures (and, by extension, orders) who both define and perpetuate these roles. Similarities (and differences) may also be traced in their juxtapositions of official and unofficial stories, as well as in their explorations of the irrational within the context of women's experience. For reasons that I discuss further in each chapter, however, I find the current pairings best suited to the focus of this study.

～～～

We saw it, we were there, as if Drusilla's voice had transported us to
the wandering light-ray in space in which was still held the furious
shadow—the brief section of track which existed inside the scope of
a single pair of eyes and nowhere else . . . the engine not coming into
view but arrested in human sight . . . then gone, vanished. Only not
gone or vanished either, so long as there should be defeated or the
descendants of defeated to tell it or listen to the telling. . . . Drusilla
said, . . . "They tore the track up so we couldn't do it again; they
could tear the track up but they couldn't take back the fact that we

had done it. They couldn't take that from us."
—William Faulkner, *The Unvanquished*

Beyond hauntingly similar analyses of the past and its relationship to the present, the texts in this study also exhibit several additional commonalities. The first is their representations of revolution, both political and social. Recurring treatment of the U.S. Civil War, the Mexican Revolution, the First World War, and the Cuban Revolution and subsequent dissemination of socialism throughout Spanish America signals a fundamental concern with the upheavals of history and the social order. Revolutions and their disjunctures, after all, by definition, usher in a change in orders, a crossing of the ways. Each text is also marked by the "double consciousness" which is the marginalized person's sense of participating in both a dominant tradition and his or her own culture. Double consciousness is the liminality of someone who looks into the mainstream from outside and sees the ideals that the center claims to uphold but experiences instead a harsher reality. It is also the urge to self-definition against the norms by which others measure it.

Finally, each of the works in this study revolves around the telling of a story, or of stories. Given the importance commanded by notions of self-definition, self-assertion, and the need for historical revisionism, it is not surprising that storytelling is a ubiquitous activity and motif in the fiction of both regions. It is common to speak of a southern verbal tradition, of southern storytelling. Southerners, Faulkner wrote in the introduction to the twice and twice again told tale of *The Sound and the Fury*, are compelled "to talk, to tell, since oratory is our heritage. We seem to try in the simple furious breathing (or writing) span of the individual to draw a savage indictment of the contemporary scene or to escape from it into a make-believe region of swords and magnolias and mockingbirds which perhaps never existed anywhere" ("An Introduction . . . ," 222). In the works in this study, the retelling of an individual or collectivity's past (and these are rarely independent of one another) is less a flight from contemporary reality than an indictment of it, and of the circumstances that gave rise to it. The prominence afforded to the activity indicates the urgency that the authors attribute to it. Whether the medium for transmitting the past is written or oral, histories or stories—and the word in Spanish is the same, *historia*—the process is central to the South and Spanish America's tasks of defining themselves in their own terms. These regions' dialogue with the historical record plays a key role in wresting the past from the colonial and neocolonial powers whose needs have dictated—*pre*-scribed beforehand and *de*-scribed, as it were, afterwards—their own. The dialogue is a means of invalidating and rectifying the official stories and miswritten histories that have been imputed to them: the northern textbooks used in the South after the Civil War that were "built around the northern legend and that either ignored the South or insisted upon the unrighteousness of most of its history" (Owsley, 64–65); or, in contrast, northern publishers' elision of the South's history as a "conquered nation," in Caroline Gordon's words, publishing instead "novels full of white columns and magnolias" (Porter, O'Connor, et al., 13); the story of racism, "that part of the human truth which we could not accept or face up to in much historical writing because of social, racial and political considerations" (Ellison et al., 70); the "history of Chile that is denied by the official textbooks of the dictatorship" (Allende, "Writing," 57). Southerners and Spanish Americans alike self-consciously reclaim their histories by telling their own stories; they simultaneously challenge the versions presented as truth by a dominant voice and call into question the voice's authority. Some authors undertake to deconstruct history by tracing the process through which an official version of an event is construed and legitimated, while others augment it by recording experiences that had not been included. Like the narrator of Gabriel García Márquez's "Big Mama's Funeral," the authors who are the subject of this study aspire to pull up a seat and tell the true story of what happened to them, "before the historians have a chance to get at it" (127–28).

Storytelling is, additionally, the practice of remembrance. "Tell about the South," Shreve McCannon demands of his southern roommate in *Absalom, Absalom!* "What's it like there. What do they do there. Why do they live there. Why do they live at all" (174). Quentin's responses are emblematic of a recurrent phenomenon in these texts: through the telling of stories and the retelling of history, characters speculate as to why they are as they are, and how they have come to be that way. The stories function as bridges: they explain the present to communities of experience through reference to the past. Accordingly, all of the texts in this study alternate between two interwoven temporal planes, a frame tale, set in the narrative present, and an embedded story, the narration of the past, thereby situating teller and audience in relation to the past. Moreover, the protagonists of the frame are deeply implicated in the story being reconstructed; often, it is their own, personal past. This formal commonality is also thematic, for the very narrative frame functions as a structural analogue to memory in its reduplication of the texts' preoccupation with the past and its legacy to the present, in the reification of the resonance of the past in its very structure. The preservation of memory keeps the past—its spirit, its spirits, and its lessons—alive, whereas, as Santayana warns, those who forget the past are condemned to repeat it. Or, as the appropriately named Jack Burden tells his wife in *All the King's Men*, "If you could not accept the past and its burden, there was no future, for without one there cannot be the other, and . . . if you could accept the past you might hope for the future, for only out of the past can you make the future" (Warren, 435). Stories about history thus also offer the possibility of change.

Wars, racial and ethnic conflicts, changing orders, urbanization and industrialization, struggles against metropolitan powers, the worship of an idealized past, the perceived sterility and stagnation of the present— the bases of correspondence between the South and Spanish America are physical, spiritual, historical, and more. Each is acknowledged in the "similar sources" enumerated by Vargas Llosa in his ascription of the fascination with Faulkner to commonalities of ambience, change, and social tensions. "There are more specific reasons," he writes,

> for which Faulkner has such appeal in Latin America. The world out of which he created his own world is quite similar to a Latin American world. In the Deep South, as in Latin America, two different cultures coexist, two different historical traditions, two different races—all forming a difficult coexistence full of prejudice and violence. There also exists the extraordinary importance of the past, which is always present in contemporary life. In Latin America we have the same thing. The world of Faulkner is preindustrial, or, at least, resisting industrialization, modernization, urbanization, exactly like many Latin American societies. Out of all this, Faulkner created a personal world, with a richness of technique and form. It is understandable that to a Latin American who works with such similar sources, the techniques and formal inventions of Faulkner hold strong appeal. (*Reality*, 75–76)

While Vargas Llosa's division of Spanish America's cultural and racial constituents into two groups is questionable, the underlying message is clear: "The world of Faulkner was not his, in effect. It was ours. . . . He wrote in English, but he was one of us" ("Faulkner," 300, 302). Or, as Borges declared: "Rivers of brown water, disorderly villas, black slaves, equestrian, lazy, and cruel wars: the peculiar world of *The Unvanquished* is of the same blood as this America and its history; it, too, is creole" (Review, 123–24). So, too, Edwards: Faulkner "belonged to another world, but he wrote about things that had a profound meaning to us" (70). And, finally, García Márquez, who recently wrote to commemorate the centennial of Faulkner's birth that

> Ever since I first read Faulkner in my twenties . . . he has seemed to me to be a writer from the Caribbean. This became more apparent when I tried to describe settings and characters from Macondo, and I had to make a

great effort to keep them from resembling those of Faulkner. . . . A few years went by before I discovered the key to the problem; the Caribbean is poorly delineated. It is not a geographical area around the sea, but, rather, a more vast and complex region, with a homogeneous cultural composition which extends from northern Brazil to the U.S. South. Including, of course, Yoknapatawpha County. Within this realistic conception, not only Faulkner, but the majority of the novelists from the U.S. South, are writers possessed by the demons of the Caribbean. But it was Faulkner who showed me how to decipher them. ("William Faulkner 1897/1997")

This is, of course, an echo of his famous declaration thirty years ago that "Yoknapatawpha County has banks on the Caribbean Sea; so in some way Faulkner is a writer from the Caribbean, in some way he's a Latin American writer" (*La novela,* 52–53). García Márquez and his contemporaries found in Faulkner and his South a set of concerns with which they could identify. Yoknapatawpha County does not just share a border with the Caribbean, it shares a history as well.

CHAPTER TWO

The Case of the Fabricated Facts

Invented Information and the Problems of Reconstructing the
Past in *Absalom, Absalom!* and *The Real Life of Alejandro Mayta*

I n 1959, the Cuban Revolution ushered in a new era in Spanish American politics and life. The 1960s were a time of possibility. What took place on the small island in the Caribbean became a beacon, a source of hope for change and renewal for nations that had long struggled with the legacy of postcolonialism. Exactly a century before, in the U.S. South, another war had put an end to a way of life that had ordered society for many years. The plantation system was delegitimized, and the downfall of an economic order was accompanied by the breakdown of established modes of race and class relations. The transitions from established forms of society to new orders have not been smooth in either case, nor have they been fully realized. While blacks, abolitionists, and northerners welcomed the changes that ensued, many southerners channeled their resentment toward the North's reconstruction of their way of life into an apotheosis of plantation society that emblematized their efforts to retain their privileges. And although Cuba sparked a flame throughout Spanish America, it gradually became apparent that improvements in social conditions had been attained at the expense of political liberty and intellectual freedom. The changes accompanying the establishment of new orders have compounded and been compounded by racial and ethnic tensions and by difficulties of modernization, underdevelopment, and poverty that have afflicted Spanish America and the South alike.

War, revolution, and their legacy lie at the heart of William Faulkner's *Absalom, Absalom!* and *The Real Life of Alejandro Mayta*, by Mario Vargas Llosa. So, too, does the question of how these events are recorded and by whom, as well as how they are understood by the present. I have chosen to compare these novels precisely because they navigate between the universal and the particular, between theoretical questions about historiography and immediate concerns with the perpetuation of the past's harmful beliefs and practices. In his novel, Faulkner uses various (and varying) versions of the South's past to call attention to racism as a constant in the region's history as well as in its present experience. Similarly, Vargas Llosa moves from an examination of the roles played by individual interpretation and vested interests in the transmission of past events to consider how the dissemination of socialism has wrought havoc throughout Spanish America. In order to demonstrate how the fictional treatment of historiography is inseparable from the authors' concern with these problems, I will begin this chapter with an examination of how both authors call into question historical discourse's autonomy, objectivity, and truth-value. My argument, of course, presupposes the recent critiques of the discourse, in particular, those proffered by Hayden White and Louis Mink. Specifically, my premise is that Faulkner and Vargas Llosa explore (and explode) the commonalities of historical and fictional discourse: they foreground the sense-making process inherent in both types of narrative and how this teleological impetus shapes the interpretation and transmission of the past. I will also focus on how their approaches to this topic reflect both the political and literary contexts that inform them. The second part of this chapter probes how the novels use the question and questioning of History to explore their regional histories and the problems that plague them. Faulkner once declared that there is "no such thing as a regional writer, the writer simply uses the terms he is familiar with best" (*University*, 95). I hope to illustrate how—Faulkner's assertion to the contrary notwithstanding—he and Vargas Llosa avail themselves of the "terms" they know best precisely in order to address the difficulties assailing their regions.

On the surface—or, rather, at the level of structure—the novels might appear quite different. *Absalom* is set up as a family saga, while the narrator of *The Real Life of Alejandro Mayta* interacts with all levels of his social milieu, but appears to be relatively unencumbered by personal ties. Also, the former revolves around the reconstruction of an event that is, technically, not historical, and whose importance is circumscribed within two families and the lives of their descendants, whereas Vargas Llosa's novel investigates an incident based on extra-literary—that is, historical—events, and whose impact is seen to reverberate throughout Peru and Spanish America. Nevertheless, *The Real Life of Alejandro Mayta* is not entirely devoid of personal implications in past events; nor is Faulkner's foregrounding of the personal and social altogether different from Vargas Llosa's exploration of political events and ideologies and their social consequences.

On the one hand, Vargas Llosa's novelist-narrator chooses to investigate the incident that he identifies as precipitating Spanish America's descent into social chaos and political violence precisely because it represented the culmination of the Marxist dreams of his youth. By casting the fictionalized Mayta of the first nine chapters of the novel as a former classmate, the narrator displaces his long-abandoned goals—as well as the responsibility for having acted upon them—onto someone that he might have been. On the other hand, *Absalom* is generally read as a novel about southern history as much as it is about personal experience. Faulkner's depiction of the Sutpen and Compson families is in keeping with that of the Civil War novel of the Southern Renaissance, in which the fate of the family was seen as "emblematic of the decline of the South since the war" (Pilkington, 358). Moreover, the event around which Faulkner's novel revolves, the fratricide that Henry Sutpen commits in order to prevent his miscegenated half-brother from marrying their "pure-blooded" sister, is inextricably bound up with issues relating to the South's secession and to its defeat, as well as to the aftermath thereof. Also, since the early decades of the nineteenth century, the desire for racial purity and segregation that had for many years been part of the fabric of white southern society had had an additional political charge. As Barbara Ladd details, it was strengthened by the fear induced by the violent overturning of the French colonial government in Haiti by blacks and mulattoes, as well as by domestic tensions arising contemporaneously from the incorporation of the Louisiana Territory (which had followed an assimilationist policy under French rule) into the increasingly segregationist U.S. These sentiments were re-evoked and reduplicated in the postbellum U.S.'s attitude toward a region that it viewed as morally "contaminated" both by the fact of slavery and by contact with the slaves themselves (see especially 347–55, 358–59). In effect, the political dispossession to which white southerners were subjected derived from a reapplication of the policies that the U.S. had used to marginalize the Creoles of color in Louisiana following its acquisition, in addition to paralleling those that the southerners themselves had used to disempower blacks in their own territory (354). Many of these issues carry over until Quentin's day, when the prospect of political equality for blacks was on the horizon, and social equality and assimilation were viewed with trepidation by many as the next step.

As I shall explore further presently, Faulkner and Vargas Llosa examine these social and political legacies by interweaving the narrative present and past. The relationship between these planes differs slightly in the two novels. In *Absalom*, it is marked by a lack of change: Thomas Sutpen insists on perpetuating the values of an order that has fallen during his lifetime, an effort that explains the survival of those values until Quentin's day. Sutpen's rise and fall and Bon's murder thus encapsulate the dynamics of the South's history and politics even as they stand in contiguous relationship to those characterizing the present. In Vargas Llosa's novel, in contrast, the relationship between past and present is one of continuity and causality: Mayta's rebellion both lays the foundation for change and initiates the trajectory that leads directly to the violence which ultimately spreads throughout Spanish America. Regardless of the mechanism bridging the temporal planes, however, both novels' juxtaposition of past and present situates the actions of their central characters in direct relation to a present that they have in some way brought about; the question of responsibility that this entails will be explored further in the second part of this chapter.

"What Happened": The Missing Plot and the Historiographical Enterprise

Absalom, Absalom! and *The Real Life of Alejandro Mayta* are arranged as investigations into an incident that was a turning point in the past, yet which, years later, remains unexplained. Consequently, they alternate between two interwoven temporal and narrative planes. The work of detection, the frame tale, takes place in the narrative present; it details the search to explain the enigma of the embedded story, that is, of the past. In this way, the two-tiered structure and plot replicate the conditions of a historical investigation: like the historian, the character-narrators compile, compare, and attempt to organize information from various sources in order to reconstruct an episode in the past. Unlike historical discourse, however, the novels refrain from synthesizing the multiple and divergent interpretations of the events that they present. They also decline (at least on the surface, as we shall see) to authorize a definitive version of what happened and instead offer what might be called a Rorschach test of history. This final irresolution undermines traditional detective-story expectations of a successful search for answers and challenges the notion of an omniscient narrator who knows (and provides) them; it also casts doubt on historical narrative's presumed truth-value by bringing to light truths that are hidden, as well as by suggesting that either there is no single truth to be discovered in the past or that it is forever inaccessible, distorted by the passage of time and subjective factors. Additionally, the fact that any single, ordered description of the past must be synthesized by the reader draws attention to the role of human participation in the writing of history. Both the obstacles facing historiographers and the histories themselves also have a decidedly regional component, for Faulkner and Vargas Llosa address concerns directly relevant to the regions in which they situate their novels. Thus the process of mediation, of filtering and selecting data, which generally prevents historical discourse from being immediately referential, is further determined by the individual informant and his or her sociohistorical context. As we shall see, the details that each source remembers and even perceives are conditioned by personal factors, cultural taboos, and the political climate.

When Yeats wrote in 1921 that "things fall apart, the center cannot hold," he expressed a sentiment shared by the generation writing in the years following the First World War. In "The Second Coming," he speaks of the apocalyptic ending of one cycle of history, the disintegration of the civilization of his time, and the advent of a new one. The modernist movement, as we have seen, was in part a response to a chaotic world in which traditional authorities no longer held all the answers: writers sought to construct a refuge out of art and controlled artistry. As Wallace Stevens wrote: "In an age of disbelief . . . it is for the poet to supply the satisfactions of belief in his measure and his style." The representation of the past in Faulkner's novels responds to many of these concerns, as well as to themes addressed by southern writers during the same years.

Like many other modernists, Faulkner sought to distill timeworn truths of human experience—his "universal verities"—from the distractions and disillusionments of everyday life. Identifying what seemed to be constants in human experience, continuities between past and present, was a means of countering the disruptions of history. Hence Faulkner's understanding of time as "a fluid condition which has no existence except in the momentary avatars of individual people. There is no such thing as *was*—only *is*. If *was* existed there would be no grief or sorrow" (Interview by Stein, 255).

The stylistic innovations of Euro-American modernism were consubstantial with Faulkner's subject matter and themes. Stream of consciousness posed alternatives to causality and chronological order as means of structuring and linking events, while the subjectivization of narrative in general reflected the loss of a shared platform from which to understand reality. Faulkner's use of what Wolfgang Iser calls an "oppositional arrangement of perspectives" is a stylistic analogue to his preference for suggestion over direct commentary and authorial—authoritative—guidance (100–102). In fact, Faulkner used to say that he opened *The Sound and the Fury* with Benjy's perspective precisely because the latter's mental capacity limited his grasp of reality to effects, to perceiving *what* was happening without understanding *why*; the reader is thus left to piece together the tale from the information presented by the four narrators. And when, as in *Absalom*, the direct frame of reference for reconstructing the past is both the nuclear family, with implicit references to the broader social context, and the battlefields of southern history, the very refusal to provide a final explanation of what has happened also calls into question the figure of the "Narrator as Nobody," the unindividuated perspective which, in historical discourse, is nevertheless omniscient and authorized to speak the truth.[1] The novel further questions authority by entrusting narratee and reader alike with the authorial task of making sense, of transforming the faded letters and the mouth-to-mouth tales of the past into a coherent narrative that stands (in) for "History." *Absalom* might, in Faulkner's words, present "thirteen ways of looking at a blackbird," but it is only the "fourteenth image of that blackbird," the one configured by the reader, that the author considers the "truth" (*University*, 273). Imagination and interpretation are thus given license to compensate for the lack of a voice that controls all knowledge.

And yet, Faulkner's claim to a universalizing humanism—his resistance of the label of "southern writer," his claim to focus on what he considered essential qualities of human behavior, and his assertions that regional history was important for what it revealed about human nature in general—is belied by the fact that his depiction of the South's turbulent past and present is highly specific. On the one hand, the treatment of personality and historical issues in *Absalom* does mirror his Bergsonian view of time as a seamless continuum in which past and future form part of the present moment. As Miss Rosa remarks of Charles Bon's death: "That was all. Or rather, not all, since there is no all, no finish; it is not the blow we suffer from but the tedious repercussive anti-climax of it" (*Absalom*, 1972, 150). Also, the novel problematizes the notion of the subject as a discrete, unique individual by casting him as the sum of his past. Quentin Compson is the quintessential "momentary avatar" of an individual: he is not "an entity," but, rather, "a commonwealth," "an empty hall echoing with sonorous defeated names" (12). And history is not a unidirectional vector composed of discrete, causally related events, but, rather, a cycle in which archetypal master plots such as love, war, and the Fall are acted out time and again, varying only in circumstantial details. On the other hand, although his regionalism invokes the world outside the South, the universal within the particular, it simply cannot be reduced to a microcosm of the general upheavals of recent history. After all, Faulkner also believed that the southerner writes about himself through his environment. The local details in his descriptions of Yoknapatawpha County evoked a determinate regional actuality, history, and set of experiences. He once commented that *Absalom, Absalom!* was about race, "a manifestation of a general racial system . . . a constant general condition in the South" (*University*, 94). Examining this "general racial system" in a specific, southern context allowed him to write about universal verities in the terms that he knew best without ever losing sight of the dynamics of racism in his South.

Much has been written on the different attitudes shaping the characters' interpretations of Bon's murder in *Absalom, Absalom!* Olga Vickery was one of the first critics to detail how each character structures his or her telling of the Sutpen family history according to the conventions of a different narrative genre and how each account reflects a different personal bias. She characterizes Miss Rosa's tale—her "demonizing"—as a gothic mystery, Mr Compson's as a Greek tragedy, and Quentin and Shreve's as a poetic drama of love (87). Lynn Levins modifies the latter classification, claiming that the boys' version is a composite of the chivalric romance and the southwestern tall tale.[2] While these categorizations tend toward the schematic, the principle motivating the division is extremely important, for it foregrounds the manner in which each narrator ascribes the events in question to entirely different ordering forces—whether God, Fate, or Fortune—and thus endows them with disparate meanings. As Richard Gray observes, "It is almost impossible to separate the meaning of the story from its medium of communication, the various narrative and linguistic frames within which it is set. . . . The different perspectives offered by the narrators furnish a means of definition and ultimately the standard of judgment also" (243). And while the novel dramatizes the search for the plot, for the personal dynamics that lead up to the murder (which are ultimately social as well), it is up to the reader to ascertain the motivations behind the variant emplotments (Levins, 35). The fact of Bon's murder is agreed on (for the most part), but its explanation and significance vary depending on the narrator. The characters know what happened but not why: they know who committed the crime, but they have no definitive motive—or, rather, given the many irreconcilable interpretations of the events, they have too many, but none that provides a satisfactory explanation. In addition to the characters, a third-person narrator also appears and reappears throughout the novel; like Miss Rosa's voice, it does not "cease," but just "vanish[es]," blending into and focalizing the characters' discourses (*Absalom*, 1972, 8). Like the other narrators, even this sometimes-omniscient perspective may be highly speculative, qualifying its statements with phrases emphasizing conjecture or a lack of knowledge[3] and thus underscoring the author's refusal to endorse a single interpretation of the past.

The perspectivist approach also illustrates how a character-narrator's degree of involvement in the action further influences his or her reconstruction of what happened, as can be seen in Miss Rosa's account, which opens the novel, and that of Mr Compson.[4] Of the novel's four direct narrators, Rosa is the only one to have actually played a role (several roles, in fact) in the story being reconstructed: she is Sutpen's sister-in-law and erstwhile fiancée, guardian of his daughter, inhabitant of his home, and pallbearer of Charles Bon. She is in the best position to illustrate how Sutpen's life was the one constant of the past, the axis around which all other lives organized themselves, adopting his trajectory as their own: "he was all we had, all that gave us any reason for continuing to exist" (154). And yet, as a result of her proximity to the events, she suffers from what Joseph Reed refers to as the "participant's handicap as narrator" (161), and what I would further specify as the participant's handicap as narrator of historical discourse. Rosa experiences events viscerally, later remembering them through a memory that is "not mind, not thought," but the brain "recall[ing] just what the muscles grope for" (*Absalom*, 1972, 143). Consequently, she is unable to distance herself and organize her experiences, or to recount them objectively.

At the same time, however, Miss Rosa's relation to key events and personages in the story is curiously secondary (Brooks, 295). Her description of Bon's murder—"I heard an echo but not the shot" (*Absalom*, 1972, 150)—is paradigmatic of her remove from the novel's action in general. Her entire existence is a series of negatives and deprivations: she never sees Bon although she loves him through Judith; upon his death, she becomes, like her niece, a widow without first having been a bride; nor does she marry Sutpen—her own "nothusband" (7)—or bear his child. Consequently, her access to information is also indirect and vicarious. And this denial of the muscle-memory that might otherwise provide some evidence of the past's truth leads her to doubt one of the few empirically verifiable facts available to her, Bon's very existence, the parameters of which are engraved on his tombstone. "I never saw it," she tells Quentin, "I do not even know of my own knowledge that Ellen ever saw it, that Judith ever loved it, that Henry slew it: so who will dispute me when I say, Why did I not invent, create it?" (147). "For all I was allowed to know," she adds, "we had no corpse; we even had no murderer. . . . [Bon] was absent, and he was; he returned and he was not; three women put something into the earth and covered it, and he had never been" (152–53). Outside and inside the vortex of Sutpen's life, then, her knowledge is either too immediate and subjective or too secondhand and contingent to stand as "fact." And yet, her attitude remains resolute: regardless of whether or not she can substantiate her accusations, she blames Sutpen in no uncertain terms for all the ills that have befallen her, her family, and the entire region. After all, according to Quentin she tells the story so that people will "know at last why God let us lose the War: that only through the blood of our men and the tears of our women could He stay this demon and efface his name and lineage from the earth" (11).

In contrast, Mr Compson, a member of the generation that came of age in the years following the Civil War, faces the challenge of resurrecting a motive from exclusively secondary sources: his father's retelling of Sutpen's story and Bon's letter to Judith. His narrative pinpoints Sutpen's rejection of Bon as a suitor as the turning point that resulted in the destruction of the design because it motivated Henry's renunciation of his birthright and subsequent disappearance, leaving the patriarch without a legitimate male heir. And yet, Mr Compson senses that the reason he adduces to explain Sutpen's action, Bon's octoroon mistress,

> just does not explain. Or perhaps that's it: they dont explain and we are not supposed to know . . . Judith, Bon, Henry, Sutpen: all of them. They are there, yet something is missing; they are like a chemical formula . . . you bring them together in the proportions called for, but nothing happens; you re-read . . . making sure that you have forgotten nothing, made no miscalculation; you bring them together again and again nothing happens: just the words, the symbols, the shapes themselves, shadowy inscrutable and serene, against that turgid background of a horrible and bloody mischancing of human affairs. (100–101)

Even allowing for the "curious lack of economy between cause and effect" that governs the Sutpen family history, Mr Compson simply cannot understand why Henry murdered Bon (119). This is, in effect, because although his deductions have produced what are, in the end, the cornerstones of Quentin and Shreve's reconstruction of events, he *has* miscalculated and brought them together in the wrong proportions—or, in this case, with the wrong referents: incest is an issue, but between Judith and Bon, not Henry and Judith as mediated by Bon. More importantly, the threat of miscegenation impinges directly upon Judith and Bon's relationship, not indirectly, by way of the octoroon mistress. Mr Compson's logical, analytical approach to putting together the pieces of history might be the opposite extreme from Miss Rosa's subjectivization of experience, but it, too, fails to account for human behavior (Fowler, 41). Only Quentin and Shreve's joint endeavor proves capable of finding—rather, constructing—a version of history that *does* explain. Only their dialogue, in conjunction with the facts that they create and invent, temporarily bridges the extremes of emotional involvement in history, the distance and the irremediable immersion separating Canadian and southerner.

Despite Vargas Llosa's profound interest in and extensive scholar-ship on chivalric romances and the traditional realist novel, Faulkner represents for him "the paradigm of novelists" (*Reality,* 75). As we have seen, modern Spanish American fiction has drawn heavily upon Euro-American modernist techniques. Vargas Llosa's works and style have, from the earliest years of his career, offered evidence of the move-ment's profound impact. Multiple narration and his trademark *vasos comunicantes* (communicating vessels), for example, are stylistic devices in the modernist tradition that challenge the notion of an omniscient narrator and break away from traditional representations of space and linear time. At the same time, Vargas Llosa and his contemporaries defy those who would like to affirm a clear distinction between modernism and postmodernism. Writers whose sensibilities were profoundly influ-enced by modernism in the earlier stages of their careers have contin-ued to write in and draw upon an intellectual atmosphere characterized by an ever-increasing distrust of the ability of history and language to function representationally. Modernism's problematization of literary realism has been compounded by directing skepticism toward discur-sive referentiality at fiction as well as history. This attitude has height-ened the metafictitious and self-conscious dimension of Vargas Llosa's work, and induced him to turn his attention toward the process of textualization and the factors conditioning it, as well as toward the events being recorded.

Vargas Llosa insists that history and fiction alike are narrative con-structs that cannot mimetically reproduce reality. It is helpful to approach *The Real Life of Alejandro Mayta* as an example of what Linda Hutcheon has described, in her *Poetics of Postmodernism*, as historiographic metafic-tion (see especially 105–57). Hutcheon asserts that texts in this post-modern mode demonstrate how both history and fiction are discursive: both dramatize the active role of language and narrative form in medi-ating experience; both organize events into a causal sequence or frame-work to endow them with meaning. As in *The Real Life of Alejandro*

Mayta, such novels trace a narrator's efforts at collecting information and trying to make sense of a past event—in other words, at undertaking the historian's task—while at the same time reflecting on this process. This emphasis on human interference—the figure of the "Narrator as Somebody," as it were—challenges history's presumption of objectivity and unmediated referentiality, as well as the truth-value that it claims distinguishes it from fiction. By interweaving historical subject matter and self-conscious aesthetic discourse, the enunciated and the act of enunciation, "fact" and fiction, these works stress the discursivity of the object depicted but also affirm that art is a part of and a participant in the world of history and politics.

Although he draws attention to narrative's non-representationality, Vargas Llosa's deeply rooted belief in the need for the writer's commitment to the public good nevertheless precludes him from adopting a nihilistic stance that would deprive his work of social relevance. On the contrary, he claims that readers in Spanish America

> are accustomed to considering literature as something intimately associated with living and social problems, the activity through which all that is repressed or disfigured in society will be named, described, and condemned. They expect novels, poems, and plays to counterbalance the policy of disguising and deforming reality that is current in the official culture and to keep alive the hope and spirit of change and revolt among the victims of that policy. ("Social Commitment," 459)

His problematization of historical discourse thus converges with his demand for historical revisionism, for rewriting Spanish America's past within an autochthonous paradigm, and for restoring to the public domain experiences which have been elided. Like Faulkner's foregrounding of the universal dimension of his work, the Peruvian's claim that his goal in *The Real Life of Alejandro Mayta* was not a political exposé but, rather, the creation of an "illusory feeling of reality," is a smoke screen (*Reality,*

144). The novel traces how Mayta inadvertently constructs an illusory reality through his attempts to transform his revolutionary ideology into a concrete plan of action and then watches the plan backfire. By demonstrating the impracticability of ideology, Vargas Llosa also claimed that he hoped to prove in *The Real Life of Alejandro Mayta* his conviction that Marxist ideology and socialist practice have been a cause of Spanish America's underdevelopment and injustice, rather than a means of correcting them. Thus he intended to reveal the mechanisms by which political philosophies such as socialism perform acts of verbal prestidigitation, creating worlds from words and misrepresenting the forces operating in history, thereby disempowering those who attempt to put the rhetoric into action.

The Real Life of Alejandro Mayta is composed of the testimony of many characters offering different insights into the unexplained failure of a 1958 rebellion in Jauja, in the Peruvian highlands. Where *Absalom* has an objective third person narrator whose sections blend into those of the characters and whose role is intentionally de-emphasized, the individual accounts in this novel are organized by a first-person narrator (or Narrator as Somebody), a writer and Vargas Llosa persona who is researching the uprising for his own novel. Various levels of time and narration weave in and through different scenarios. Critics generally identify only two temporal levels, past and present (e.g. Berg, DeGrandis, Reisz de Rivarola), but I would like to propose three instead. In the narrative "present" of 1984, which is ultimately revealed to be a construct, we find the novelist's interviews with his informants. Another level, set in the past and narrated primarily by a third-person voice, focuses on the preparation and execution of the rebellion. These are, presumably, excerpts from the narrator's novel and are generally interspersed with the interviews, pursuing leads suggested in them; occasionally, they contradict the given information or explore possibilities that raise doubts about an informant's credibility. The novelist-narrator's own meditations on the inaccessibility of the details and motives constitute the final narrative frame, also set in the narrative present. On this level, he questions the information gathered from his interviewees. He juxtaposes different versions of the incidents, points out their discrepancies, and voices his confusion as to which he can trust. These metafictional—and transparently metahistorical—sections also trace his creation of information to substantiate a hypothesis which will, in turn, make sense of the few undisputed facts in his possession. That is, they follow the steps in his transformation of testimony into fiction.

The narrator approaches his project with a postmodern skepticism about the accessibility of the past and the truth-value of what is labeled history. "I wonder if we ever really know what you call History with a capital H," an informant remarks to him, voicing his own doubts, "Or if there's as much make-believe in history as in novels."[5] He responds by insisting that he does not plan to write "the real story" but, rather, a novel only loosely based on historical reality and licensed to modify its details at will (66). As his investigation proceeds, however, he finds that even the basic facts are uncertain, for each deposition reveals details that call into question the veracity of the preceding ones; every question elicits many answers, each of which, in turn, raises new issues that are never resolved. "The more I investigate," he comments, "the less I feel I know what really happened. Because, with each new fact, more contradictions, conjectures, mysteries, and incongruities crop up" (139). What really happened at Jauja? Why did key players fail to perform their assigned duties? What was Alejandro Mayta's role in the rebellion—adjunct or instigator? Also, the narrator watches as his informants themselves puzzle over how an event may appear to have one explanation at the moment it takes place, while the subsequent disclosure of additional information, temporal distance, retrospection, and imagination may suggest other possibilities. To proceed with his novel, then, the novelist-narrator must first reconstruct the episode from the many contradictory interpretations thereof; that is, contrary to what he had planned, before he can write his fiction, he must identify history.

The validity of the narrator's data becomes more tenuous as he realizes that each narrative is tailored to portray the informant's actions in a favorable light. This is particularly evident in the accusations, partial revelations, and contradictions of the former members of Mayta's revolutionary cell, which exemplify the knowledge-destroying rather than fact-finding direction of the narrator's research. Both Moisés Barbi Leyva and Senator Campos disclose censorious evidence about Mayta even as they conceal their own involvement in the insinuations. Barbi Leyva describes Mayta as an idealist who had changed his allegiance from one faction of the Left to another throughout the 1950s in an abstract search for perfection, for the revolution that would put an end to all injustice. His assessment of Mayta's motives is not as neutral as it might seem, though. Later, the reader learns of Campos's claim that Barbi Leyva had ordered Mayta's expulsion from the RWP(T)[6] for being a CIA infiltrator. The senator hints that Barbi Leyva has edited his contributions to the narrator's investigation in order to protect the interests of the development organization that he heads and funds with donations from every political group on the spectrum.

Campos, however, has his own reasons for restricting the information that he discloses. "Sooner or later, the story will have to be written. . . . The true story, not the myth," he begins his interview, hinting at willingness to assist the narrator in his efforts (81). Yet his candor is immediately qualified with the declaration that this moment has not yet arrived. He suggests that Mayta had planned the almost-forgotten rebellion in conjunction with the CIA as a pretext for justifying an official repression of the Left. He supports the Peruvian Left's censorship of the incident from the records and fears that restoring it to the public domain now could only jeopardize his party and its move toward reunification, which he views as the country's only hope in the current political crisis. Campos only concedes to the interview, in fact, because it is for a novel, and fiction does not wield the same authority as a political report. Nevertheless, he protects himself by demanding that the narrator distort the information that he provides and honor his condition of anonymity. Yet the novelist-narrator surmises that political motives alone do not account for the senator's withholding of information, his hatred of Mayta, and his unsubstantiated accusations. Mayta's homosexuality at first appears to explain a multitude of unresolved issues. Campos attributes Mayta's supposed duplicity to it: on the one hand, he claims that knowledge of Mayta's homosexuality was the leverage that had enabled the CIA to co-opt him; on the other, he declares that being an "incomplete" person predisposed Mayta toward "weakness" and that treason was a natural consequence (95). In either case, he concludes that this social "deviance" is incompatible with being a loyal revolutionary. Nevertheless, the narrator remains unconvinced. Only in the embedded novel does the senator's personal reason for defaming Mayta become clear. Here, the reader learns that the senator had been Mayta's lover, one of those facts, presumably, that he tells the narrator that he would never reveal, "even if they were to skin me alive" (101). Both his integrity and his political standing would be compromised if it became known that he had been guilty of the same unacceptable behavior as Mayta.

Several charges are proposed to explain Mayta's expulsion from the RWP(T), none of which is ever definitively corroborated. Was he expelled for informing to the CIA? for attempting to enlist the support of enemy Communist factions? Was it his homosexuality after all? Or was all this just an excuse, a moral discrediting that provided his cell with grounds to refuse to participate in the rebellion? The issue is further complicated by Mayta's announcement of his expulsion as a self-imposed renunciation. According to Campos, the open letter that Mayta placed in the RWP(T) newspaper was "a fiction," while the Trotskyists' former enemy, Blacquer, explains that neither the sender nor those who published it believed its contents. Ultimately, however, there is no one and nothing to challenge it, since, according to the narrator, several comrades, despite critical discrepancies among their versions, agree that Mayta submitted his renunciation by mail and deny that a session was called to discuss his expulsion. The narrator's information is inconsistent on this point, confusing rather than clarifying the issue. He includes Barbi Leyva and Campos among these informants, but this contradicts their own testimony: Campos states that Mayta was expelled but decided to publicize it as a renunciation, while Barbi Leyva also vaguely remembers Mayta's departure as an expulsion. In the end, the letter is the only proof of his withdrawal from the RWP(T), and so, despite assertions to the contrary, its contents are the most likely to be accepted as fact. "That's how history is written," Blacquer and the senator alike affirm (89, 168). In spite of a lifetime of political rivalry, both men find common ground in their disbelief in history's omniscience, as well as in its immunity to ideological manipulation.

Politically motivated distortions of information are complemented in the private sphere by self-justifying intentions that make the testimony of other informants equally suspect. All offer nonincriminating explanations of their actions. According to the narrator, Professor Ubilluz and don Ezequiel fabricate excuses to avoid confessing that they reneged on their responsibilities. Likewise, Quero's former Justice of the Peace claims to have accompanied the rebels unwittingly, rather than as an attempt to escape blame when the police reached the town. Noting the careful elaboration of his informants' testimonies, the narrator despairs of ever determining what happened during the uprising. The truth has been buried: all the interviewees have interpreted the events of the rebellion from their own personal and political standpoints and, moreover, have come to believe their own concocted excuses.

The interview with Mayta at the end of the novel provides the ultimate confirmation of the inaccessibility of the past. After concluding his research, the narrator seeks out his protagonist's biographical counterpart, hoping that he will resolve once and for all the discrepancies in the various versions of the incident. To his disappointment, however, he finds that not even Mayta is a sacred repository of the truth. He, too, suffers from the participant's handicap as narrator and is subject to the same weaknesses—partial knowledge, the need for self-justification, the attenuation of time and memory—that afflict the other informants. "I realize that you know more about it than I do," Mayta confesses, ashamed, and defers to the narrator's more complete knowledge (295). The narrator can never piece together an incontrovertible version of what happened that day in Jauja. He discovers that there is no single, verifiable, or absolute reality waiting to be discovered. By the end of *The Real Life of Alejandro Mayta*, then, the two meanings of the word *historia*, "history" and "story," both of which are implicit in the novel's Spanish title, *Historia de Mayta: Novela*,[7] have become inseparable and indistinguishable, leaving the narrator and the reader tormented by their awareness of the always already-mediated nature of the past.

WITHHELD INFORMATION AND CREATED FACTS

Within the context of their searches for the past, *Absalom, Absalom!* and *The Real Life of Alejandro Mayta* exhibit a curious dialectic between the concealment of information and the imaginative creation of "facts" to compensate for a gap in verifiable knowledge. Narrative withholding in both novels entails the delayed disclosure or the suppression of critical information, without which the explanation of past events does not cohere. Since disclosure necessitates the reevaluation and reinterpretation of previously analyzed data, the technique may easily be seen as another strategy for problematizing historiography through underscoring the tenuousness of reconstructions of the past. Where the novels differ—significantly, as we shall see—is in the moment at which withheld information is restored or revealed and, additionally, in the reader's and character-narrators' access to these "facts."

In *Absalom, Absalom!* this narrative strategy has a social correlative. Charles Bon's putative black blood is the sense-making information absent from Miss Rosa's and Mr Compson's ventures at explaining his relations with the Sutpen family. What goes unsaid is the unspeakable:

the white southerner's fear of relations between a white woman and a black man cannot be admitted under any circumstances. That "something" that is "missing" from Mr Compson's historical-chemical formula thus corresponds to what is excluded by and from the social order. The absence—or absenting—of the possibility of miscegenation in Judith and Bon's relationship thus makes the first two emplotments of the story socially acceptable, but deficient from a hermeneutic standpoint. In effect, what James Snead has described as "withholding the black" is the literary correlative of Bon's social marginalization (see "The 'Joint' of Racism"): Bon's black blood is effaced from narrative and society alike. Moreover, he must for the same reason be eliminated from history as well before he marries Judith;[8] the southern myth of racial purity must be preserved. So strong is this impulse that it even takes precedence over the primal taboo of incest. Henry can "justify" Judith's incestuous relationship with their half-brother but is unable to reconcile himself to the possibility of miscegenation. More important than the fact that Bon is Henry's brother is the threat that he poses as "the nigger that's going to sleep with your sister" (358).

Bon's very person incarnates the potential for social chaos implicit in the mixing of races. Like Joe Christmas in *Light in August*, he displays no physical feature that would identify him as black. Both men challenge the division of society into clearly differentiated—because visually distinguishable—groups. They conflate and therefore undermine categories that must be kept separate to allow the white aristocracy to maintain its hegemony (Sherry, 73). It is thus no accident that it takes the collaboration of southerner and Canadian, insider and outsider to this legacy, to conjure Bon's racially mixed parentage. Acknowledging the repressed element or entity—restoring the black, as it were—makes sense of what happened and is indispensable to Shreve and Quentin's reconstruction (Snead, *Figures*, 141).

Quentin, who is immersed in a culture that is "always reminding us to never forget," is the purveyor of information, the bearer of the tale

(*Absalom,* 1972, 361). His heritage, an "entailed birthright . . . of never forgiving," makes it impossible for him to approach his material objectively (361). Mr Compson speculates that this same legacy is precisely what caused Miss Rosa to tell Quentin the tale in the first place: "So maybe she considers you partly responsible through heredity for what happened to her and her family through [Sutpen]" (12). Additionally, until Quentin takes an active role in history, breaking into Sutpen's Hundred and likewise into the story that he carries, he is also unable to question or alter it. He must accede to the authority of the tellers, the last vestiges of an older order, in both his passive listening and exact transmission of the tale. He cannot interrupt and may only listen reluctantly to the voices that sound like his father's or answer Miss Rosa with a mere phatic "yes'm" or "no'me."[9] Shreve, in contrast, is able to approach the tale of the house of Sutpen without Quentin's submissive reverence. Rather than a fixed ritual of authority, he sees the telling as "play," a game in which he must be allowed to participate (*Absalom,* 1972, 280). He punctuates his roommate's recitation with questions about what he does not know or understand, as well as sarcastic and (to Quentin) sacrilegious comments. Shreve's demands to be allowed to speak gradually transform the monologue into a collaborative dialogue wherein both boys listen, both talk, and, most importantly, both add and revise. In addition to refusing to accept the truth-value of the tale as it has been transmitted, Shreve's ludic approach to narration also challenges the presumption that the data used to reconstruct history must be empirical. Instead, it requires the conjunction of reason and imagination that best explains the past (Donnelly, 116). Comprehension of this point, and virtually this alone, prompts Shreve to mitigate his disparaging treatment of Miss Rosa with an implicit concession of agreement. "What," he asks, "was it the old dame, the Aunt Rosa, told you about how there are some things that just have to be whether they are or not?" (*Absalom,* 1972, 322). And so, together, the boys distill the Sutpen story to its essence, searching for the absolute in the contingent. As Vickery observes, the tale evolves through the various tellings "from the factual to the mythic, leaving Quentin and Shreve free to interpret, imagine, and invent so long as they remain true to what they believe is the spirit of the past" (87). The boys' account transforms the past into a timeless and invariable tale of love, holding at bay the overwhelming—to Quentin—fact of a world whose security and stability had long since vanished. Neither Quentin nor Shreve believe that the Civil War had been fought over the issues of race and nation, but, rather, between "two young embattled spirits" who believed that "wars were sometimes created for the sole aim of settling youth's private difficulties and discontents" (*Absalom*, 1972, 336).

For a brief while on the cold December night, then, the Canadian's playful attitude toward history briefly rouses the southerner out of his paralysis (if not entirely out of the racist preconceptions that are his heritage). The act of jointly elaborating upon the outlines of the past—of creating facts, actions, and "people who perhaps had never existed at all anywhere" (303)—allows them to transcend their differences and ushers them into a "happy marriage of speaking and hearing" (316). The final explanation of Bon's murder is not discovered in preexisting information but, rather, contrived. It is made possible by the synchronizing of details and difference—of genres, latitudes, and speakers—effected by the collaboration. In their joint narration, Quentin and Shreve "forgave condoned and forgot the faulting of the other—faultings both in the creating of this shade . . . and in the hearing and sifting and discarding the false and conserving what seemed true, or fit the preconceived—in order to overpass to love, where there might be paradox and inconsistency but nothing fault nor false" (316).

That is, the boys adopt the historian's methods of analyzing data and determining their relevance, but with significant differences. First, their reconstruction uses the information they have received in order to invent "facts" that will compensate for a dearth of substantiated evidence. In this manner, Shreve and Quentin establish Bon's genealogy, "create" Eulalia, her home, the lawyer, and the many permutations of her, his,

and their counter-designs for reinserting Bon into the Sutpen household; they even speculate that Eulalia and the lawyer may have created
Bon himself as an instrument for exacting the former's revenge. Second,
because they fill the lacunae and corroborate the boys' archetypal tale
of love, their fabricated "facts" are ultimately deemed true—or, at least,
"probably true enough" (335). Finally, in the course of their project,
Quentin and Shreve themselves overpass to love, to that "happy marriage" which brings them together and allows them to go beyond the
dry dust and factual constraints of history. Critics have commented
on the analogous functions of design making and storytelling as means
of establishing posterity in the novel (e.g., Brooks, 292; Donaldson, 23).
Everyone is involved, like Sutpen himself, in the battle against time, and
so all the character-narrators lend their voices to the transmission and
deciphering of his biography in order to "weave [their] own pattern into
the rug" and so be remembered (*Absalom*, 1972, 127). Yet neither
strategy is guaranteed success. On the one hand, Sutpen's design defeats
itself, leaving no untainted line of descent. On the other, there are no
guidelines either for telling the story or for mastering its interpretation (Brooks, 292). Nevertheless, the boys deign to transmit passively
the "rag-tag and bob-ends of old tales and talking," and instead fill in
gaps and tie pieces together (*Absalom*, 1972, 303). In this manner, simultaneously talking and listening, they transform the incomprehensible
monologues handed down by history into a more egalitarian and intelligible dialogue.

Narrative form's implicit promise of a final resolution dominates
the listener's expectations to such an extent that it prevails over the material that it emplots (Brooks, 303). The details that Quentin and Shreve
invent to compensate for the dearth of information and the hermeneutic insufficiency of the available facts are, in effect, by-products of the
needs of the plot (303). Since empirical evidence and logical analysis fail
to apprehend the meaning of the past, imagination is given free reign.
Perhaps, then, *Absalom* may be construed as dramatizing Faulkner's

statement that "fact is not too important and can be altered by law, by circumstance, by too many qualities . . . but truth is the constant thing" (Interviews in Japan, 145). Truth, here, is that which explains. As Quentin and Shreve proceed, they qualify their speculations less and less frequently, for the progression of their story presupposes and, indeed, depends on the "facticity" of previous conjectures. Their search for answers culminates with the discovery—or creation—of Miss Rosa's "might-have-been which is more true than truth" (*Absalom,* 1972, 142). They supplement history, in the Aristotelian sense of events that have happened, with poetry, what ought to have happened. The fabricated fact of Bon's black blood and the concomitant threat of miscegenation solve the mystery and render moot the distinction between what "was" and what "must have been." Because it provides a satisfactory explanation of the past, and because it is the offspring of the union that allowed the boys to overpass, their interpretation of the Sutpen family's destiny becomes truth, Faulkner's fourteenth blackbird. Closing the novel, it endures and prevails.

Although Vargas Llosa credits Faulkner with having taught him the potential of withholding information as a narrative strategy, he utilizes the technique in a very different manner (*Reality,* 51). The problematization of history in *The Real Life of Alejandro Mayta* demonstrates how political ideology as well as personal and social factors are responsible for the creation and withholding of evidence. The rebellion itself was deleted from the historical record. The informants' knowledge was limited to the duties that they were supposed to carry out. Additionally, their testimonies reflect twenty-five years of speculation, suppression, transformation, and forgetting of information: Professor Ubilluz contradicts himself, don Ezequiel lies, don Eugenio has convinced himself of his own self-justifying explanation, and even Mayta is unable to confirm whether or not the rebellion was sabotaged. The narrator reveals his own vulnerability to the tendency to interpret events to support his own political beliefs—to "fit the preconceived," as it were—when he tells how in the late 1950s, he and his fellow "café revolutionaries" had misconstrued news of grass-roots land reappropriations in Peru as the beginning of the organized socialist revolution that they awaited (128). Concrete details such as scenery and physical appearances might be reconstructed, then, but the desires and meanings motivating past actions may only be recreated. The past can be explained solely by dismantling the traditional opposition of history and fiction and affording equal privilege to their narrative forms (Muñoz, 108–9).

Unwilling to wait indefinitely for his questions to be answered "when history clears its books and establishes the truth" (*HM*, 281), when it finally reconciles the kaleidoscopic information and opinions circulating about the event into a single, coherent explanation, the narrator takes matters into his own hands and resorts to his imagination (placed at the service of his ideology) but deliberately conceals his fabrications from the reader—a technique that Gérard Genette has labeled "paralipsis" (52, 195–96). The invented data here, however, obfuscate rather than elucidate: paralipsis is compounded by paralepsis, the presentation of superfluous information which, in this case, is both false and misleading. This is illustrated most dramatically at the end of the novel, when the reader learns that Mayta's homosexuality, his friendship with the narrator, and, lastly, the apocalyptic political situation are the narrator's embellishments. The entire frame story as well as the embedded novel hinge on the truth of these data. The fact that they are fabricated invalidates most of the testimony furnished by the informants, almost all of the personal background that the narrator provides on Mayta, and, in fact, his stated motivation for writing about the rebellion in the first place—creating as a means of surmounting despair. The fact of fabrication also causes the reader to question whether some of the interviewees even existed. Adelaida's entire deposition, for example, centers on how her reaction to her former husband's homosexuality has determined the course of her life. Two of the three levels of narration are conflated: the supposedly historical present of research into the rebellion is shown to be as fictional as the novelistic reconstruction of the past, shattering all of the reader's illusions of referentiality. As in *Absalom*, the correlatives to narrative withholding and fabricated facts are regionally determined here. Above all, the invented apocalyptic Peru complements Vargas Llosa's criticism of the Spanish American Leftist movement. The fictional crisis is a speculation on the extremes of destruction toward which he sees the Left's strategies and its legacy propelling Peru. Thus, the narrator's novel condemns Mayta's project for the violence that it unleashes.

Within the shared recourse to the interplay between invented and withheld information, the novels differ in their relative points of fabrication and disclosure. Whereas the creation of "facts" is the final step in Quentin and Shreve's collaboration, and is simultaneous with their revelation to the reader, the narrator of *The Real Life of Alejandro Mayta* starts his project by fabricating data that he does not divulge as invented until the end of the frame tale. Additionally, the boys' goal is constructive; that is, they adopt and creatively adapt historiographical methodology to compensate for a lack of information and to resolve ambiguity. Vargas Llosa's novelist-narrator also relies and elaborates on the historian's catalogue of activities: "My job is to listen, observe, compare stories, mix it all together, and weave a fantasy" (123). His addition of the element of imagination, however, ultimately undermines the credibility of all levels of narration. The "something" that is "missing" in *Absalom*, the withheld invented information preventing other facts from resolving into a coherent explanation, is inverted in *The Real Life of Alejandro Mayta*. Here it is instead something whose facticity is never questioned by the reader, and whose negation causes the preceding narrative to cease to make sense. The narrator seems to demonstrate, both in theory (his metahistorical comments throughout the novel) and in practice (his final coup de grace, the disclosure of the withheld information) that uncovering the truth of history is impossible, for it simply does not exist.

The relationship between the created and withheld information becomes apparent in both novels under the same set of circumstances: the meeting in the narrative present between the narrator and a protagonist of the events that he is trying to reconstruct. While the actual dialogue between the representatives of past and present proves disappointing, the "missing link" nevertheless becomes available as a result of the encounter (Brooks, 295). Quentin's conversation with Henry is brief and palindromic, disclosing nothing that might solve the mystery. Experiential knowledge, though, compensates for the inexpressiveness of words. Seeing Clytie and her "Sutpen face" during his visit to Sutpen's Hundred shows Quentin that the patriarch had fathered other children who were racially mixed. This allows him to deduce Bon's parentage and provide Mr Compson with an "awful lot of delayed information awful quick" (*Absalom*, 1972, 266). The exchange between Vargas Llosa's novelist-narrator and his protagonist has a dual effect on the information provided until this point. On the one hand, it discloses information that undermines facts previously considered true by readers, challenging their knowledge. On the other, it leaves the narrator feeling disillusioned precisely because he had expected (and not received) critical information. Toward the end of the interview, the narrator realizes that he has lost interest in their conversation: "I know I'm not going to get from my false fellow student anything more than what I've already got: the depressing confirmation that he is a man destroyed by suffering and resentment, who has even lost his memories" (302).

For the principal character-narrators of the two novels, then, fabrication is a potent tool in the reconstruction of the past. Creation in *Absalom* brings about the fusion of narrator and narratee, the storytellers and their subjects. Readers, too, are allied with Quentin and Shreve and watch over their shoulders as they jointly resurrect Sutpen and his brood and learn at the same time the "why" of what happened, the "fact" that finally allows them to explain Bon's murder. The sense-making capability of their creation supersedes the information provided by the narrative voice. In its silence, authorial power is transferred to those who were originally addressees of the story—narratee and readers alike—compelling them to assume a more active role in its transmission (Brooks, 303). The readers' access to fabricated information in *The Real Life of Alejandro Mayta* and, by extension, their role in the process of creation and their position in relation to the narrator are diametrically opposed to those presented in *Absalom*. Until the very end of the novel, the narrator's musings on his informants' lapses and lies, and on his own inability to extract a single satisfactory explanation for the rebellion's failure from conflicting testimonies, have led readers to believe that they are being included in the investigation and are privy to sources of accurate knowledge and thought processes. However, the final chapter reveals that the narrator has instead been creating, conjecturing, and concealing all along. It is a masterful stroke: the culmination of his knowledge coincides with and, in effect, brings about the loss of readers' epistemological certainty and the realization that they have not, after all, been joined with the narrator in collaboration. The narrator officially ends his investigation by accepting the power of fiction as a contingent form of compensation for the lack of absolutes in history. He has attained a measure of control over the past—and over his readers, as well—by altering what he does and does not know in the novel that he is writing. Readers, in contrast, have learned firsthand the power of discursive authority and the need to be skeptical of it. Left facing a void, the readers' task is just beginning. They must now review the facts and separate them from the fabrications on their own, analyzing and revising for themselves the information received from their informant. Or they may accept—albeit guardedly—the possibilities suggested by the narrator.

The Accessibility of the Past and Narrative Authority

I have found in one facet of Faulkner's *Light in August* what seems to me an interesting counterpoint to the quests for history depicted in *Absalom, Absalom!* and *The Real Life of Alejandro Mayta*. At any given moment in the former, each character has multiple conflicting and interrelated thoughts in his mind.[10] At the level of the community, knowledge is a compilation of many perceptions, often incomplete and contradictory, and subject to revision by the disclosure of new information.[11] The search for answers—in this case, for a killer—is a collective enterprise, undertaken to protect the interests of Jefferson's white society. Construed as "an anonymous negro crime committed not by a negro but by Negro," Joanna Burden's murder transforms a shared primal fear into a reality (*Light*, 315). To exorcise the threat that it poses, Jefferson synthesizes a single, self-justifying truth from many competing inner and outer voices: the townspeople accept gossip as fact in order to confirm their speculations about the killing and convince themselves that Joanna demands revenge from beyond the grave because the idea "made nice believing" (317). Their fear is powerful enough to bring southerner, "casual Yankee," and poor white together in defense of a common cause, as well as directing their actions toward a single goal, the elimination of the perceived destabilizing element.

Absalom, Absalom! and *The Real Life of Alejandro Mayta* likewise presume an initial state of disorder, the dispersed knowledge at the individual and collective levels that renders history inaccessible. However, where *Light in August* focuses on the configuration of a legitimating voice and the almost simultaneous execution of its commands, the other novels seek instead to impose order on chaos retrospectively by reconstituting the past events and the forces that had given rise to them. In a sense, the lack of a coherent plot in the embedded tale generates the frame story. This shared strategy, though, belies a fundamental difference in the novels' conclusions about the role of the narrator in the organization of historical and fictional narrative, as well as about who or what may replace the absent authority. Each would seem to respond— albeit from different sides—to the claim that the novel is a form of narrative that grants the fiction writer absolute power over materials, a power not afforded to the historiographer.

The final step in *Absalom*'s problematization of the referentiality of historical narrative is the disclosure of the information necessary to solve Bon's murder in the scene that is furthest removed from historical reality and most deeply embedded in fiction. The narration of both the bivouac scene and the preceding moments is apocryphal. Parentheses frame the former, setting it apart from the preceding text, attributable to the third person narrator; in the latter, the omniscient narrator states that Shreve has stopped speaking and that now there is "no talker," but it, too, gives way to an unidentified voice (351). Both passages are printed in italics, used primarily in the novel for a kind of indirect discourse and to indicate speeches by one character embedded in those of another. This typography, in conjunction with the fact that these scenes incorporate information that the boys have invented, suggests that perhaps they are transcriptions of Quentin and Shreve's wordless recreation of the confrontation between father and son. After all, their attempts to resurrect the past are said to have culminated in the brief moments when both are "thinking as one, the voice which happened to be speaking the thought only the thinking become audible, vocal" (303). In addition to the fact that the relevant data are presented by an unidentifiable perspective emerging out of the collaboration, this process fatally undercuts a basic component of historical discourse: the authority of the monologic viewpoint that structures and legitimates it. The anonymous but authorized "History as Nobody" here cedes before a narrator who is, truly, nobody. The boys' joint endeavor further challenges the genre's authority by annulling narrative conventions of time, space, and subject, and eliminating the distinctions upon which it depends. The act of telling transports the boys from the time and space of the enunciation to that of the enunciated. The segment's provenance is thus called into question both by the lack of an authorized narrative voice and by the fact that it is not, supposedly, even being told but, rather, relived: "Because now neither of them were there. They were both in Carolina and the time was forty-six years ago, and it was not even four now but compounded still further, since now both of them were Henry Sutpen and both of them were Bon, compounded each of both yet either neither, smelling the very smoke which had blown and faded away forty-six years ago" (351). What "WAS" and now "is not because it is dead" comes to life again in the resurrection of the bivouac scene, the only italicized, remembered episode of the Sutpen story narrated in the present tense (131; Donnelly, 118). The boys live and feel history; its transitions, turbulence, and pressures impact directly on their senses. Here the boundaries between characters, narrators, and narratees collapse, and the two boys are conflated, first into one another and subsequently into Bon and Henry, in preparation for a face-to-face confrontation with the man in whom they also existed. Purged of rhetorical conventions, and of the mediation of language, of words themselves, this section would have the truth of history become immanent, and the past once again immediately present.

These challenges to historical discourse are reinforced by discrepancies between the text of the novel and the appended historiographical materials. Some information in the chronology, genealogy, and map of Yoknapatawpha County—signed "William Faulkner, sole owner and proprietor" and therefore attributable to the "author" himself—is incomplete, while other material conflicts with that presented in the novel, not by the characters, whose knowledge is, as is already evident, fallible but by the omniscient narrator.[12] While these traditional schema for ordering time and space supposedly, because of their provenance and their situation outside of the novel's fictional parameters, fall within a domain of greater authority, they, too, fail to exhibit superior knowledge (Parker, "Chronology," 194). The author would thus seem to have fashioned himself as subject to the same limitations as his characters, to the same "barriers of circumstance and medium that make all authority suspect in *Absalom*" (192).

In its skepticism of historical knowledge and facticity, and its ostensible challenging of an authoritative, monologic viewpoint, *The Real Life of Alejandro Mayta* resembles Faulkner's novel. In practice, however, the conception of narrative authority presented here opposes that of *Absalom, Absalom!* as well as many tenets of postmodern aesthetics, which the novel had appeared to uphold. The narrator's machinations ultimately give the lie to the novel's polyphonic form, dispelling the illusion of a neutral transcription of equally valid interpretations competing for posterity. Although the narrator repeatedly declares that he, like history itself, is at the mercy of his informants, he nevertheless stakes a claim to superior authority and knowledge. As researcher and novelist, he controls his reader, synthesizes information, and filters the testimonies that he collects through his own perspective; he compares them and points out their lacunae and discrepancies. Additionally, his status as a Vargas Llosa persona "guarantees" his credibility. Although the author is nowhere explicitly identified with or as his character, as various critics have observed, his knowledge, opinions, and numerous biographical experiences inform both novel and narrator, narrowing the distance that separates narrator-novelist from author-novelist (Newman, 218; Castro-Klarén, 132). In effect, by authorizing his narrator's point of view with his own autobiographical—and authorial—authority, Vargas Llosa suggests the truth-value of his text. "History as Nobody" has given way to a narrator with recognizable features.

The careful arrangement of the narrator's discourse attests to his having assumed control over his materials. In both the embedded novel and in *The Real Life of Alejandro Mayta* itself, one scene blends into the next, collapsing the differences between characters and events that are distant in time and place, and seemingly (as in *Absalom*) actualizing the past: the narrator's questions in the interviews are answered by voices from the past, most frequently by the informant in his or her earlier role as participant; Spanish grammar's lack of a marker distinguishing between the first and third persons of the imperfect tense is exploited to create maximum ambiguity about a subject's identity; and, midway through the embedded story, the narration of Mayta's thoughts and emotions begins to alternate between an omniscient voice and a first person narrator, suggesting an incipient conflation of the novelist-narrator and his protagonist. The thematic parallelism between the juxtaposed scenes clarifies rather than confuses: actions and words in the embedded narrations suggest explanations and motives that are not given in the interviews. Also, despite the apparently unpredictable alternation between present and past, the action in both the frame and embedded stories is narrated in strict chronological order, with suspense increasing as both the rebellion in Jauja in 1958 and the current invasion of Peru build toward their respective climaxes, belying any impression of structural disorder gathered by the reader (Oviedo, 23). The scenes are not disjointed fragments but, rather, pieces in a puzzle that shed light on one another and explain the larger picture. Whereas in *Absalom* the manipulation of conventions of time and identity complements the weakening of the omniscient narrator's authority and the transfer of authorial power to the narratees, *The Real Life of Alejandro Mayta*'s subversion of boundaries reinforces both the author's and the narrator's power and their agenda (Newman, 218).

Vargas Llosa forsakes authorial indirection and, instead, endeavors to compensate for the uncertainty of historical knowledge, the lack of an absolute framework for understanding the "paradox and inconsistency" of experience, by offering his own message as constant and authoritative. And while the narrator faults his informants for lying and concealing information, he offers his own product as a constructive act, an attempt to make sense of the horrifying present. In effect, his strategy dramatizes the author's belief that "literature is always a contradiction of reality more than an exposé or chronicle of reality . . . what it presents as reality is fundamentally a fiction, that is, a lie" ("Maestro," 157). The attention given in the frame story to the act of enunciation constantly reminds the reader that this is a work of fiction and thus challenges the text's ostensible historiographical pretensions. The narrator also discredits history by defining both it and fiction in terms of their recourse to the same principal materials: "In a novel there are always more lies than truths, a novel is never a faithful account of events" (287); at the same time, all histories ("historias") are also stories ("cuentos"), for they, too, are made from truth and lies (118). Once again, the use of the word "historia," with its dual meanings of "story" and "history," in reference to both narrative forms further narrows the distance between them. What distinguishes historical and fictional discourses in the narrator's mind is not their relative proportion of truth and lies, but, rather, the former's claim of truth-value and the latter's overt rejection of any pretension to veracity.

Vargas Llosa holds that self-consciously non-mimetic works that deny their own truth-value—what he refers to as "literary fictions" (*Reality,* 149–53)—are nevertheless able to reveal basic truths. Specifically, he claims that they counteract so-called "ideological fictions," that is, they uncover the illusions propagated by political philosophies—namely socialism—which claim to describe society and the forces of history, yet which, in actuality, misrepresent them. He blames the failure of such ideologies to coincide with the objective world for rendering their adherents unable to correct the injustice and poverty that afflicts them. The analogy between historical discourse and Vargas Llosa's "ideological fictions" is evident in the false rhetoric of public records in the novel. I have already discussed the confusion surrounding Mayta's letter renouncing his affiliation with the RWP(T). An even more telling example of this, however, is the section interweaving text from the RWP(T)'s newspaper with the television broadcast of the current invasion of Cusco. The years separating the two texts are erased, placing them in a direct cause-effect relationship: the articles exhort the working class to rebel, while the news report describes the disastrous consequences of its having done so. Yet even the suggested truth-value of current journalism, which provides a corrective to the idealism of the 1950s by showing the underside of Communism's utopian promises, is immediately qualified: the narrator confirms that the reports of revolutionary activity in one town had greatly exaggerated—had themselves been "fictions," bearing no resemblance to the "real Quero." " I'm not surprised that reality contradicts these rumors," he comments, and continues:

> Information in this country has ceased to be objective and has become pure fantasy—in newspapers, radio, television, and ordinary conversation. "To report" among us now means either to interpret reality according to our desires or fears, or to say simply what is convenient. It's an attempt to make up for our ignorance of what's going on. . . . Since it is impossible to know what's really happening, we Peruvians lie, invent, dream, and take refuge in illusion. Because of these strange circumstances, Peruvian life, a life in which so few actually do read, has become literary. [13] (246)

Reality simply cannot be represented objectively, a situation that is aggravated when political interests are at stake. The sign of historical narrative has become irremediably estranged from its referent.

In contrast, the narrator uses the distinction between the two types of discourse to reassure his informants that he will transform their testimony through the addition of "a large dose of fancy" (81). "Because I'm a realist," he explains (using the term somewhat differently from its traditional definition), "in my novels I always try to lie knowing why I do it. . . . And I think the only way to write stories is to start with History—with a capital H" (67). This self-proclaimed "untruth-value," as it were, dovetails with the author's notion of "literary fictions," and his belief that it is incumbent upon fictional discourse to acknowledge that it has been codified. Qualified by the recognition of its non-referentiality, he declares that fiction may assume the truth-value traditionally ascribed to historical discourse. Literature may be a "lie," but it is nevertheless "a lie through which a deep truth may be seen" ("Maestro," 157). The narrator's novel, as well as *The Real Life of Alejandro Mayta* itself, are to function as antidotes to ideology's descriptions of reality couched as fact. Vargas Llosa's distrust of master narratives is thus directed at history but stops short of depriving fiction and its cultivators of authority. "Writers," he avers, "instead of being basically creators and artists must be above all politicians, agitators, reformers, social publicists, moralists. . . . For better or for worse, in Latin America, literature has for centuries been the only medium for exposing problems" ("Utopía," 5). In a backhanded way that constitutes a marked departure from postmodern theory, then, his "aesthetics of the lie" implies that the truth may be accessible after all: to the writer of fiction.

In the absence of an absolute, impersonal guarantee of truth, the narrator assumes contingent authority through and in his fictional text and his interviews. His capacity as a writer offers him tools that help to compensate for his uncertainty as to the cause of the rebellion's failure. By comparing the speculations, locating their incongruities, and drawing his own conclusions, he is able to identify the general outlines of the plan for the rebellion, purging it of the "web of distortions and fantasies" that had obscured it (*HM*, 237). And although he is unable to clarify the details surrounding Vallejos's death, he claims that he has heard so many hypotheses about it that "I know that no one can tell me what I don't already know" (*RL*, 269). Somehow, too, he can detect when his sources are distorting the truth. His role has gradually evolved from impartial—or at least non-contestatory—scribe to judge: he even challenges an informant with information from other interviews, accusing him of treachery in the past and prevarication in the present. Rather than affirming the historian's lack of omniscience and the fallibility of his products, his claim to actually *be* history— "I, in this case, am history, and I know that . . . time doesn't always let the truth come out" (253)—insidiously foreshadows his manipulation of his readers and materials.

Absalom, Absalom! challenges and expands traditional understandings of historical discourse and explains what happened with the assistance of another type of master narrative, the "old universal truths lacking which any story is ephemeral and doomed" ("Nobel Address," 120). And so the addressees of the Sutpen tale solve the mystery with invented details; they distill from it those constants that, unlike "facts," do not vary, and explain what happened in terms of the "old verities and truths of the heart" which apply to all and which transcend the passage of time. In contrast, Vargas Llosa's assumption of narrative authority in order to illustrate a historically specific point excludes readers from the process of literary creation. It precludes them from participating in the search for meaning—from finding their own "fourteenth image of that blackbird"—and instead renders them passive addressees of a moral tale: the story of how the rebellion "was the first of many. It charted the process that has ended in what we are all living through now" (59).

Sutpen's and Mayta's Designs: The Burden of History and the Question of Responsibility

And as he talked about those old times and those dead and
vanished men of another race from either that the boy knew,
gradually to the boy those old times would cease to be old times
and would become a part of the boy's present, not only as if they
had happened yesterday but as if they were still happening. . . .
—William Faulkner, *Go Down, Moses*

Although the frame stories of both novels call into question historical narrative's referentiality, they nevertheless hold sacred history's traditional role as *magistra vitae* and, moreover, rely on it to draw attention to issues that are of vital importance to the South and Spanish America. The lessons to be learned from the negative exemplary tales of Sutpen's and Mayta's great projects and even grander failures address both the object of their aspirations and their strategies for attaining it. The men endeavor, respectively, to perpetuate and change the prevailing social structures in their homelands by dedicating their lives to a single goal: the design and the revolution. For both, however, reality refuses to comply with their plans. When put into action, their calculations go awry and bring about effects contrary to those that they were supposed to achieve. In this demonstration of the distance that separates idea from action and theory from practice, they resemble Miss Rosa's initial description of the Sutpen family: when her words are transubstantiated into a visible portrait, something goes wrong, giving the image "a quality strange, contradictory and bizarre; not quite comprehensible, not . . . quite right" (*Absalom*, 1972, 14). While the failure of their short-term plans comprises the plot of the embedded stories, the lasting effects of the protagonists' projects give rise to the circumstances in which their reconstruction, the frame tale, takes place. The retrospective narration thus situates their actions in relation to the present, demonstrating the harm inflicted by the practices that they reproduce or initiate. Thus, although the novels' enmeshment of two time periods and stories has very different implications for the issue of narrative authority, it accomplishes a similar purpose thematically: by identifying precursors of their region's current circumstances in an episode in the past, Faulkner and Vargas Llosa acknowledge the burden of their history, its legacy to the present.

Sutpen's design operates according to an intricate dialectic of repudiation and replication of the extant social system, revenge by emulation, as it were. He hopes to acquire the same possessions and privileges as the antebellum plantation owner who rejected him, in order to let the "boy-symbol" of who he was into his own "white house" and thus undo the original affront (*Absalom*, 1972, 261). Paradoxically, the success of this act of inclusion hinges on instilling in his son the class awareness and race consciousness that constitute the basic axes of the Old South's plantation society. That is, instead of redressing the wrong, the design reproduces the very circumstances that made it possible in the first place: Sutpen may only gain entry to the system by passing on the belief that all people are not equal, the very belief that had justified his own initial exclusion as a poor white and thus precipitated the "Fall" which made him aware of his "innocence." As in evolutionary theory, then, ontogeny recapitulates phylogeny: where the elite of the plantation system refuse to grant equal status to other social groups in order to safeguard their privileges, Sutpen's monomaniacal innocence similarly allows him to ignore anything that might interfere with his advancement. Even when it seemed as if all options for transmitting his name had been exhausted, "it (the old logic, the old morality which had never yet failed to fail him) was already falling into pattern, already showing him conclusively that he had been right, just as he knew he had been, and therefore what had happened was just a delusion and did not actually exist" (279–80). His self-justifying "morality" is like a dysfunctional motor that induces him to pursue his plan unconditionally. He dies unaware that his design is as incapable of channeling reality as Mr Compson's chemical formula is of explaining it afterwards.

The West Indies serve as a precursor to the social structure that Sutpen strives to replicate. The "shifting sands" at the foundation of the South's social and economic edifices were brought over from the islands' beaches, where the practice of acquiring wealth through racial exploitation and at the cost of justice originated (260). Nature's attempted rehumanization of economic transactions does not, however, figure among the imported practices. Where nature in the islands had "held a balance and kept a book and offered a recompense" for the white man's reduction of precious human life to dollar sums, the protocapitalist order that Sutpen ushers into the South's society and economy is based exclusively on monetary exchanges (250). After the foundational crime, in Marx's terms, of original accumulation—contemporaneous with the mythical creation of Sutpen's Hundred "out of the soundless Nothing" (8)—each item required to accomplish Sutpen's design, "money, a house, a plantation, slaves, a family," may be assigned a price or value proportionate to the importance of its role, rather than to any abstract notion of intrinsic worth (263): hence the acquisition—in truth, the purchase—of the "proper" wife and children as if they, too, were live-stock or slaves. Even language is not immune to Sutpen's pecuniary cal-culations. Critics have preferred to focus on the reassuring description of it as "that meager and fragile thread . . . by which the little surface cor-ners and edges of men's secret and solitary lives may be joined for an instant now and then before sinking back into the darkness" (251). How-ever, Sutpen's description of

> the patois he had to learn in order to oversee the plantation, and the French
> he had to learn, maybe not to get engaged to be married, but which he would
> certainly need to be able to repudiate the wife after he had already got her
> . . . and how . . . he discovered that all people did not speak the same tongue
> and realized that he . . . would have to learn to speak a new language, else
> that design to which he had dedicated himself would die still-born (248)

suggests instead that the role of language in Sutpen's design has far more to do with acquiring wealth and power than with establishing emotional bonds. It follows that redressing injustice is also treated as a monetary transaction. The "conscience" which excludes Charles and Eulalia Bon from participating in the design considers Sutpen's "moral ledger" balanced by his offer of material compensation (297).

In the end, however, human life refuses to comply with Sutpen's cal-culations, for his financial agreements fail to satisfy the injured parties. Bon rejects the lawyer's scheme to translate his desire for vengeance into a monetary settlement because it operates according to the same financial ethics as Sutpen's morality. He wants neither the formal recog-nition nor the wealth that are the axes of the design, merely the "father and security and contentment" (340) that Henry has and he feels "his due," in the lawyer's terms, but which may not, after all, "be had only in exchange for hard dollars" (337–38). However, when the "boy-sym-bol" finally arrives at the "white house," Sutpen does not reverse the orig-inal insult but, rather, exactly repeats it, sending a "message" to Bon through Henry, "like you send a command by a nigger servant to a beggar or a tramp to clear out" (341); ironically, the one Sutpen child deemed worthy of inheriting (by racial "purity" and gender alike) is cast here in the role of "nigger servant." In turn, Bon exacts his revenge by precluding the fulfillment of the central requirements of Sutpen's design. His engagement to Judith threatens to taint the purity of the family line, and his friendship with Henry causes the latter first to renounce his heritage and, ultimately, to fail to perpetuate it. The design self-destructs, then, because financial ethics do not apply—and therefore may not be applied—to human relationships. That is, it fails when Sutpen tries to buy himself a legitimate male heir and to buy off those whom he has treated unjustly. Human beings do not behave like elements whose reaction may be predicted when brought together by a formula or equation. The business methods that Sutpen relies on to repay the debts in his "moral ledger" are the "logical steps" that pervert the course of his life, leading him to "a result absolutely and forever incredible" (263). His ledger, it seems, will never be cleared, nor will his design be fulfilled. Moreover, in the end, Sutpen is unable to compensate for the years "spen[t]" with—and on—his first wife (264). He loses his race against the one force necessary to accomplish his design that may not be purchased or controlled. Father Time, in the guise of Wash Jones and his rusty scythe, puts an end to his scheming, finishing the job that Bon had begun. And Shreve calculates instead that Sutpen's sole surviving descendent, the racially mixed Jim Bond who is doubly marginalized by race and mental capacity, will prevail. His illegitimate offspring will conquer the world, forever rendering impossible Sutpen's desire to establish a "pure" genealogy, and at the same time failing to pass on his name.

Absalom, Absalom!'s portrait of the South's economic and social practices, of which the "general racial system" that characterizes them is a by-product, belies Faulkner's claim that he is not a regional writer. It is impossible to overlook the centrality of the South's history to his work and, especially, to this novel. In 1951, in fact, Malcolm Cowley described the novel as "a tragic fable of Southern history":

> most of the characters and incidents [in the novel] have a double meaning
> ... besides their place in the story ... Sutpen's great design, the land he stole
> from the Indians, the French architect who built his house with the help of
> wild Negroes from the jungle, the woman of mixed blood whom he mar-
> ried and disowned, the unacknowledged son who ruined him, the poor
> white whom he wronged and who killed him in anger, the final destruc-
> tion of the mansion like the downfall of a social order. (Introduction, 13)

Vickery characterized Sutpen himself as "a mirror image of the South" and
adds that "his career in Jefferson merely repeats in a foreshortened form
the rise of many families whose longer tenure of the land has given them
respectability. Through his single-minded preoccupation with the 'design,'
he effects consciously and in the span of a few years what other Southern
families accomplished over a period of generations" (93). *Absalom* also
narrows the distance thought to separate the Old and New South. Sutpen's
reliance on the dehumanizing financial ethics commonly associated with
the New Southerner suggests the latter's kinship with the gentlemanly
plantation owner (Dale, 324). The treatment of humans as commodities, after all, is not new to capitalism but, rather, is the very cornerstone of
a slave-based economy. In the Old Order and the later, more openly mate-
rialistic, value system alike, one person's possession—whether of land or
of other human beings—entails another's dispossession (Sherry, 57).
Corinne Dale claims that "the destruction of Sutpen's family coincides with
and epitomizes the collapse of the Old South" (334). Given the overlap
in practices and premises between the two orders, perhaps the would-be
patriarch's downfall suggests the weaknesses of the New South as well.

Whether Sutpen's modus operandi corresponds more directly to
the values of the Old or New South, it reflects the values of a social organization based on racial inequality that did not change substantially
over time. As Parker notes, the violent response to the threat of mis-

cegenation within the family, that is, the fact of murder over racial issues, emblematizes the reasons for the South's involvement in the Civil War and casts a different light on claims of states' rights and the defense of southern nationalism (*Questioning*, 153). The public arena of war, in turn, indicates that Sutpen's actions were part of a widespread effort to retain privileges that were thought to be endangered (153). The Sutpen family is, literally, a microcosm of the "house divided" that pit brother against brother and father against son. The dialectical relationship between public and private spheres of action further provides a corrective to self-justifying explanations of southern history. The dynamics of the War and racial system alike, then, are "condensed and concentrated" in the representation of the Sutpen family. And the past, Faulkner believed, is never dead. The continuing vitality of these issues is reflected in Quentin's recourse to the miscegenation motif to solve the mystery; his choice is, as we have seen, both a regional marker, a reminder that the drama took place in the South, and an indication that racism is still a widespread problem in the turn-of-the-century South—and in the 1930s, when the novel was written, as well (Ladd, 361–65; Levins, 44). Even Quentin may only extricate himself with difficulty from the racist ideology that has alienated both him and the region that he calls home from the national ideals.

The revolutionary ideology that drives Alejandro Mayta operates in a similar manner as the morality that tells Sutpen that "he [is] right in the face of all fact and usage and everything else" (*Absalom*, 1972, 287). Mayta is an "armchair revolutionary," what Vargas Llosa calls an ideologue. He is also an anti-hero, a negative exemplary figure: he is politically, sexually, socially, and economically marginalized. His Marxist doctrine provides him with pat explanations of the mechanisms governing society that will supposedly enable him to determine how to change his circumstances. His plan of action is like a formula: provided certain conditions are met, the revolution will commence. Like the approach of the professors who had so disappointed him in his university years, though, his theory is merely "vain science, sterile erudition separated from life" (48). Mayta does not have the practical skills or the preparation necessary to carry out his plans: he does not know how to shoot a gun, nor, more importantly, does he have any contact with the masses, any means of involving them in the revolution planned for their benefit. Additionally, he has no strategy for redistributing power and resources and instead expects that reform will come about of its own accord once the revolution is underway.

The failure of the rebellion dramatizes the impracticability of Mayta's theoretical approach, that is, how reality refuses to conform to human calculations. "The plan was perfect," one of its organizers declares, but he cannot explain what went wrong, why key players refused to participate or simply did not show up and left the others unable to carry out their duties (144). And yet, even when the viability of the uprising is in doubt and the only revolutionaries left are a handful of untrained adolescent cadets, Mayta still, in the author's words, "finds a theoretical justification to move forward" (*Reality,* 153). His unconditional dedication justifies the recourse to any means that might spark the revolution and usher in a socialist government. Instead of saving the country, though, two participants are killed, and Mayta himself is incarcerated. Mayta thus exemplifies the power that Vargas Llosa attributes to ideology as a self-justifying force and dramatizes how ideology's estrangement from reality may make things worse. By basing his actions on abstract theoretical principles, Mayta fails to reorient history and implement a program for reform. Worse, his plan boomerangs: the rebellion sets a precedent for the use of violence as a means of effecting change. In this sense, Mayta's biography dramatizes the novel's (and Vargas Llosa's) premise that the Left has legitimized terrorism and, in the long run, wrought havoc throughout Peru and Spanish America.

The narrator invokes Faulkner's strategy of revealing the universal in the particular to explain why he has chosen to research the rebellion: "it's . . . possible that the whole historical context has no more importance than as decor and that the obscurely suggestive element I see in it consists of the . . . marginality, rebelliousness . . . which all came together in that episode" (44). However, his obsession with the rebellion's "precursory character"—"[It's] true that it inaugurated a new era in Peru"—belies this answer (44). Vargas Llosa, too, has a design in mind. The uprising in the novel is based on a historical rebellion that took place in 1962. The author moved the date back to 1958 for *The Real Life of Alejandro Mayta* so that it would mark Jauja as the spark that preceded and precipitated the Cuban Revolution, therefore making it responsible for socialist activity throughout Spanish America. The interwoven narration of the uprisings of 1958 and 1984 collapses two cycles of history. Events of the intervening years are elided from Vargas Llosa's record, causing past and present to appear to be cause and effect, action and immediate repercussion (Huston, 113; Zapata, 192–93). As in the aforementioned interweaving of newspaper articles and radio reports, Marxist ideals are juxtaposed with shortcomings of the reality of socialism and attempts to implement it; the condensation of time reinforces Vargas Llosa's contention that the Sendero Luminoso, which terrorized Peru from the 1980s into the early 1990s, was the culmination of the violence unleashed by the Left in the early years of the revolutionary movement. References to the events at Jauja as a portent of the present predicament trace an uninterrupted path of political turmoil from the rebellion to the fictional revolution, showing the narrator "how we have come to be what we are, why we are in the condition in which we find ourselves" (109). They also refute the narrator's claims that the earlier incident is of little consequence in comparison with the apocalyptic present. Additionally, as Roger Zapata has observed, the multiple perspectives comprising the novel's polyphonic form unanimously endorse the narrator and author's point of view (194). One informant after another traces the origins of Peru's predicament directly back to the "forgotten" episode of 1958. Rather than denying the possibility of an authoritative historical narrative, as is the case in *Absalom*, the multiple narration is synthesized by an unchanging point of reference that reinforces the author's political message at the same time that it obviates any voice which might challenge it. Despite the narrator's ostensible challenge to history's status as an authoritative genre, then, in practice he ignores its limitations and uses his thwarted research as a pretext for exposing the relevance of this particular event to the present.

Cause and effect converge in Mayta's person as well. His political trajectory as "In APRA, an APRA dissident; in the Communist Party, a Communist Party dissident; finally, a Trotskyist," is a metonymy of that of the Left in the 1950s (50). At the same time, as "an X-ray of Peruvian misfortune," he embodies the consequences of the movement's fractiousness and violent strategies (15). Mayta also exemplifies the intellectuals whom the author holds responsible for disseminating the Left's doctrine and carrying out its agenda. Writers and intellectuals in Spanish America have long wielded political influence. Many, Vargas Llosa included, have campaigned for and occupied important positions in government, while he, Isabel Allende, Carlos Fuentes, and Gabriel García Márquez, among others, are often sought out for their opinions on matters of social and political consequence. Their fame and prominence, their affiliations with official institutions and the media give them valuable opportunities to publicize their ideas. *The Real Life of Alejandro Mayta*'s revision of the past shows intellectuals putting socialist ideology into practice on a large scale for the first time. The novel's dramatization of intellectuals' aggravation of Peru's political predicament is a fictional expression of Vargas Llosa's condemnation of the Left's legacy and an admonition to be more cautious when making political propositions and pronouncements.

Thus, the novel's postmodern distrust of historical discourse is conditional: it only challenges historiography to the extent that doing so strengthens the narrator and author's position (Zapata, 194). The disclosure of the withheld information is a masterful blow that leaves the reader in a state of profound uncertainty as to which of the facts about the rebellion are "true." It does not, however, invalidate the problems plaguing Peru that are identified in the embedded story. The descriptions of the garbage piles, violence, and crime taking over Lima and the entire country are constant throughout the various levels of narration in *The Real Life of Alejandro Mayta*. These motifs forge a link between the embedded and frame stories, a continuity which is foregrounded in the novel's final sentence, the narrator's statement that "I'll remember that a year ago I began to concoct this story the same way I'm ending it, by speaking about the garbage that's invading every neighborhood in the capital of Peru" (310). The attribution of these conditions to the actions of the Leftist movement also remains undisputed. The difference between the "fictional" and "historical" Perus is one of degree, not kind. Both presents are marked—and marred—by the unforeseen consequences of past efforts to change the course of history.

Both Sutpen and Mayta attempt to program the future, one in the hope of replicating and the other of overturning a rigid and hierarchical social system. The long-term repercussions of their projects constitute the bridges that link past and present, the novels' embedded and frame stories. In both cases, the pressing issue of responsibility for the present takes precedence over the more esoteric problem of the inability of verifiable facts and causality to elucidate the meaning of the past. "Maybe nothing ever happens once and is finished," Quentin thinks as he listens to Shreve; "Maybe happen is never once but like ripples maybe on water after the pebble sinks, the ripples moving on, spreading" (*Absalom*, 1972, 261). Faulkner was less interested in history, in the Aristotelian sense of a record of specific events, than with the past itself, and with its encroachment upon the present (Millgate, "Faulkner and History," 26). Similarly, although Vargas Llosa deliberately foregrounds the general problem of discursive non-representationality, he never loses sight of local and regional issues in need of being addressed and redressed. His narrative strategies short-circuit standard causal and temporal conventions in order to foreground the direct bearing of the past on the present. In the final analysis, both authors avoid the nihilistic dispersion of historical discourse into non-referentiality, and of historical events into fictionality, by holding the past accountable to the present for its racism, suffering, injustice, and violence. History might only be accessible to us now in various conjectural and conflicting interpretations, but ultimately, so they affirm, that which was—or that which might have been—has determined that which is.

CHAPTER THREE

To See or Not to See

Invisibility, Clairvoyance, and Re-*visions* of History in
Invisible Man and *The House of the Spirits*

F rom Harlem to Santiago, from a race riot to women's rights, a socialist revolution, and a military coup d'état, the distance that separates
Invisible Man from *The House of the Spirits* might seem, at first glance,
unbridgeable. But perhaps the bond of commonality lies deeper than
the more obvious surface disparities. In a 1988 interview, Isabel Allende
hailed the end of the Pinochet regime with the simple recognition that
"[o]ne cannot keep the people oppressed forever and profit from that.
. . . It's unjust—as obscene and perverse as slavery ever was. And people have to get up and say 'No'" ("Responsibility," 123). The comparison of conditions in Chile to slavery is particularly suited to the subject
of this chapter, for the focalization of Allende's first novel through the
perspective of women in Spanish America coincides with Ralph Ellison's depiction of an African American's experiences of U.S. society—

both southern and northern—in that both articulate realities traditionally absent(ed) from historical writings that claim to bear the truth of the past.

I analyze the novels in this chapter as fictional works and as projects for self-empowerment conceived by and about members of social groups in the South and Spanish America that have suffered from injustice and inequality. Like Colonel Sutpen and Alejandro Mayta, the invisible man in Ellison's eponymous novel and the women of the Trueba family in *The House of the Spirits* are inhabitants of regions that have been relegated to peripheral status. While the former are posited as outsiders, men living in but not quite of their societies and striving toward the center, Ellison's and Allende's protagonists are removed yet again from access to power by race, class, and gender. If the white southerner felt excluded from the mainstream following the Civil War, segregation and other modes of treating blacks as second-class citizens exacerbated the plight of the latter. Similarly, the distance between women, denied the rights and privileges afforded to men, and the patriarchal hegemonic discourse in Spanish America reduplicates at an intranational level the region's remove as a whole from international centers of power. Blacks and women in these cases are not exactly barred from the larger social corpus, but, rather, "inscribed within it as *nonparticipants*" (Brenkman, 98; emphasis in original). The goal of this chapter is to delineate how, by telling the tales of such "nonparticipating" members of society, these novels endeavor to redress the invisibility of blacks and women in their respective regions. It is a task that Toni Morrison describes as "rip[ping] that veil drawn over 'proceedings too terrible to relate,'" and which she claims is "critical for any person who is black, or who belongs to any marginalized category, for, historically, we were seldom invited to participate in the discourse even when we were its topic" ("The Site of Memory," 302). I will first examine the use of nonrealist discourses in both works as a formal counterpart to their challenge to the systems that have marginalized these groups. I will follow this with an exploration of the novels' related and shared concern with finding a mode for writing history that will reinscribe these groups in the social body both past and present.

The question could be raised as to whether it might be preferable to compare works from the two regions in which *either* race (or ethnicity) *or* gender is the primary concern. One might, for example, compare *Invisible Man* to Manuel Scorza's *Garabombo, the Invisible,* a novel written in the magical realist mode in which the protagonist has been disenfranchised and literally rendered invisible by the centers of power in Peru because he is an Indian; like Ellison's narrator, he, too, tries to reappropriate his invisibility, transforming his liability into an asset in order to resist his oppressors and reclaim the rights of his community. Ellison's work might also be paired with another novel within the Spanish American indigenist tradition, *Deep Rivers,* by José María Arguedas, which also asserts ways of knowing deriving from a mythical, indigenous worldview over the Western perspective espoused by Peru's dominant classes. Alternatively, there are parallels in the notions of womanhood in the South and Spanish America that have yielded numerous similarities in experiences and roles of women, as well as in efforts to transform these, seen in the points of contact in the works of Isabel Allende and Katherine Anne Porter delineated in the introduction. And yet, I would argue that despite the divergent grounds for marginalization, the common experience thereof has, in the works that I discuss in this chapter, a fundamental deep structure that generates common surface manifestations and effects. These common grounds include similar strategies of resistance, of debunking official versions of the past, and for proposing alternatives, in addition to other sometimes uncanny structural, textual, and thematic parallels.[1]

For this reason, in fact, one finds in the social attitudes and literature of the South and Spanish America a long-standing tradition of what Michael Moon and Cathy Davidson have called a "concatenation of blacks-and-women" (4), a symbolic equation of the plights of these groups, which has also been extended to indigenous populations and oppressed classes. As Susan Bassnett has noted, the filtering of a critique of generalized social oppression through the depiction of women's lives is "a device that has been used by women novelists since Aphra Behn wrote *Oroonoko* in 1688 and compared the oppression of slavery with the oppression of women in the marriage market" (258). The use of this device in Spanish America may be traced back to *Sab*, the first Hispanic antislavery novel, published by Gertrudis Gómez de Avellaneda in 1841. In this novel, the author's abolitionist message was also an implicit and explicit protest against society's subjugation of women (Kirkpatrick, 158). In the antebellum South, many white women similarly found it difficult to support slavery and, indeed, privately came to oppose it, in large measure because they saw concrete similarities between the demands placed on them by the code of southern womanhood and the slaves' own circumstances (A. Jones, *Tomorrow*, 29). Consequently, as Anne Goodwyn Jones has observed, literature written by southern women often exhibits a strong critique of the denial of freedom and equality on the basis of race, gender, and/or class. The sense of common cause became even stronger in the 1960s, when the participation of white southern women in the Civil Rights movement focused attention on the parallels between sexual and racial oppression, compelling them to direct their energies toward what later became the feminist movement (22). While I treat racial and gender issues separately in this chapter, this tradition of concatenation, of the perceived coincidence of the fundamental sources and ultimate effects of inequality, in addition to both authors' declared intentions of exposing and eradicating them, underlies my choice of texts for comparison here.

Barbara Smith has argued that black women authors exhibit a common approach to writing as a result of shared social, political, and economic circumstances (416). It is this chapter's premise that, by virtue of the common experience of double marginalization, Ellison and Allende, too, participate in a broader but nonetheless similar "identifiable literary tradition." One of the predominant features of this tradition is to be found, as we shall see in greater detail presently, in the recourse to nonrealist discourses that are grounded in dual and dueling codes of reality. These, in turn, correspond to the "double vision" or "double consciousness" often marking the worldview of groups whose participation in both the dominant tradition and their own allows them to develop both an insider's and an outsider's perspective, to see the rules and ideals that the center claims to uphold even as they experience a reality where these do not hold (hooks, 341). W. E. B. DuBois first described the phenomenon as characterizing the African American's experience in an oft-quoted passage from his *Souls of Black Folk* (1903):

> The Negro is a sort of seventh son, born with a veil, and gifted with second-sight in this American world,—a world which yields him no true self-consciousness, but only lets him see himself through the revelation of the other world. It is a peculiar sensation, this double-consciousness, this sense of always looking at one's self through the eyes of others, of measuring one's soul by the tape of a world that looks on in amused contempt and pity. One ever feels his two-ness,—an American, a Negro; two souls, two thoughts, two unreconciled strivings; two warring ideals in one dark body. . . . (3)

Henry Louis Gates has claimed, in fact, that dualism is the essential trope of black discourse (313). Others have argued that postcolonial cultures are characterized by a double consciousness that stems from the displacement and replacement of indigenous languages by those of the colonizers, ultimately leaving the subaltern populations with only the medium (and corresponding structures of reality and possibility) of their oppressors with or through which to express themselves (Slemon, 411; Tiffin, 32), while others still have identified dual and dissenting perspectives within the context of gender studies and cultural criticism: Elaine Showalter has posited that a "wild zone" exists, uncodified, outside the dominant ideology, which potentially applies to all of the "muted" groups—racial, ethnic, regional and/or gendered—generated by each dominant culture (264); Gerda Lerner has commented on women's duality as a result of participation in both the general culture and their own (52); and Octavio Paz speaks of the Spanish American's eccentricity (or ex-centricity) as "a European eccentricity: it is an other way of being Western. A non-European way. Both inside and outside the European tradition" (quoted in King, 101). Within this framework, then, I would like to examine Ellison and Allende's novels as emerging out of literary traditions concerned with exploring how the burden of history has fallen even more heavily on certain groups within the South and Spanish America, alienating them from the structures of power and, in some cases, from self-knowledge; this focus will supersede the discussions of the frustrations and failures of a regional past that were so prominent in *The Real Life of Alejandro Mayta* and *Absalom, Absalom!*

To see America with an awareness of its rich diversity and its almost magical fluidity and freedom, I was forced to conceive of a novel unburdened by the narrow naturalism which has led . . . to the final and unrelieved despair which marks so much of our current fiction. . . . There must be possible a fiction which, leaving sociology to the scientists, can arrive at the truth about the human condition, here and now, with all the bright magic of a fairy tale. . . . Our task then is always to challenge the apparent forms of reality—that is, the fixed manners and values of the few, and to struggle with it until it reveals its mad, vari-implicated chaos, its false faces, and on until it surrenders its insight, its truth.

—Ralph Ellison, "Brave Words for a Startling Occasion"

> Authority is not always successful in its desire to tie words
> down. Forbidden words . . . are able to transmit ideas and write
> the secret history, the hidden and true story of reality. In Latin
> America, we have proven this.
>
> —Isabel Allende, translated from "La magia de las palabras"

As was discussed in the introduction, challenges to dominant descriptions of reality may be correlated with the recourse to nonrealist discourses, explaining the recent proliferation thereof in southern and Spanish American fiction. This is in keeping with a general tendency in recent criticism to associate magic realism with marginalized and postcolonial literatures. Stephen Slemon, for example, has argued that, as a mode appearing most prevalently in literary traditions that have been excluded from the literary and cultural "mainstream," magic realism provides a basis for comparative studies of these literatures (408–9). He identifies three fundamental characteristics of magic realist texts produced within this context:

> the representation of a kind of transformational regionalism so that the
> site of the text, though described in familiar and local terms, is metonymic
> of the postcolonial culture as a whole . . . the foreshortening of history so
> that the time scheme of the novel metaphorically contains the long process
> of colonization and its aftermath . . . [and] the thematic foregrounding of
> those gaps, absences, and silences produced by the colonial encounter and
> reflected in the text's disjunctive language of narration. (411–12)

Each of these aspects is present in both *Invisible Man* and *The House of the Spirits*; in both novels, moreover, the use of spatial and temporal frames, which are microcosms of the experiences of an entire marginalized population, intersects with the novels' key projects of rewriting history to restore what has been omitted from the official record.

The debate over magic realism has raged in Spanish America since Alejo Carpentier posited it as a literary correlative to the region's extraordinary reality, a mode able to elude realism's inability to describe an ex-centric experience.[2] It represented an indigenous and endogenous means of expression rather than one that had been imported and imposed. "The Latin American returns to his own world," Carpentier wrote, "and begins to understand many things" (83). The marvelous real was seen to emerge out of conditions of life on this side of the Atlantic. It was identified in cultural artifacts, rituals, and natural reality; it was also to be found in supernatural feats, further mythologized by the collective memory that preserved and transmitted them. The enumeration of its distinct manifestations was inextricably linked to ongoing efforts to characterize *americanidad*, what was authentically and essentially Spanish American. P. Gabrielle Foreman considers the dynamics of the black population in the U.S. to be similar to the multicultural, multiracial circumstances of Spanish America and has proposed that magic realism is a key feature bridging Spanish American and African American literature (370). Black writers in the U.S. have, in fact, often granted beliefs and events outside the parameters of Western definitions of reality a privileged position in their texts. Morrison, for example, avers that African Americans are "practical" but that "within that practicality we also accept what I suppose could be called superstition and magic. Which is another way of knowing things" ("Rootedness," 342). In *Song of Solomon*, she uses a matter-of-fact, non-apologetic style to naturalize these elements and draw her readers into the text and the beliefs that it presupposes, that is, into the "amplified reality" that she views as such an important part of African American culture (341; Foreman, 382).

Carpentier speaks of a marvelous reality; Morrison, perhaps echoing him, of one that is "amplified." Ellison challenges "the apparent forms of reality," while Allende records "incredible or magnificent facts—which, in Latin America, are not hyperbole, because that is the dimension of our reality" ("Writing as an Act of Hope," 45). Each of these authors also links the need to recognize otherly experience to the act of writing. "[O]ur crucial problem," Gabriel García Márquez proclaimed to the world in his Nobel Prize acceptance speech, "has been a lack of conventional means to render our lives believable. . . . The interpretation of our reality through patterns not our own serves only to make us ever more unknown, ever less free" (89). Each of them (and, as we have seen, many of the others who inscribe their works in the same genre) is motivated by the sense that the referent of supposedly mimetic realist narrative, as well as that of history, does not include the experience of groups that have been excluded from mainstream reality and deprived of its benefits. Thus does Ellison's invisible man declare that

> history records the patterns of men's lives . . . : Who slept with whom and with what results; who fought and who won and who lived to lie about it afterwards. All things, it is said, are duly recorded—all things of importance, that is. But not quite, for actually it is only the known, the seen, the heard and only those events that the recorder regards as important that are put down, those lies his keepers keep their power by.[3]

For these reasons, Ellison and Allende draw on "nonrealist" or un"real" discourses that undertake to correct biases in the recording of history and to carve out a space and mode for representing populations subject(ed) to the control of a center but not recognized within its perimeters. As part of their efforts to challenge cultural hegemony and thereby reclaim both their heritage and the present, they attempt to turn their outsider's vantage point to their advantage. Their protagonists' activism entails a search for justice and recognition as individuals with rights— a goal whose accomplishment will entail rearticulating prevailing social systems, renegotiating current ideologies, and redefining what these have labeled "reality."

Ellison excoriated the aesthetic imperatives of social realism, especially as they related to the depiction of African Americans.[4] He denounced the demand that protest and fighting ideological battles take precedence over art and craft, for the mandate to "express 'black' anger and 'clenched militancy'" does not permit the writer to speak of his or her personal experiences.[5] Moreover, he found that the presumed contiguity between life and art was often manipulated in such a manner as to aggravate the circumstances that social realism purported to combat. He claimed that realism's reliance on "facts" and exterior details denied blacks their individuality and, instead, reproduced skewed images from the stock comprising the white world's construction of reality. "To white Americans' claims to represent 'American reality,'" he wrote, "the Black American answers 'Perhaps, but you've left out this, and this, and this. And most of all, what you'd have the world accept as *me* isn't even human" (*S&A*, 26). The exogenous perspective for representation thus compounded society's objectifying and discriminatory practices. For these reasons, as Gates points out, Ellison's novel signifies upon Richard Wright's fictions precisely in order to expose the latter's approach "as merely a hardened conventional representation of 'the Negro problem,' and perhaps part of 'the Negro problem' itself" (294).

Thomas Schaub has noted that some of Ellison's views on social realism coincide with those held by white liberals disenchanted with the Left in the 1940s (*American Fiction*, 91). However, he continues, while the latter take a universalist view of contradiction and irony as basic operating principles of history, Ellison asserts that they reflect the specific African American experience of a political system that has failed to fulfill its obligations, to live up to its promise of "liberty and justice for all." A constant state of social invisibility had given rise to a generalized feeling amongst blacks in the U.S. that they simply did not exist. Hence the narrator's sense of alienation from the American flag, for it reminded him "that *my* star was not yet there" (*IM*, 342). His task, then, and that

of his race, became one of compelling the nation "to live up to its ideals.
. . . It is [the black American] who insists that we purify the American
language by demanding that there be a closer correlation between the
meaning of words and reality, between ideal and conduct, our assertions
and our actions" (*Going,* 111). Accordingly, *Invisible Man* was conceived
as an antidote to the traditional realist and the social realist novels, which
Ellison found too limited and limiting to apprehend the narrator's experiences. In order to correct the disjunction, he sought to invalidate the
constructs upon which realism is predicated, including causal relations
and a fixed, substantial reality. This, in turn, would enable him to
redefine reality and restore referentiality to both literature and politics—
with a twist.

Various critics have correlated the stages of the invisible man's social
and geographical journey and those of black history in the U.S.[6] Briefly,
from segregated southern society and the black college that emblematizes its race relations (modeled on the Tuskegee Institute in Alabama,
where Ellison studied in the 1930s), the invisible man travels to the industrial North, where he takes a job with Liberty Paints and then becomes
a spokesman for the predominantly white Brotherhood.[7] Whether the
focus is the African American experience as a whole or the frustrations of its leadership, the analyses essentially concur that the link between
novelistic biography and collective history is to be found in the experience of invisibility and in the disparity between the narrator's expectations and the results of his actions. "How had I come to this?" he
asks himself; "I had kept unswervingly to the path placed before me, had
tried to be exactly what I was expected to be . . . yet, instead of winning
the expected reward, here I was . . . holding on desperately to one of my
eyes in order to keep from bursting out my brain against some familiar object swerved into my path by my distorted vision" (*IM,* 131).
The "boomerang effect" of his efforts to change his personal and communal realities belies the notions of causality in his experience and of
history as linear progression (Strout, 85). Nor can logic and reason obtain

in an environment where the material self is rendered invisible, treated as if it did not exist. The narrator inhabits a world that is "unreal" both because it is governed by different laws and because it is not recognized by dominant society. Elsewhere, in fact, Ellison has described Harlem as haunted by a "sense of unreality," a world "so fluid and shifting that often within the mind the real and the unreal merge, and the marvelous beckons from behind the same sordid reality that denies its existence" (*S&A* 302, 296). Accordingly, he prioritizes psychological and social factors, rather than economics or class consciousness, as the primary agents and targets of change (Schaub, *American Fiction,* 91). His belief that only an interiorized discourse offers the possibility of a more accurate depiction of his race is emblematized in the narrator's loss of a physical self (Schaub, "Ellison's Masks," 128): at the end, he is pure subjectivity, "invisible and without substance, a disembodied voice" (*IM,* 503).

Shifts in literary mode correspond to changes in the protagonist's lifestyle, "express[ing] both his state of consciousness and the state of society" (*S&A,* 178). Enveloped by the relatively stable, traditional life of the South, the narrator accepts unquestioningly its categories and its presumption of white superiority. In these "pre-invisible days" (*IM,* 47), nonconformity is carefully compartmentalized, set aside in figurative and literal enclaves and marked as deviations from the normative order: the grandfather who encourages the narrator to sabotage the dominant order while feigning acquiescence is labeled crazy by the rest of his family; Trueblood's incestuous relations with his daughter ostracize him from the black community even as they validate whites' construction of black reality; and educated black professionals who have used their skills but been denied success in white society are shunted and sent off to the Golden Day asylum. As the narrator moves to the constant change of industrialism in the North, however, the narrative becomes more surreal. Here he is forcefully separated from all that he has learned, thrust into an unknown world where his structures of certainty no longer

obtain. The sole continuity with his past is to be found in the social hierarchy, only now the "old freezing unit" that had conditioned him to
accept his status begins to melt (226). Subsequently, the immutable laws
of reality mandated by the Brotherhood—an organization with "a
policy for everything" and the novel's most thorough example of a total-
izing ideology, as we shall see in the following section (352)—are juxtaposed with and overpowered by subjective visions, hallucinations, and
dreams that conflate time and space and blur the boundaries separating exterior from interior reality.

Invisible Man is "realistic," then, in the sense that its style accommodates a different form of experience, and that it undertakes to demonstrate the shortcomings of official institutions' rigid and self-serving
definitions of the past and present. Viewing the world from "inside of
his opponent's sense of time" (12), as it were, the narrator is at first unable
to comprehend the self-imposed exile from the Brotherhood chosen by
Ras the Exhorter, the novel's advocate of black separatism, by his former friend Tod Clifton, and by the black youths whom he sees forging
their own style on a subway platform. From the perspective authorized for him by the organization, their dissociation is tantamount to
plunging into the nothingness outside of the history that it also defines,
where they have no voice and will not be remembered. Not until his own
actions clash with the organization's plans does he understand that he,
too, is still invisible and that his plight is that of the African American
excluded from the frame of another's picture of reality. The Brotherhood is thus revealed as yet another manifestation of the whites, who
control reality and dispossess others of their pasts by defining the way
the world is supposed to operate and by not recognizing alternatives.
The invisible man's lesson, then, is that the truth of history may—indeed,
must—be transmitted by someone who is outside of "history."

Ellison claims that awareness of the discrepancy between authorized
and unofficial histories has made African Americans skeptical of the
truth-value and objectivity of written records of the past (Ellison et al.,

69). Since slavery, popular traditions that do not challenge the dominant order in its own written terms have served blacks as alternative
vehicles for preserving their experiences.[8] They thus offered Ellison a
particularly apt vehicle for re(-)presenting his section of American life.
In the novel, this vital, emic form of communal expression and history stands in opposition to the ideologies that vie for the narrator's
subservience. The author afforded a prominent role to different folkloristic forms, from figures such as Peter Wheatstraw and Rinehart the
trickster, to music, dreams, speech, and sermons. Jazz in particular stands
out as a mode of cultural expression defined by its anti-repressive
spirit. Slaves, Ellison reminds us, substituted music for freedom (*S&A*,
255). Throughout *Invisible Man*, music serves as a metaphor for history. The boys that the narrator sees in the subway station are not just "out
of time," they are "outside the *groove* of history"; their names would be
forgotten, but the music of the blues would "be *recorded* . . . the only true
history of the times" (*IM*, 9–10, 383; emphasis added). Here, then, in
the "invisible music of my isolation," the author finds a supplement to
existing systems of expression (16). Words can neither describe nor contain experience. Additionally, they form part of a legacy of dispossession. The inexpressive lyrics of the song that he listens to are thus likened
to the "lies" that the historian records to help him keep his power (379).
In contrast, as with the spiritual "There's Many a Thousand Gone," it
is the unnamed "emotion beneath the words" which, the narrator discovers, constitutes a true expression of self and collectivity, in the
same manner that the unseen, the unheard, and the unknown complete
the historical record (392). Music thus offers a way to expose the dominant ideology, call into question its image of reality, and propose an
alternative.

Having gained awareness of his invisibility, the narrator realizes that
his true job had not been to get others into the "groove of history"—the
Brotherhood's history, that is—but, rather, to let the "unheard sounds"
exist in their own terms and time (9–10). Being invisible gives him a

"different sense of time," which allows him to extricate himself from the music's regular beat and instead explore the "breaks" of its linear progression (11). The dialectic between the song's forward movement and its still points and silences foreshadows the narrator's final insight. He will only be able to find his identity by deviating from the imposed "straight white lines" of mental vision (297) and learning to see "around corners" into the future. This nonlinear mode of perception will sharpen with his awakening sense of a shared black experience and its traditions of expression, a sense previously precluded by his acceptance of the dominant ideologies. In preparation for starting anew, the narrator stops perceiving his experiences as raw materials to be shaped to someone else's program and instead assimilates them into his own identity:

> They [the Brotherhood] had set themselves up to describe the world. What did they know of us, except that we numbered so many . . . offered so many votes. . . . And now all past humiliations became precious parts of my experience, and for the first time . . . I began to accept my past and, as I accepted it, I felt memories welling up within me. It was as though I'd learned suddenly to look around corners; images of past humiliations flickered through my head and I saw that they were more than separate experiences. They were me; they defined me. (439)

Like Morrison's other "way of knowing," the invisible man's new perspective both derives from and leads him back toward collective racial consciousness and at the same time helps to clarify his own situation. Thus, at the end of the novel the protagonist acknowledges from his basement that he has "boomeranged," arriving at a point quite distant from the standing to which he had originally aspired (496). On the one hand, as in *Notes from Underground*—and Ellison openly proclaimed Dostoyevsky as a literary model—the narrator is situated underground in a literal, physical sense, emblematic of his dissociation from dominant culture.[9] The site chosen for the rejection of imposed white ideologies, coupled with the reaffirmation of black values, is additionally charged with the subversive connotations of the slave railway. On the other hand, the orator who had disseminated white accommodationist ideology to his people through their own traditional, oral forms, now inverts his betrayal: he resorts to the written tradition and "makes music of invisibility," expanding the fixed novelistic form to include his own experiences (16). If realism is like authorized history, whose recording of the "truth" is both partial and partisan, then *Invisible Man* focuses on those parts of reality that have traditionally been denied representation and thus offers a more "realistic" expression of black experience.

The issue of referentiality and finding a more representative means of representation is also a primary concern in Allende's novel. Many critics have catalogued Allende's variations on literary realism—e.g., magical, political, and historical—as part of her search for a mode that will capture and convey at a thematic level the enmeshment of the fantastic and the real that is characteristic of the prodigious region that is her subject.[10] Where *Invisible Man* posits literary style as as analogous to historiography's exclusiveness, *The House of the Spirits* suggests that prevailing discourses for constructing and depicting reality are additionally handmaidens of a patriarchal system whose pseudo-objective voice likewise claims to stand for the past but, in truth, reproduces only that which affirms and perpetuates its own norms. Accordingly, magic realism is refigured here from a feminist perspective to describe women's experiences and strengths within a male-dominated system. The novel attempts to provide a corrective to the official view of history by emphasizing its female protagonists' "second sight": Clara's clairvoyance, of course, but also, and perhaps more importantly, the peripheral vision—the vision of and from the periphery—shared by the women of the Trueba family.

The power dynamics behind the competing visions of reality in the novel are concretized in the structure and remodeling of the family house. Potentially as disruptive to society and its institutions as her mother's activism on behalf of women's suffrage and the legal recognition of illegitimate children, Clara's magic is circumscribed within the house, first by her father and, subsequently, by her husband. However, she sets a precedent for the women of her family by marking off a space for herself—both figuratively and literally—within Esteban Trueba's domain. Initially as a child and later in her anger at her husband, Clara resists patriarchal authority by recuperating as a source of power over her family the silence traditionally associated with women. She compensates for her silence by writing in notebooks which, after her death, are the sole remaining testaments of the magical realm that she once inhabited. Together, these written and ethereal spaces place Clara beyond her husband's desire to possess her in body and soul, since he cannot control or even enter them. "I tried to share those aspects of her life," he confesses, "but she didn't like anyone to read her notebooks that bore witness to life, and my presence interfered with her [inspiration] when she was talking with her spirits, so I had to stop."[11] Moreover, Clara's metaphysical territory is reified in the sections of the house that she takes over, and which are actually partitioned off during Trueba's terms in office. In the same manner that her notebooks defy historical convention, narrating events in terms of their importance rather than in chronological order, she turns the house, constructed in a uniform, classical style as the public image of the senator and his family, into a twisted aberration. It gradually becomes an enchanted labyrinth whose architecture breaks municipal laws made on earth, while the activities that it shelters defy the laws of physics and logic ordained in the heavens. In the magic universe of her own devising, she holds court with her friends and carries on conversations with the other world; here, "time was not marked by calendars or watches and objects had a life of their own" (82).

Alba's sections of the novel repeatedly designate Clara's heyday as "the days of the spirits," part of "a magic world that no longer exists." Critics have seized on these and other references to the departure of the spirits to postulate a gradual transition in the novel from one order of reality to another, and, concomitantly, from magic realism to a politically realistic style.[12] That is, as the Trueba family becomes more involved in events outside the house, and as these become more appalling, they claim that Clara's magic recedes from Alba's experience. While I agree that the world invoked by the former does not survive her death intact, I would argue that it was not a hermetically sealed refuge even during her lifetime, nor had it ever been. "The world has changed," Clara remarks when she returns to the house in the city and finds it devoid of spirits and eccentrics alike (*LCE,* 162). Moreover, both magic and tragic historical realities are present in the narrative from the very beginning. Rosa's death officially announces the violence—at first anonymous, but, later, engendered by Trueba himself—which is to mark the family's destiny. The relationship between the two orders of being, then, is not progressive, but instead has enchanted periods punctuating starker moments. The spirits might abandon the house, but they do not go far away. The narrative owes its very existence, in fact, to their actions. First Clara, herself a ghost, visits her granddaughter in the concentration camp and bids her to write to surmount the horror of her circumstances. And finally, Clara's notebooks, repositories of the past and sources for Alba's text, escape the pyre that destroys the other family papers only because they are "[s]muggled out by certain friendly spirits" (*HS,* 432).

The novel's political history, conversely, is not itself lacking in "unreality"—and not, simply, because the evil that it engenders is too horrifying (diabolical, as it were) to be believed. The dictatorship seemingly renders the benevolent spirits impotent only to appropriate their powers for its own purposes. It actively exploits the public's need for something to worship, for "the magical side of things" that had not been satisfied by the atheistic, pragmatic Marxist doctrine of the deposed regime (307, 382). It uses magic to support its illusions of order and prosperity: overnight, gardens appear as if "by magic," promoting the "fantasy" of a peaceful spring (*LCE,* 361). And it is successful in creating a sector of reality able to lead a fairy tale existence: the upper class returns to the bounty of the era preceding the socialist government, and the city had never appeared more beautiful. This prestidigitation, however, makes the lives of some surreal. Reality becomes a "nightmare" when Jaime sees the pistol in his doctor's life-giving hands and again, later, when Alba is taken captive (*IIS*, 368, 403). Additionally, Trueba, unable to trace the latter's whereabouts, cannot explain her disappearance except "as if by magic" (419). It is under these circumstances that Clara's warning that "your spiritual protectors are powerless when it comes to major cataclysms" proves true, and twice they fail to rescue Alba when she calls upon them (365).

And yet, even though the women's alternative spaces and activities are largely overpowered by male-dominated forces—and it is extremely important to keep in mind Allende's repeated conflation of patriarchy and military, her characterization of a military dictatorship as "the most macho society that you could possibly imagine" (Interview by Montenegro, 114)—they still succeed in channeling their subversive strategies in other directions. In addition to an unbridled imagination, each woman also passes on a strong sense of social justice to her children, a compulsion that drives the women to confront forces of victimization and that does not allow them to remain enclosed in a fantasy world (Rojas, 920). Consequently, throughout *The House of the Spirits* a continuous dialectic goes on between the women's metaphysical undertakings and their earthly missions. One critic's claim that Clara's magical powers recede when she is devoting her energies to a worthy cause and are fullest when she is engaged in frivolous activities (Mora, "Ruptura," 73) is overly reductionistic.[13] It is true that when circumstances are most dire, her supernatural resources wane, and she draws on other skills:

> Within a few hours, the earthquake had brought her face to face with violence, death, and vulgarity and had put her in touch with the basic needs to which she had been oblivious. Her three-legged table and her capacity

to read tea leaves were useless in protecting the tenants from epidemics and disorder . . . her children from abandonment, and her husband from death and his own rage. (*HS,* 165)

And even though she strives to maintain a "delicate balance . . . between the spirits of the Hereafter and the needy souls of the Here-and-Now" (164), her greatest accomplishments and, later, Alba's are achieved through her interaction with the latter. Nevertheless, the spirits are still granted indispensable—if adjunctive or secondary—roles in her projects. Her power to "see what was invisible," for example, points out to her the hatred and resentment seething at Las Tres Marías (105). It awakens her to social reality and precipitates her activism among the women of the ranch. Thus it is responsible for drawing her out of a sheltered life and compelling her to redress the legacy of the patriarch's abuse, even as it temporarily puts an end to her contact with the spirits.

Clara gradually erases the boundaries between public and private, the spaces between "masculine" and "feminine," and, along with those, the distinctions between her earthly and otherworldly enterprises. When the welfare system fails, she brings her beneficiaries into her home, sheltering them alongside the eccentrics already in residence. Her daughter and granddaughter follow her precedent, appropriating more and more of the patriarch's domain, but at the same time displacing most of the final remnants of her magic. They use the rooms first wrested from Trueba's power and set aside for séances to spirit away, as it were, political refugees, including Pedro Tercero, the senator's lifelong enemy. As Marcelo Coddou notes, Allende's female protagonists achieve greater independence from the patriarch and the patriarchy as they participate more actively in history and politics ("Dimensión del feminismo," 52). And women eventually become a pressure group for mobilizing others to collaborate in transforming society. Like the hens in Pedro Tercero's revolution-inciting song, they rebel and band together against a common aggressor, the fox who since time immemorial has robbed them of their offspring and products. The women's project is both symbol and part, metaphor and metonymy of the larger movement, for the system's analogous treatment of women and the poor brings about the convergence of their struggles, in the same way that the dictatorship's subsequent (mis)treatment of both has a similar result. Thus does the designation of political dissident bridge the distance previously separating Alba, nicknamed "the Countess" for her wealth and social standing, from her revolutionary classmates; the shared experience of torture levels differences of class, allowing her and Ana Díaz finally to become friends. And when Alba returns from having been disappeared, rendered invisible by the regime that similarly erases all official evidence of the horrors that it commits, she moves to expose and denounce it in order to prevent it from doing the same to others. The strength to prevail and to force the world to take note, will, in the end, be found in this solidarity and in the determination that it inspires. And while, as a spirit, Clara is powerless to remove Alba from Esteban García's physical clutches, her encouragement—her own spirit—and her notebooks reinforce this strength and help Alba to survive and, ultimately, work through her own experiences.

Finally, then, at the end of the novel, the difference between "spirits" and "spirit" becomes clear. Offered shelter by one of the myriad stoic women whom she views as the source of the country's strength, Alba realizes that "the days of Colonel García and all those like him are numbered, because they have not been able to destroy the spirit of these women" (429). The dictatorship temporarily renders the spirits impotent, but together the women are able to surmount the difficulties that they face and take action. The regime may harness their spirits, but their spirit, like Alba's, is beyond its reach. Even more so than the ghosts, then, I suspect that it is the bearers of this strength, the women who inhabit "the big house on the corner" and the dissidents who pass through it, whom Allende honors in her title. It is an homage rendered explicitly in her dedication of the novel to her mother, grandmother, "and all the other extraordinary women of this story."

Carpentier's original formulation of the marvelous real emphasized the power of blacks' belief in the supernatural to mobilize revolution and social change. So, too, do these two authors' similar extra-literary projects correspond to their depiction of an alternate reality and, in turn, bear directly on their mode of representation. Subjectivized, sur-real, magically and politically real, Ellison and Allende write unofficial stories, as it were, which challenge conventional(ized) referentiality and which they feel more accurately correspond to their otherly realities. The novels' denial of linearity and teleology reduplicates this intention at the level of form. The boomerang that represents the trajectory of the invisible man's life doubles as the structure of his tale. "[T]he end is in the beginning," he tells us in the prologue and echoes toward the novel's conclusion. This statement is made literal in Allende's novel, which opens and closes with the same sentence: "Barrabás came to us by sea." And Clara's notebooks themselves also deny historical discursive form: they are not arranged in chronological order but, rather, according to the importance of the events they detail. Both novels, then, dramatize Robert Stepto's remark that "any step outside what others call reality requires an accompanying step outside what others call literary form" (190).

"I once was lost, but now am found; / was blind but now I see." These final lines from the chorus to "Amazing Grace" encapsulate for me the invisible man's trajectory, his journey from innocence to experience, the realization of his blindness and the revalorization of his invisibility. His disillusionment is an exemplary tale directed after the fact at those who, like himself, go unseen and at those who refuse to see. Allende's female characters, in contrast, are conscious from the very beginning of their active nonconformity with society's plotting of their lives. *The House of*

the Spirits thus becomes a tribute to their self-assertion and a testament of horror that even the willfully blind must acknowledge. I will now examine more closely the role of self-awareness (or the lack thereof)—specifically, in relation to the group—in the two novels. A focus on self-awareness reveals how the two novels differently treat the relationship between individual and collectivity and the ramifications of this difference on the marginalized group's quest for recognition and empowerment.

In a recent article, Lois Parkinson Zamora characterized ghosts as reifications of collective memory (both of course being equally intangible) and as reminders of a shared past and its traditions and transgressions, as well as of the community itself ("Magical Romance/Magical Realism," 497). Their presence, she avers, is often a sign of the "slippage from the individual to the collective to the cosmic," of transformations and instabilities that challenge the fixed conventions of character, time, and place in realist narrative, and that are by the same token hallmarks of magic realism (501). But Zamora makes a critical distinction between the counterrealist traditions of the U.S. and Spanish America. "[M]ost contemporary U.S. magical realists," she writes,

> find a way to bring their ghosts above ground, that is, to integrate them into contemporary U.S. culture in order to enrich or remedy it. . . . Isaac Bashevis Singer, Leslie Marmon Silko, Maxine Hong Kingston, and Toni Morrison imagine reestablished communities after disruptive cultural transitions and political abuses. . . . Most contemporary Latin American magical realists, on the contrary, refuse such consolation: magical resolutions are considered, then canceled by crushing political realities. (542–43)

She singles out *The House of the Spirits* as an exception that proves this rule, leaving me to wonder where Ellison's protagonist—not exactly a ghost, but a man who is, after all, "invisible and without substance, a disembodied voice" issuing from underground (*IM,* 503)—may be seen in relation to the rule.

The problematic dialectic between individual and community, solitary and solidary, lies at the heart of *Invisible Man.* It is played out in the African American protagonist's struggle to construct a role which acknowledges both his individuality and his ethnic heritage in a society that recognizes neither. In this sense, the autobiographical form that Ellison chose for his tale is the perfect frame, for the narrator's progress participates simultaneously in the two fundamental movements that Stepto has identified as the slave narrative's legacy to African American literature: it is both an ascent to self-awareness and an immersion in group consciousness (168). Toni Morrison has described this navigation between the private and the public as "provid[ing] an instance in which a writer could be representative, could say, 'My single solitary and individual life is like the lives of the tribe; it differs in these specific ways, but it is a balanced life because it is both solitary and representative'" ("Rootedness," 349). Implicitly rendering homage to the collective dimension of his identity, the protagonist embarks upon the symbolic journey northward, toward enlightenment, that is a central trope in this autobiographical form. Also, as Ellison has noted, his final emergence from underground will likewise follow the path "upward" whose destination, in folktales, is always freedom (*S&A,* 173). Hence the invisible man's belief that when he discovers his identity, that is, when he arrives at his personal "north," he will be free. And yet, throughout much of the novel, the balance that Morrison refers to is lacking; the narrator's solitude, isolation, and lack of affective ties completely preclude him from being considered a representative figure. Additionally, until the end, he feels that his identity would be hampered by identification with the African American community, and so he casts off his ties to it and casts his task as an individual quest for power and success within society's mainstream institutions.

The invisible man's journey, as we have seen, takes him through several institutions that force him to forsake his ethnicity, heritage, and his own past in favor of the belief systems, names, identities, and goals—that is, the dominant ideals and definitions of American reality—that they offer to him. He accepts them all, for he looks to these frames to emplot his life with meaning, but each ultimately proves to be no more flexible than—and, indeed, is revealed to be subordinate to—the prevailing power structure. All of them moreover deliberately deny his experiences as an African American: they condition in him cultural amnesia, an implicit recognition of the fact that cultural and spiritual consciousness will be a potent resource for a leader emerging from within the black community. At the paint factory hospital, in fact, dispossession is literal: he is subjected to shock treatment, which induces him to forget both his name and identity.

The maneuverings of the Brotherhood show in greatest detail the mechanisms by which these institutions claim control of what was and will become history. Like Fredric Jameson's strategies of containment, the modi operandi of ideology, the organization's image of the world is a frame imprisoning the part of reality that it controls, and this frame draws attention away from what lies outside its boundaries. Within the organization, the acceptance and execution of an assigned function determines social visibility which, in turn, decides an individual's incorporation within what the organization designates as "historical time" (381). To become one of the Brotherhood's leaders and thereby enter its history, the narrator must give up his own, for race in the eyes of the Brotherhood supposedly does not "count," only dispossession (340). And yet, the committee's explicit goal of turning him into the next Booker T. Washington both denies its assertion that only economics is important and also delimits the path that his career is to follow: compromise, concession to (white) authority, and conformity to the dominant (white) ideology. Separate but equal, the blacks were told in 1865, and again by Washington in his 1895 Atlanta Exposition Address, known colloquially as the "Atlanta Compromise." "[U]nited with others of our country in everything pertaining to the common good," the narrator parrots early in the novel, "and, in everything social, separate like the fingers of the hand" (19). An anonymous note sent to the narrator at his Harlem office—later revealed to have been written by his Brotherhood sponsor—reiterates this message, cautioning him not to overstep his bounds, for "this is a *white man's world*" (332; italics in original);[14] it is fitting that this lesson, first learned in his native South, is the only memory of his past that the Brotherhood allows him to retain. The restraints on the invisible man become even more explicit when he is reprimanded for organizing a funeral for a former (black) leader and friend who, after publicly renouncing and denouncing the organization, had been shot by a white policeman. The narrator's action is deemed reprehensible because it allows the crowd to express sympathy for a peer wrongly killed by white authority, a sentiment that cannot be redirected to serve the organization's goals. Rather than reflecting the Brotherhood's interests, the funeral draws (on) the boundaries of race: Tod Clifton is mourned as an African American "brother," not as a member of the organization.

Harlem's black population ultimately has no say in deciding and decisive historical issues because assigning it a voice does not support the Brotherhood's interests. Additionally, the negative response to the protagonist's initiative and the final sacrifice of the Brotherhood's local (black) chapter to its larger plan demonstrate unequivocally that the organization does not hesitate to promote its projects at the expense of its (again, black) constituency. This brings the narrator to the realization that outside of the Brotherhood and the roles that it authorized for African Americans, "we were outside history; but inside of it they didn't see us" (432). Too late, he comprehends that he is only invested with power—in other words, visible—as long as he serves the interests of the white hegemony and that attempting to define himself in its terms has only resulted in self-effacement. He has no need of his sponsor's oculist, for he has long since learned to "not-see myself as others see-me-not" (412). In this manner, the engagement in politics on behalf of a shared cause that affords the women in *The House of the Spirits* a measure of independence has the opposite effect on Ellison's narrator, whose activism for the Brotherhood leaves him without self-knowledge, renders him powerless to effect change, and, moreover, makes him dangerous as a leader of the African American community (Harper, 138).

His failure to understand that he is the incarnation of the Sambo puppets that symbolize the organization's manipulation of blacks and racial issues—that by towing the party (or Communist Party) line he is maneuvering the Brotherhood into a position where it will betray his constituents—places him at the front of the march toward the race riot, which is the novel's climax. Realization of what his role has been is accompanied, finally, by comprehension of the prediction-*cum*-accusation made by Ras, who had warned him that the whites would use him to do their dirty work and then betray him, leaving him to betray his own. The invisible man also realizes at this point that he is at least partly responsible for his own disenfranchisement, for he has striven for success in the terms authorized by society's institutions, accepting the path placed in front of him without question and opting not to search for others; like his fellow students at the southern university, conditioned by the same race relations that enslaved their predecessors, he, too, has "come to love the symbols of [his] conquerors" (100). Thus do his intentions always "boomerang," bringing about effects opposite to those he intends, and even his efforts to undermine the Brotherhood from within fail him: as long as he acts within its framework, whether for or against it, he supports its goals and not those of the black community that he aspires to represent.

Ellison's denials notwithstanding, the Brotherhood appears to represent the radical and non-mainstream Communist Party; paradoxically, its role in the novel is to represent the white hegemony and its marginalization of African Americans. The protagonist's early intuition that his participation in it gives him a "glimpse [of] how the country operated" (265; see also 308) is confirmed in his final revelation: "And now I looked around a corner of my mind and saw Jack and Norton and Emerson merge into one single white figure. They were very much the same, each attempting to force his picture of reality upon me and neither giving a hoot in hell for how things looked to me" (438). The organization's actions thus serve as a representative instance of white American political activists using blacks for their own ends, reiterating the lesson learned at each of the previous stages of the invisible man's journey: the fact that he lives in "a white man's world." The South's unchanging belief that "white is right" (87) became in the university the knowledge that "[t]hese white folk have newspapers, magazines, radios, spokesmen to get their ideas across. If they want to tell the world a lie, they can tell it so well that it becomes the truth. . . . You're nobody, son. You don't exist" (128). In the industrial North, that knowledge became the revelation that he had been programmed to acknowledge in accommodationists "the same quality of authority and power in your world as the whites before whom they bowed" (197).

The narrator only becomes Harlem's true leader with his final disillusionment and alienation from both community and organization (Harper, 138). The resulting distanced perspective allows him, finally, to distinguish "between the way things are and the way they're supposed to be" (*IM,* 126)—that is, to see *with* the double vision of the periphery, and to see *through* the illusion that is presented as reality. As he comes to acknowledge his racial identity, he will recognize that his problems and their solutions are part of a collective plight. This will, in turn, give him access to the lessons learned by others before him—that is, access to the heritage, condensed in his own passage through the different stages of black history in the U.S., that the Brotherhood forced him to forsake. At the same time, he will also define his own strategy for self-authentication, his own "plan of living," to keep at bay the competing ideologies imposed on him by those who would make him invisible.

Perhaps, then, Ellison's "ghost," who remains underground at the end of the novel but has acquired self-awareness and is moving toward group consciousness, may also be considered an exception that proves Zamora's rule.

The perception of a different, or un"real" reality in *Invisible Man* stems, in Ellison's words, from the black's "sensation that he does not exist in the real world at all ... [that he] seems rather to exist in the nightmarish fantasy of the white American mind as a phantom that the white mind seeks unceasingly ... to lay" (*S&A*, 304). Thus it resembles the type of magic realism that Roberto González Echevarría characterizes as epistemological (113), that is, as deriving from the observer's apprehension of reality, which in this case is the outgrowth of a group's exclusion from what is considered by the dominant center to be "the real world." In contrast, Allende's invocation of the "incredible or magnificent facts" constituting "the dimension of our reality" would seem to indicate a branch of magic realism more ontological in nature, in which reality itself is governed by a different set of rules, as in Carpentier's marvelous real ("Writing as an Act of Hope," 45). In *The House of the Spirits* an alternate world is generated, a parallel universe which, like the reification of the women's dissenting perspective in the architecture of the family home, is accessible to all of the dispossessed. Whereas the enlightenment of Ellison's protagonist is a gradual process, here the incompatibility of dominant descriptions of life with the outsider's experience is demonstrated synchronically: the individual's struggles to achieve self-definition take place within and explicitly reduplicate the more widespread struggles against the patriarchal system and its various incarnations. Thus, rather than following a movement from ignorance to awareness, the trajectory of the four generations of women in the del Valle and Trueba families traces the development of a preexisting female consciousness in Spanish America over the course of the twentieth century, as well as a trajectory of rebellion against the prevailing social structure. And as Allende develops the parallels in the predicaments of several mar-

ginalized groups, the women's consciousness, solidarity, and self-assertion are seen to extend to socialists and the poor as well.

In the Spanish American system, patriarchy or fathers rather than a
"Brotherhood" dominate, but their role in prescribing "the way things
are supposed to be" is virtually identical. Men have the power to determine which individuals merit recognition and which groups' pasts
will be recorded. Women's roles are narrowly defined in this world: their
main function is to produce legitimate male heirs; their space is the
home. As Férula's case demonstrates, any abnormality is vehemently
opposed; the "deviance" of Nívea del Valle is likewise condemned as
threatening to Church, country, and family, in the same way that knowledge of Clara's magical powers is kept from the public realm by her father,
who fears that it might jeopardize his political career. Poverty further
curtails women's potential and rights: the peasant women at Las Tres
Marías are merely objects of sexual gratification for Trueba, who acknowledges neither their maternal role nor their—his—offspring. The
patriarch, like Faulkner's Sutpen, endeavors to predetermine his line
of descent and declares that only those children born within a marriage
sanctioned by the Church—and to a woman of his own class—may bear
his name. After all, the narrator writes, "the only ones who really count-
ed were the ones who bore their father's surname; the others might just
as well not have been born" (52). That is, they were invisible to the society and history that he represented.[15]

The dialogic relationship between dominant male views of reality
and those of women and the lower classes is reduplicated structurally
in the novel's assignment of opposing perspectives to separate narrators: Trueba, the incarnation of the patriarchy, and his socialist granddaughter, Alba, the voice of subversion. The former's order is shown
to reproduce the power relations of the ruling classes and gender and is,
in turn, replicated in the governing institutions of the military regime.
In the same way, his most outstanding qualities—"He was fanatical, violent, and antiquated, but he represented better than anybody else the

values of family, tradition, private property, law and order" (307–8)—
both qualify him for political leadership and are the paradigm out of
which the regime (which both emulates and perpetuates his abuses)
emerges. On the one hand, as senator, Trueba tries to transpose the social
organization from his *latifundio* to the nation: his compatriots require
"a strong government, with a strong [*patrón*]," while his tenants, like
children, need someone to dictate their actions (64). On the other, he
censors from his early letters home all mention of his enjoyment of
his patriarchal "rights," as well as the children, poverty, and resentment that result, and dismisses all alternatives to his rule as "Communist." Meanwhile, the dictatorship likewise fabricates an official story in
which world history is rewritten, its own brutality and the city's misery
are hidden from sight, and international Communism is blamed for
attempting to sabotage its order and progress. Moreover, the patriarch
and the military alike count on the complicity of the upper class—"those
who preferred not to see" (381), "those who did not want to know"
(414)—to consent to the use of violence to protect its privileges and
ensure a return to the heyday of land ownership that had ended with
the Marxist government. The dictatorship's version of reality is simply
that of Trueba projected on a wider screen. Ultimately, though, the military turns this system and its official story against its creator: after
abducting Alba and ransacking the house, soldiers force him to sign a
paper declaring that they have adhered to proper procedure. And in Esteban García—the regime that he personifies, and the revenge that he
exacts with tools honed by Trueba himself—Allende further dramatizes
the "boomeranging" of the senator's design, his unspoken word made
flesh, as it were.

As a foil to the patriarchal ideology, the novel details how the women
of Trueba's family—none of whom, in the end, bears his surname[16]—
defy his authority by refusing the roles he has allotted them and further
link their efforts to rearticulate their positions with the class struggle.

Nívea, Clara, Blanca, and, finally, Alba, "break away from tradition," in Allende's words, and claim agency in a realm beyond male control ("The World," 18). Each proposes a different resolution to the conflict between a patriarchally determined "life plot" and her own urge to self-definition. Despite their shortcomings, Nívea's campaigns nevertheless set a precedent for challenging society's most powerful institutions. Blanca, in turn, raises her child as a single mother, refusing her father's financial assistance and marriage to her lifelong lover; also, she encourages Alba to pursue an education, to be prepared to earn a living "like a man," rather than having to rely on one (*HS*, 307). Alba and Clara's efforts to repossess and redefine their lives are directly interwoven with the reclaiming of the power of the word and with the task of reinscribing history. Change, a different future, would seem to depend on a reappraisal of past and present. Clara's notebooks become her excuse for wresting from the patriarch the privilege of naming children and, by extension, of founding a lineage that "counts." As we have seen, the notebooks also constitute a space that he can neither participate in nor control. And writing, in addition to magic, is the principal legacy that Clara bequeaths to her granddaughter: Alba records her experiences—which are also those of the other women at the camp—at her grandmother's suggestion and with her encouragement. On the one hand, she writes in order to survive and, on the other, to expose and denounce the government's lies. The writing that began during her childhood as an exercise in preserving the fairy tales made even more fantastic by Blanca's "poor memory" is now a bond between women and classes, and through time (303); in its goal of forcing collective historical awareness, it is also a means of thwarting a more insidious type of "poor memory" (432).

Alba's testimony challenges the patriarch(y)'s claim to authority through both structure and content. It disproves the supposed truth-value of Trueba's first person narrative and thereby reveals how his version is, as Sharon Magnarelli has noted, far more subjective biography than objective history (55). On the one hand, the senator situates himself at the center of his story, with his voice overriding and distorting all others, and presents his goals as beneficial to all society:

> [T]hese poor people are completely ignorant and uneducated. They're like children, they can't handle responsibility. How could *they* know what's best for them? Without me they'd be lost. . . . What you need here is a strong government, with a strong [*patrón*]. It would be lovely if we were all created equal, but the fact is that we're not. . . . I had to come in order for there to be law and order here, and work. (*HS*, 64–65)

On the other hand, Alba's self-effacing, third-person account draws attention away from the subject of narration to events and other external referents. She restores what has been excised and provides a corrective to her grandfather's legitimating discourse (Magnarelli, 55). And, because of the microcosmic relationship of the patriarchal order and the military regime, Alba's narration of her own experiences has ramifications in the public sphere. It is

> a testimony that might one day call attention to the terrible secret she was living through, so that the world would know about this horror that was taking place parallel to the peaceful [and orderly] existence of those who did not want to know, who could afford the illusion of a normal life . . . ignoring, despite all evidence, that only blocks away from their happy world there were others, these others who live or die on the dark side. (*HS*, 414)

As in testimonial literature, Alba's individual, autobiographical concerns (already attached to a political cause), are also caught up in a shared plight and in a project for collective empowerment (Masiello, 54).[17] Thus, where recourse to a first-person narrator in *The Real Life of Alejandro Mayta* indicates a claim to contingent historical authority, it serves an entirely different purpose in the novels treated in this chapter: throughout *Invisible Man* and in the epilogue to *The House of the Spirits*, the first-person is used to debunk official history's authority and to move toward the creation of an identity that defies conventional authority and the controlling images thrust upon marginalized groups (Schaub, "Masks," 150).

Through its privileging of women and other marginalized groups with the double vision of the outsider, *The House of the Spirits* demonstrates that it shares with *Invisible Man* the broader goal of laying bare the ideologies and exclusionary tactics employed by the hegemonic order. In the words of Ellison's protagonist, "Being invisible and without substance, a disembodied voice, as it were, what else could I do? What else but try to tell you what was really happening when your eyes were looking through?" (503). It is telling that both novels culminate in a similar sequence of events, proceeding from a funeral to a state of violence and chaos, and, finally, to the narrators' retreat to a protected space where they record their experiences. The funerals of Tod Clifton and the Poeta—the one "outside of history," and the other, like the friends who could not join him as he lay dying, "outside of the law" (*IM*, 376; *LCE*, 367)—mark not only the end of a life but the end of a way of life for those who had had faith in them. After Clifton's death, the invisible man can no longer deny the Brotherhood's opportunistic manipulation of race issues and begins to cast off the ideological blinders that it had imposed on him. Rather than viewing his audience as numbers or votes, he is finally able to see them as individuals who, like himself, also share a collective identity rooted in a common set of experiences. And out of this bond issues the means for preserving the past despite having been denied a voice in history, for affirming the identity of the group against efforts by dominant institutions to erase it, and for forging ahead into the future: out of the crowd, a voice begins to sing the spiritual, "There's Many a Thousand Gone," expressing a transcendent sentiment shared by the narrator and his audience, one "for which the theory of Brotherhood had given me no name" (392).

Where Clifton's funeral represents both a revelation and a release, that of the Poeta evolves into "the symbolic burial of freedom" (*HS*, 388), inverting the euphoria which had followed the election that brought the Left to power. The marginal populations that had participated in the celebration have once again been hidden from sight—literally as well as figuratively—by the regime. The burial of the man of words and of the word *liberty* itself, which many had already censored from their vocabulary, emblematizes the dictatorship's appropriation of meaning, its manipulation of systems of signification to render communication useless for everything but its own designs. In the end, even Trueba is unsure whether the regime is trying to suppress Communism and its infiltrators in the country, or the country itself. The only facts that are unequivocal are those of war and destruction. The loss of the word, in turn, entails the loss of the world. Alba's tale, coupled with Trueba's recognition of Esteban García's paternity and, by extension, of his own responsibility for her brutalization, signals the end of the order that he thought he had known. And yet, those following the Poeta's procession refuse to accept the fate that they have been assigned. Many a thousand might have gone, but here, too, a single voice arises to express the crowd's shared emotion, the hope that "a people united will never be conquered" ("el pueblo unido jamás será vencido" [*LCE*, 367–68]). Perhaps both novels' advocacy of collective, non-violent resistance, implicit here in the coup's aftermath and in the apocalyptic resonances of the race riot, indicates a source of renewal after historical disaster.

Motivated by a need to speak for others and to publicize their ordeals, Ellison and Allende champion collective action and solutions and empowerment by race, gender, and class as means of promoting social change. The invisible man's need for self-authorship, though, his initial aspiration to establish an individual identity for himself apart from that of his race and as part of the dominant order, contrasts sharply with *The House*

of the Spirits, where conflict at the level of the individual is emblematic of larger dynamics and telling one's own story dramatizes the struggles between marginalized groups and the hegemony. Perhaps these positions with respect to the common goals of individual and community bear some relation to the moments of intense solidary activity during which the novels were written. *Invisible Man* was published just two years prior to the landmark decision of *Brown vs. Board of Education*. The Civil Rights movement and its efforts to recover and revise American history arose out of this and other groundbreaking events of the 1950s. In earlier years, though, disillusioned by the black leadership and community's frustrated efforts at surmounting racism and injustice, Ellison had turned to communism as a means of redressing the inferior position to which society had relegated him. He was soon disabused of his enthusiasm, however: the Party had failed to resolve racial problems because, like the invisible man's Brotherhood, it had neither recognized the needs of the black community nor afforded it the opportunity to exercise effective leadership. Race simply could not be subsumed within economic issues defined—and with strategies of resistance devised—by white political groups implicitly working to defuse and disarm the struggle for racial justice. Allende, in contrast, stresses the transformative potential of Marxism in Spanish America. She began writing *The House of the Spirits* during the revolution in Nicaragua and finished in the midst of the activity and the waves of hope that followed. The novel was, not surprisingly, barred from distribution in Chile during most of the Pinochet dictatorship, but, like the spirits whose tale it tells, it circulated in a clandestine manner.

Despite these differences, however, implicitly and explicitly, both authors explore shared situations of injustice and exploitation and set out to validate different realities, or different experiences of reality. Both emphasize responsibility, commitment, and the social function of literature, and, accordingly, both have declared their revisionist goals, censuring official institutions for censoring history.[18] This integration of social and literary projects is what Cornel West has labeled a "cultural politics of difference," a tendency that he identifies in writers who, through their works, "desire to align themselves with demoralized, demobilized, depoliticized and disorganized people in order to empower and enable social action" (19–20). Although Ellison's narrator begins his tale by declaring that "responsibility rests upon recognition, and recognition is a form of agreement" (*IM*, 16), he would seem to arrive at a different conclusion by the novel's end, speculating that even an invisible man may carry out a socially responsible role. Precisely because invisibility causes him to go unrecognized in society, it obliges him to dissent and, through writing, to shatter the "dream world" of those who refuse to see (17). Allende, too, views her task as an obligation to challenge the tacit and willed consent to the status quo. "You cannot," she contends, "live in a bubble away from the problems you think are not yours . . . you are responsible . . . and we cannot ignore reality. We cannot say, 'I didn't know.' We bear the responsibility to know! And I know, as a writer, I bear the responsibility to tell and convince you that all this is happening" ("Responsibility," 118). The need to remember and to know is, of course, at the core of both authors' desire to have their fiction interact with and rearticulate the contemporary social context. By reinterpreting the past, they cause the present to be seen from a different perspective, and hope to prevent history from repeating itself.

Also, by making the invisible visible and speaking for voices that have been muted, Ellison and Allende show their readers what lies beyond the dominant structure. And, of course, knowledge—acknowledgment—precedes action. Both novels have been criticized for the "passivity" of their endings, in which the narrators are writing in isolation, disengaged from society and sheltered from its violence (see Cooke, "Ellison and García Márquez," and Mora, "La mujer como ciudadana"). I would argue instead that writing is both the authors' and their protagonists' chosen mode of subversion. The epilogues do not suggest a final refuge in escapism. Rather, they are deliberately left open, with the possibility of movement outward (and upward, in the case of Ellison's protagonist), and are pervaded by a sense of expectation, in the etymological sense of *hope* as well as *awaiting*. Both meanings are implicit in Alba's "expectant" state, while the invisible man's underground "hibernation" is actually "a covert preparation for a more overt action" (*IM,* 16). The process of thinking through, shaping, and writing his experiences is not just the representation of action. It is, as Gates suggests, an action in itself and one that demands his (and Alba's) final emergence (293). The invisible man can continue to wage his war against Monopolated Light & Power "without their realizing it" (*IM,* 9), just as Bledsoe, the accommodationist president of the southern black university, wields his power in the dark. This option, on the one hand, is acquiescence, even complicity, for the fight is still being carried out in terms that have been given. On the other hand, he may choose to reappropriate the light and use it to "confirm [his] reality" (10). The invisible man's text thus joins forces with Alba's narration in its role as an antidote to "poor memory" and its selective transmission of the past. Also, by preventing knowledge from being "filed and forgotten," both keep alive the "possibility of action," and thus of change (501).

Through writing, the protagonists additionally exorcise their own hatred, rather than using it as a justification for seeking vengeance and thereby reducing history to an endless cycle of destruction. The invisible man and Alba's trajectories, as well as their final realizations, are eerily similar on this point. For the former, writing is a process of "disarmament," anticipating Martin Luther King's nonviolent resistance and advocacy of a love-centered revolution (502). "I've set out to throw my anger into the world's face," he writes, "but . . . even before I finish I've failed. . . . The very act of trying to put it all down has confused me and negated some of the anger and some of the bitterness. . . . In order to get some of it down I have to love . . . [T]oo much of your life will be lost, its meaning lost, unless you approach it as much through love as through hate" (501). Alba, in turn, states that

When I was in the doghouse, I wrote in my mind that one day Colonel García would stand before me in defeat and that I would avenge myself on all
those who need to be avenged . . . And now I seek my hatred and cannot
seem to find it . . . It would be very difficult for me to avenge all those
who should be avenged, because my revenge would be just another part of
the same inexorable rite. (*HS,* 431–32)

In both cases, love becomes a personal and a political sentiment, again
underscoring the integration of individual and communal experience
(Callahan, 75). In this manner, the historical record that is revised—
both in the sense of *corrected* and of *re-vised,* or *seen again*—and the
very act of rewriting it become, together, a means of achieving a future
different from the past, Faulkner's reason to "endure and prevail."

The invisible man's invisibility and Alba's liminality enable the
respective narrators to narrate what, on the one hand, the invisible man
had at first been unable to perceive—the difference "between the way
things are and the way they're supposed to be" (*IM,* 127)—and, on the
other, to record reality without reproducing the bias of history. The
invisible man is, in fact, the living antithesis of all norms and centers:
he is *anonymous,* face*less,* voice*less,* living *under*ground in a forgotten
basement, somewhere in a "*border* area" near the "*jungle* of Harlem" (9;
emphasis mine). And both narrators speak with a figurative clairvoyance or "second-sight" that assists them in reclaiming the visual metaphorical field from which they have been excluded by those who have blinded
themselves in order not to see. That is, the unspeakable and unspoken
unofficial stories are told by the unsaid, those people whose presence
and voices have been suppressed, restoring their histories to visibility.
Whereas the goal of Ellison's protagonist is to "tell you what was really
happening when your eyes were looking through" (503), so, too, does
Alba, following Clara, "call attention to the terrible secret she was living
through, so that the world would know" (*HS,* 414). These endeavors
to re-present and reclaim misrepresented historical experiences are in

keeping with the goals and strategies of numerous other marginalized and postcolonial texts. Ellison was well aware of this potential as early as 1955, when he compared the U.S.'s racial difficulties to problems faced by colonial and postcolonial nations worldwide and hailed the power of the marginalized experience to apply pressure to society and hasten the "achievement of democratic ideals" (*S&A*, 182).

By speaking as a subversive voice from outside history, then, the invisible man meets the challenge of trying to improve our peripheral vision. Similarly, it is the spirits in *The House of the Spirits*—whom I have come to think of as reifications of Ellison's ghostly protagonist—who protect Clara's notebooks, the Trueba family's unofficial story, from the pyre that destroys so many other documents. Things fall apart, the center cannot hold. The act of writing itself constitutes an exorcism of hatred and a threat to cultural hegemony; its power is matched by that of its addressees, for whom reading is a means of defiance. As in African American autobiography and Spanish American testimonial literature, Ellison and Allende's first-person narrators are both solitary and representative; each constitutes a nexus between private life and public action. Both novels have enjoyed tremendous popularity nationally and internationally, inspiring efforts to break down the authority of a dominant ideology, to move the margins toward the center, and, ultimately, to make their subjects visible.

Paradise Lost and Regained

The Old Order and Memory in the
Miranda Stories and *Pedro Páramo*

Katherine Anne Porter's Miranda stories[1] and Juan Rulfo's *Pedro Páramo* speak to issues stemming from the transition from an agrarian society to new systems of social and economic relations and from the concomitant breakdown of traditional social structures. The succession of orders was a subject of immediate concern in the 1920s and 1930s both in the South and in Mexico and related to events taking place internationally. Porter's and Rulfo's childhoods were spent in the shadow of violent civil wars that marked turning points in the regions' histories but did not immediately alter the prevailing modes of social organization, even though their ends (falsely) announced the onset of new orders. Instead, the plantation system remained a fundamental paradigm for the regions' social structures and relations in the years following the U.S. Civil War and the Mexican Revolution. Porter's stories of the Old Order and Rulfo's *Pedro Páramo* afford a prominent role to collectivities whose decline in fortune is catalyzed by a change in social orders, but whose patriarchal, authoritarian social systems escape restructuring following the civil wars. They also foreground the plights of characters caught between the old ways and the new: Miranda struggles to escape from a fossilized and stifling milieu and create a place for herself as an independent woman and a writer, while the town of Comala is disenfranchised by the cacique's dismantling of its traditions.

Porter's and Rulfo's works differ in many considerable respects. The regions that they depict are neighbors, but they are separated by far more than the Río Grande: they are situated on either side of a border that is national, political, cultural, linguistic, and much more. Additionally, Porter's stories center on experiences specific to the development of a female protagonist, while *Pedro Páramo* has neither a center, in the sense of a traditional, linear plot, nor a single protagonist. It is not my intention to overlook or underplay these differences. And yet, in the end, I find that despite the divergences, the texts exhibit striking and highly significant commonalities. Lois Parkinson Zamora attributes similarities shared by Rulfo, his compatriot Elena Garro, and Texan writer William Goyen to "shared cultural sources," that is, to the fact that until 1848 the Río Grande was *not* a border between two nations but, rather, simply cut across what was then the broader territory (and common history) of Mexico ("The Animate Earth," 63). I do not believe that a similar cultural framework unites Rulfo's and Porter's communities, in part because the class and society that Porter depicted and with which she identified were more generally associated with the Deep South than with the state from whence she hailed, and in part because the South's history and belief systems do not have roots in the Hispanic and mestizo cultural substrata that Zamora identifies in works by Goyen (with whom, coincidentally, Porter had a tempestuous relationship during 1951–1952). As we shall see, however, Porter's attitude toward the South was colored and even changed by her travels in Mexico. Also, her interest in Mexican culture and politics imbued many of her other writings with a hope for and, ultimately, disillusionment of the prospect of change following the revolution that are strongly reminiscent of Rulfo. Additionally, because of their acute consciousness of recent historical trauma and change, both the Rhea family and Comala are strongly bound to traditions and belief systems stemming from their pasts and exhibiting a common insistence on upholding these—characteristics that I will explore in detail in this chapter. In keeping with numerous other scholars (including—but not limited to—Mexican writers Octavio Paz and Carlos Fuentes), Zamora argues that Rulfo's—and Mexico's—worldview is both informed and defined by a profound consciousness of the nation's history, culture, and cultural disruptions; additionally, she believes that this awareness is in contraposition to the U.S.'s image of itself as an innocent land (the "New World") without a past, an image from which the violent dispossession of Native American and African American populations has been erased (75–77). Fuentes has characterized this attitude by claiming that North Americans act as if they

> don't have history. This country was founded out of nothing. . . . The dream of a nation with no past, the great eighteenth-century utopia, 'Let us exist without any reference to the barbarous past, as a total promise for the future. . . .' There is a Pollyanna mentality at the very foundation of the U.S., one in which you avoid all mention of genocide or crimes. The Indians were killed: forget it. . . . They threw a veil over history, history does not exist. We have a future that is our history. . . . This has been a country postulated on the absence of the past and on the hiding of the past when it is disagreeable.[2] (Interview, 52)

It has been my contention throughout this study, however, that, like Mexico, the southern U.S., because of its experience of defeat, because of the legacy of that "peculiar institution," because of the stigma and ostracism that it experienced during Reconstruction, has also been unable to escape from the burden of its past and, consequently, has been excluded from the national discourses of innocence and progress, as well as from its future-oriented mentality. This rootedness in (or outside) history marks Porter's Rhea family as much as it does Comala; in fact, as I shall detail presently, in both cases rootedness becomes a search for refuge in the past which, in turn, condemns both groups to their would-be sanctuaries.

Not only do both authors address similar issues but also similar constellations of issues. In the first part of this chapter, I will discuss their depictions of the struggle between traditional and new ways of life. This entails a contrastive analysis of the characters' relationship to their communities and the values they share. I will subsequently compare the texts' discussions of wars (the First World War and the Mexican Revolution) and their role in precipitating social change and breakdown, or, conversely, continuity. Finally, I will examine Porter's and Rulfo's depictions of pasts prolonged through idealized evocations of fallen orders and their assertion that the continued presence of the past denies the communities access to the future. I will also show how both additionally harmonize form and content by employing narrative strategies that use modernist techniques to express these predicaments.

Beauty and the Beast: Plantation Society, *Caciquismo*, and the Crossing of Ways

Many of the authors' thematic convergences may be understood within the context of the comparable social organizations, the plantation and the (extended) *hacienda*, in which the works are set. The fundamental role of the plantation in shaping societies in various areas of North and South America has received much attention in recent years. Sidney Mintz posits that the Caribbean is a "societal area," a group of nations exhibiting parallel socioeconomic structures determined by the ubiquity of the plantation and its formative force in the islands' development (915). In his ground-breaking study, *The Repeating Island: The Caribbean and the Postmodern Perspective*, Antonio Benítez-Rojo similarly analyzes the plantation as a primary paradigm for society and literature. Despite differences between the system's determination of social organizations in the Caribbean, northeastern Brazil, and the southern U.S., the paradigm's constituent elements are remarkably constant throughout these regions and in Mexico's *hacienda*—as, I will argue in this chapter, is its legacy (38). And Gilberto Freyre's description of the planter's residence, or *Casa Grande*, which was the cornerstone of the plantation system of northeastern Brazil and a basic structuring model for much of Brazilian society, might easily be applied to the agrarian societies depicted by Porter and Rulfo (to say nothing, of course, of Faulkner):

> The Big House completed by the slave shed represents an entire economic, social, and political system: a system of production (a latifundiary monoculture); a system of labor (slavery); . . . a system of religion (a family Catholicism, with the chaplain subordinated to the paterfamilias, with a cult of the dead, etc.); a system of sexual and family life (polygamous patriarchalism); . . . and a system of politics (*compadrismo*). (xxxiii)

This is the social organization that the Rhea family sustains beyond its official collapse and that Miranda is forced to reject, for the patterns that it sanctions for women's lives simply leave no room for her desire for independence. These are the elements that the cacique consolidates into the perverse order that destroys Comala and frustrates the completion of Juan Preciado's quest.[3] Accordingly, within the common frame of plantation societies staving off or undergoing fundamental transformations, I will now contrast Miranda's self-definition as an individual outside of her community with Juan's search for reintegration in a traditional communal structure.

Katherine Anne Porter was at once a product of the South and a rebel against it. On the one hand, she was attracted to the image of the plantation promoted by the Agrarians; its sense of the past and of community appealed to her. The biographical information that she disclosed to the public—apocryphal in many cases—was, in effect, a rearticulation of the agrarian myth, an outward display of allegiance to traditions that she had in practice repudiated: she transformed her impoverished antecedents into a "good old family of solid wealth and property" and recast herself as a belle, the disinherited descendant of a "nobly unreconstructed" aristocratic lineage.[4] Porter's feelings toward the grandmother who raised her (after whom Miranda's grandmother, Sophia Jane Rhea, was modeled) expresses this facet of her attitude toward the South as well: "The real break-up did not occur immediately after the [Civil] war, but with the death of my grandmother, an old woman who almost single-handedly held the thing together until her last day. . . . I belong to the generation left stripped and homeless . . . not my father's generation . . . because they still had the land and they still had the tradition" (quoted in Titus, 196). And yet, despite the fact that Porter expressed her sense of alienation from the present in terms of yearning for the lost South, the plantation was nevertheless the domain of the white patriarch. For Porter, who aspired to be a writer, as well as an authority on literature and politics, the subservience demanded of the southern woman was intolerable. It is understandable that the woman who lauded Thomas Hardy for opposing society's most powerful institutions should bristle at a culture that ostracized those who desired to search for their own answers.[5] Porter left the South—and her first husband—at an early age because, she claimed, "I didn't want to be regarded as a freak. That was how they regarded a woman who tried to write. . . . It was a confining society in those days" ("Portrait of an Artist," 17). She returned infrequently thereafter, never again living in Texas for an extended period of time.

The stories comprising the Miranda cycle are unified by a single protagonist and follow her development as a child, her initiations into adulthood, and her search for a satisfying role in society. Miranda's trajectory illustrates many of the problems commonly found in the female *Bildungsroman*, problems which stem from the collision of the protagonist's desire for self-realization and social resistance to deviations from conventional notions of femininity.[6] The traditions with which Porter's semi-autobiographical heroine struggles are precisely those that form the basis of the Rhea family's identity and that represent the perpetuation of the Old Order's practices into the early twentieth century. Miranda comes to realize that even in her day, the only roles sanctioned for women are those of belle and matriarch, while romance, marriage, and maternity are still the only permissible life plots. Thus, as Jane Flanders has pointed out, the conflicts developed in the Miranda stories reflect the transition from one order to its successor and are at the same time a function of the protagonist's experiences as a woman (48n.1).

To the degree that the Miranda stories reflect Porter's own struggles to free herself from patriarchal society, they support Mary Titus's assertion that autobiographical fiction written by women during the Southern Renaissance can be read as a gender-inflected response to the Agrarians' idealization of plantation society (195). Joan Schulz, too, has shown how male and female authors of the renaissance positioned themselves differentially with respect to the family and the traditions that it offered to its members (see also Fox-Genovese): women protagonists and authors often implicitly rejected the "Southern way of life" (structured around men and their goals) by cutting themselves off from the community rather than by futilely seeking fulfillment through integration into it. This is in keeping with Sandra Gilbert and Susan Gubar's observation that texts written by women modernists tend to express pleasure at the same social breakdown that was a source of anxiety for male writers, and that often their heroines' search for identity necessitates the renunciation of ties to a social order that has not allowed them to pursue their ambitions (3).

In the following pages, I examine five female characters in the Miranda stories who essay the limited options available to women: Sophia Jane, Cousins Amy and Eva, Great-aunt Eliza, and Nannie.[7] Subsequently, I turn to Miranda's negotiation of her own identity in relation to the models available to her. The Grandmother best represents Miranda's (and Porter's) ambivalence toward the Old Order; as Janis Stout observes, she "provides the measure by which Miranda can assess herself and the world, but she provides also the standard that must be resisted if the child is to achieve autonomy" ("Estranging Texas," 92). On the one hand, she offers security and a sense of belonging to the motherless grandchildren that she raises: the children see her as "the only reality . . . in a world that seemed otherwise without fixed authority or refuge" (*CS,* 324). On the other hand, the antebellum order that she upheld also had obvious and significant flaws. As the story "The Old Order" details, in addition to hierarchical race and gender roles, plantation society fostered destructive social and moral values in the men who oversaw it (Flanders, 55). Many of the trials that Sophia Jane faces are attributable to the men of her family, and although she recognizes this, her adherence to a code that deemed that "it was the business of a man to make all decisions and dispose of all financial matters" prevents her from challenging their authority (*CS,* 337). Similarly, although she wonders "how so much suffering and confusion could have been built up and maintained on such a foundation" as God's plan, she nevertheless has "no doubt as to the utter rightness and justice of the basic laws of human existence" (327–28). In her world, all know what their roles are, and all are to accept their lot without question. "This way and no other," she declares, as she organizes her family's life as well as her household (354). Her traditionalism also extends to intellectual pursuits: she vigorously discourages curiosity because discoveries represent change and therefore threaten the established order.

Although Sophia Jane offers her family stability, then, her order is mono-lithic and sacrifices the present on the altar of tradition: "nothing remained of life as [she and Nannie] had known it, the world was changing swiftly, but by the mysterious logic of hope they insisted that each change was probably the last; or if not, a series of changes might bring them, blessedly, back full-circle to the old ways they had known" (327).[8] There is no place in her world for any type of change that does not represent a return to the past.

Several women in the stories do rebel against conventional female life-plots but are unable to determine viable (or even attractive) roles for themselves. Miranda's Aunt Amy prefers to exercise her charms as a coquette rather than observing the propriety demanded of the south-ern belle. She stays out dancing, rides to the border of Mexico with her brothers, and resists marriage. Jane Krause DeMouy notes that she also struggles against her own biology, which seems to compound the social restrictions on her activities (153): it is suggested that the potions Amy drank to suppress her menstruation so as not to miss parties result-ed in her becoming consumptive and, moreover, that the attacks were strongest when she flouted permissible feminine conduct. Ultimately, Amy's only escape consists in determining the time and manner of her death: she scripts her marriage as a romantic tragedy, her wedding as a funeral, and commits suicide while still on her honeymoon. Even this final act of self-assertion is short-lived, though, for the family rewrites her ending posthumously and reestablishes her in legend as a paragon of beauty and grace, the unsurpassable standard for judging all future belles.

Sophia Jane's sister, Eliza, and Amy's Cousin Eva choose paths that may not be reconciled with traditional images of southern womanhood. In contrast to the Grandmother, Eliza is an "Inquirer" who searches for answers and for whom nothing is exempt from question. Her legacy, however, is mixed. On the one hand, she shows Miranda at an early age that there are alternatives to Sophia Jane's law. Whereas Shakespeare's

Miranda exclaims at the "brave new world that has such people in't," so, too, does Porter's find "another world" when looking at the moon through Eliza's telescope and her inquisitive eyes (361). And yet, both sisters' refusal to concede when arguing suggests that Eliza's religion of science might ultimately be as narrow and authoritarian as Sophia Jane's emphasis on tradition. The unattractive Eva leads the stereotypical life of the old maid: she is a Latin teacher, a suffragette, and is overbearing and bitter. Haunted by Amy's legend, which deformed her character as much as her own appearance condemned her to spinsterhood, she searches for vindication by fighting for women's right to vote. She also tries to avenge herself by destroying Miranda's illusions about the beautiful belle. Amy, however, remains on her pedestal in the family's hall of legend, while Eva remains "a blot [who] belonged to [the] everyday world of dull lessons to be learned . . . and disappointed expectations" (178). Eva's cause gains Miranda's sympathy, but her bitterness induces the younger woman to wonder if personality is the price that must be paid for independence.

Only in Nannie, the slave who remains with the family after emancipation but eventually redefines her role in relation to it, does Porter offer Miranda a positive female model. While Sophia Jane lives, Nannie is her double and shadow. Both women faithfully perform their duties as mothers, nurturers, guardians of the past, and strongholds of their families. Critics have commented on the mutuality of their experiences of oppression in a patriarchal system. In Nannie's case, racial and gender inequality operate in collusion when her owners wed her to another slave and present them both to Sophia Jane as a wedding gift. However, the death of the grandmother frees Nannie, who begins to distance herself both socially and spatially from what is left of the Old Order. Now she exchanges the "place in the world" that it had assigned her (328)—"faithful old servant Nannie, a freed slave," "a real member of the family, perfectly happy with them," "the amiable, dependent, like-one-of-the-family old servant" (349, 350)—for a "place of her very own" (348). She moves into her own home, rejecting the white family's claims to power over her and the identity that those claims had imposed. She also refuses to let her former husband live with her, declaring that she will serve no man, white or black, in her last years. Her actions openly challenge the Rheas' ideas of the world by revealing that the "happy slave" is but one of the many myths that they used to justify their way of life. The weakening of her once powerful and resilient spine in her old age suggests that she had provided the strength behind Sophia Jane's iron rule. In turn, her absence from the family's daily life exposes the fissures in the order that Sophia had struggled to hold together: "almost immediately after she went, everything slackened, lost tone, went off edge. Work did not accomplish itself as it once had. They had not learned how to work for themselves, they were all lazy and incapable of sustained effort or planning" (350). In effect, Nannie uncovers the discrepancies between the family's illusions of itself and its actual circumstances, and proves that without slaves, servants, and Sophia Janes, its code is not only defunct, but the values and conduct that it had sanctioned are simply untenable.

Porter once wrote to a friend that the artist "sees, he is the witness, the one who remembers, and finally works out the pattern and the meaning for himself, and gives form to his memories" (quoted in Brinkmeyer, *Artistic Development,* 181). Miranda's development in the stories of the Old Order would seem to follow this trajectory: in "The Witness," she bears witness to Uncle Jimbilly's tales of suffering; in "The Grave," she wants to see and to know; and "The Grave" and "Old Mortality" depict her efforts to distill meaning from the memories that she has inherited from her family and gathered from her own experiences. Like Quentin Compson, who did not have to be told stories of the past because he "knew it all already, had learned, absorbed it already without the medium of speech somehow from having been born and living beside it" (*Absalom,* 1972, 212), Miranda and her sister Maria, too, "felt they had lived a long time. They had lived not only their own years; but their memories, it seemed to them, began years before they were born, in the lives of the grown-ups around them" (174). As DeMouy has observed, Miranda's childhood desire to be like her cousin Isabel, the prototype of prevailing standards of beauty, attests to the fact that she internalizes the Old Order's prescriptions for femininity at a young age (155). Nevertheless, unlike Quentin, Miranda refuses to accept unquestioningly her family's explanations of the social order and of the past itself: the child who always "wanted to know the worst," and who stands out from the other grandchildren as "the little quick one" is destined to be an Inquirer who will search for her own answers (*CS*, 342). Thus, Porter's treatment of the pervasiveness of history and tradition, and their role in shaping the present, can be seen to focus an additional concern of Southern Renaissance authors through the prism of women's experience.

The stories that Miranda hears from former slaves lead her to doubt the grandmother's fairy tales of slavery and her idealized vision of contemporary race relations. By serving as counter-witnesses to the family's legends, Uncle Jimbilly and Nannie set precedents for Miranda's rejection of its views, while Nannie's actions foreshadow her own distancing of herself from a system that has become entrenched. In "Old Mortality," Miranda tests her family's "distorted images and misconceptions" of the past against the "visible remains" thereof and finds the former lacking (176). Like Platonic shades, the legends bear less resemblance to their originating forms as they gain distance from them; along with Amy, they, too, belong in a world of poetry that "was true but not real" (194). Miranda chips away at the armor of family legend until it breaks down and reveals that even Amy was neither as beautiful nor as content as she was held to be. When she finally meets her Uncle Gabriel and sees that he is a thoroughly unlegendary man, the few illusions that she still cherishes are shattered, and she realizes once and for all that she must rely on her own perceptions to correct the memories that falsify the past and betray the present. Stout details how Miranda's tendency to keep her own counsel sets her apart from her family in the same manner that her critical acceptance of their code does (*Strategies*, "Guarded Speech"). Her fears, queries, and revelations are not shared; gradually, they contribute to her alienation, setting the stage for her decision to set out on her own.

Miranda learns of the biological concomitants of womanhood at the same time that she is being socialized into a system that denies them, and the discovery further increases her awareness of the constructed nature of the code governing her society and its failure to accommodate her experiences. In "The Fig Tree," Miranda first glimpses her potential role as life giver. The story is dominated by images of birth, death, and renewal: the fig, a time-worn symbol of female sexuality; the tree of knowledge, which hearkens back to the primal moment of enlightenment; the tree frogs that shed their skins and eat them; the baby animals at the farm. However, these biological realities are absent from the ideal of femininity that initially captivates her in "The Grave." The wedding ring her brother finds is symbolic of a womanliness that is untainted by suffering or death, as well as a synecdoche of the family's—and the South's—myths of its past as a life of comfort and leisure. As Miranda places it on her finger, she feels herself succumbing to the "law of female decorum" associated with the role of belle (364): her interest in hunting wanes, and she wants to exchange her tomboyish clothing for a pretty dress and sit idly under the trees. The "law," however, is a chimera. The ring, like the civilization that it represents, is *buried* treasure, coextensive with a time that had come and gone with the wind, as it were.

Both the pregnant rabbit that Miranda's brother kills and its attendant symbolism confront her with a more realistic image of what womanhood entails and appeal to the curiosity that makes her seek her own answers. Looking at the dead baby rabbits in the mother's womb, Miranda is once again an Inquirer who wants "most deeply to see and to know" (366). Here as elsewhere in the stories of the Old Order, blood imagery accompanies the revelation of a truth, for the sight of the bloodied baby rabbits precipitates Miranda's awareness of her reproductive capacity and sexuality.[9] The forbidden knowledge is disturbing, as is the conflation of womb and tomb, which offers a lesson in mortality as well. Additionally, Miranda's fear of having violated her life-giving capabilities in "The Fig Tree" comes true here in her participation in killing the rabbit—a universal symbol of fertility—and its unborn babies.

In the final section of "Old Mortality," we learn that Miranda, like Porter herself, has eloped and left home. Her rejection of the narrow roles allowed her and of the idealized vision of society upon which they are predicated demands that she extricate herself from the collective memory through which they are transmitted as well as break free of the region of which they are a metonymy:

> Her mind closed stubbornly against remembering, not the past but the legend of the past, other people's memory of the past, at which she had spent her life peering in wonder like a child at a magic-lantern show. . . . I can't live in their world any longer, she told herself, listening to the voices back of her. Let them tell their stories to each other. Let them go on explaining how things happened. . . . At least I can know the truth about what happens to me. . . . (221)

By the time "Pale Horse, Pale Rider" begins, Miranda has divorced and moved to Denver. Her profession is hardly fortuitous: as a journalist in the New Order, she carries on the southern woman writer's struggle with social and literary traditions that define women as voiceless and passive, a struggle that reduplicates women's fight for liberation from the ideal of the belle (A. Jones, *Tomorrow,* 39–40). Her decisions reflect several of the modes of self-orphaning in women's writing that are discussed by Schulz: separation from community, spiritual and intellectual reconstitution, and the plotting of new directions for one's life

(104). As we shall see, though, how well Miranda succeeds in breaking free from inherited models for women's lives, and whether she reinscribes the past or repeats it, remains undetermined.

In a sense, Rulfo's novel inverts the situation presented in the stories of the Old Order, as well as the effects of the crossing of ways on individual and community. Where the Rhea family perpetuates a code of conduct supposedly delegitimized by the Civil War, Pedro Páramo deposes tradition. He implements a new order, which severs Comala from its past and renders its modes of exchange and social interchange ineffective. The transformation accompanying his assumption of power is in keeping with what Fredric Jameson has characterized as the social rupture induced by the advent of capitalism, which dissolves older rules and forms of collective relations without replacing them (69). As Jean Franco and others have noted, the order that Pedro Páramo ousts is based on a feudal system wherein the lord is to offer support in return for fealty, but the cacique reneges on his reciprocal obligations (see Franco, 768–72 in particular); service does not guarantee protection, and the lawyer Gerardo's hope of a bonus to compensate him for years of loyal assistance goes unfulfilled. Through the accumulation of property and money, Pedro Páramo expands his authority from the material to the immaterial, gaining control over Comala's judicial and religious institutions and, by extension, over its inhabitants' morals, lives, and spiritual beliefs (Monsiváis, 837). Whereas Miranda actively seeks to liberate herself from outmoded rules and traditions, as well as from family and community, Comala's inhabitants are disempowered by the new order's refusal to fulfill the traditional expectations once governing their actions.

Pedro Páramo replaces the old social and moral orders with a code in which money and force invalidate all prior obligations and absolve their wielder of the moral consequences of his actions (Franco, 772). The death of the cacique's father marks that of the old ways as well: "Lucas Páramo is dead. They must make new deals with me," he tells the manager of his estate, as he redraws the boundaries of his lands and rewrites the law to sanction his actions.[10] He proceeds to implement a system whose resolution of moral and spiritual grievances bears a striking resemblance to Thomas Sutpen's approach to balancing his "moral ledger": Pedro Páramo, too, "started a new account," canceling all previous debts ("hizo cuenta nueva" [*Páramo,* 133]). Prior to his reign, Comala's economy had been in harmony with the natural cycle, with the townspeople repaying their debts after the harvest. The Páramo family was the first to deviate from this state of relative equilibrium and thus set a precedent for the cacique's distortion of the town's patterns of exchange. When Pedro takes over the family's accounts after the death of his father, Fulgor Sedano, the family's estate manager, warns, "Your family ate it all up. They borrowed and borrowed without ever returning any of it" (*PP,* 36). The warning that such transgressions must be "paid" for, with the meaning of "redressed,"[11] is accompanied by the realization that there is "nowhere to get the money to pay" in a literal sense (*PP,* 36). This crucial dialogue is dominated by the verbs "pagar" and "pedir," *to pay* or *repay* and *to request*. To repay his debts, Pedro Páramo asks for Dolores's hand in marriage. However, he knows that this final favor will not increase his obligations to his greatest debtors, but, rather, will cancel itself out, as well as voiding his previous debts to the family. With this one action, then, he mercantilizes human relationships, reduces women to the status of commercial goods, and overturns an economy that requires repayment of debts incurred. His act of original accumulation destroys established meanings of terms of exchange, as well as the agreements that they entail, and introduces the rules that become the paradigm for social and spiritual relations in Comala.[12]

The semantic transformation that gradually becomes systemic parallels the expansion of the cacique's power from the physical to the metaphysical. The abrogation of territorial rights that takes place when he annexes his neighbor's land also brings down the laws which had protected them. As he tells Sedano, "From now on, we're the law" (40). Thus begins the path by which Pedro Páramo becomes "dueño" of Comala (*Páramo,* 93), in the etymological sense of *lord,*[13] a religious and secular ruler and one who dominates, as well as the standard usage meaning of *owner.* In the new order, the only value recognized is quantifiable, "measured" in monetary terms rather than according to any abstract concept of intrinsic worth; "non-quantifiables" such as familial obligations are not honored. Pedro Páramo casts his wife and legitimate son off without financial support, denies alms to Abundio (whom he does not recognize literally or legally as his son), and secures Susana San Juan's return as a financial transaction, through the offer of a home and provisions. Her father, Bartolomé, who understands that charity does not exist in the cacique's world and that nothing is ever offered without a demand for payment in kind, tells Susana that "I was willing to give him the benefit of my toil, since we had to repay him somehow" (*PP,* 83; "estaba dispuesto a que se cobrara con mi trabajo, ya que teníamos que pagar de algún modo" [*Páramo,* 107]). What he has yet to learn, however, is that Páramo does not want the revenues from the miner's labor, but his daughter, whom he classifies as "his crowning achievement" (*PP,* 83.; "su mejor trabajo," *Páramo,* 107).

The Church, too, is incorporated into the new system when Pedro Páramo renders Father Rentería's services commodities by promising to remunerate him for performing his marriage. Indeed, in the same way that he "cancels" his obligations to the Preciados, he also reneges on his debt to the Church. Father Rentería, who is contaminated by the cacique's "values," later tries to justify his denial of service to the poor because "prayers don't fill a stomach," that is, because the faith that they offer cannot be redeemed, as it were, for what he needs to survive (*PP,* 30). Even salvation is given a price tag: Rentería considers Eduviges's kindnesses toward her fellow men goods ("bienes" [*Páramo,* 41]) that she has put toward her salvation, but he claims that she forfeits them with her suicide. And while granting forgiveness literally costs him nothing,[14] he will only intercede for her by saying masses, for which he does charge. Heaven and hell, good and evil, are empty formulae because the priest's allocation of reward and punishment does not correspond to conduct but, rather, to wealth, and thus perpetuates the inequities of the current social system into the afterlife (Franco, 771).

Rentería is eventually denied absolution for having, in effect, sold his soul. However, the suspension of his powers takes place outside of the sphere of Pedro Páramo's influence—outside of "reality," as he calls it (*PP*, 73)—and once he returns to Comala, he resumes his practice, authorized as before by a closer and more immediately powerful lord. The cacique will be held accountable to no one but himself for his actions. Like Thomas Sutpen, he is a vortex, the figure around whom all others' lives revolve and upon whom they are dependent since all other powers and institutions have been subsumed into his will. He even betrays and destroys Comala's faith. Juan Rulfo once commented that although the characters of *Pedro Páramo* "continue to be believers, in truth, their faith is vacant. They have no handle, nothing to grab on to" (Interview, 106–7). Their predicament would seem to exemplify that of the modern Mexican, as described by Octavio Paz in his famous essay, *The Labyrinth of Solitude*, published in the same period as *Pedro Páramo* and drawing on similar issues arising from the contemporary debate over *mexicanidad*: "To Christians death is a transition, a somersault between two lives, the temporal and the otherworldly; to the Aztecs it was the profoundest way of participating in the continuous regeneration of the creative forces . . . [However,] death . . . lacks meaning for the modern Mexican. It is no longer a transition, an access to another life more alive than our own" (57). Hence Dorotea's literal assertion that "[a]fter so many years of never lifting up my head, I forgot about the sky ['el cielo']"—the Spanish meaning both *sky* and *heaven*—acquires metaphorical significance (*PP*, 65). Told by the priest that she will never enter heaven and will instead be condemned for all eternity to a town already situated at the entrance to hell, she must recreate both heaven and the sky for herself: "For me . . . heaven ['el cielo'] is right here" (66).

And Eduviges's suicide preempts God's prerogative of giving life and taking it away, confirming that even the most sacred of decisions has been taken into human hands.

Miguel Páramo, the only son that the cacique formally recognizes, fully realizes his paternal legacy. He, too, alters the law and subverts traditional codes of conduct to accommodate his transgressions. After murdering Father Rentería's brother, he visits the dead man's daughter, ostensibly seeking her forgiveness. She allows him into her room, heeding the Catholic doctrine that has taught her not to hate. However, instead of apologizing, he rapes her. He couches his illicit intentions in terms sanctioned by the Church, while Ana's adherence to these teachings disempowers her. The code guiding her actions has been disarmed, leaving her and the townspeople unable to protect themselves from the Páramo family. The cacique, in turn, offers compensation for his son's misdeeds in his own economic terms. When a woman accuses Miguel of killing her husband, Sedano "measures" her grief in kilograms and offers her an appropriate quantity of corn as compensation, as well as to prevent her from pursuing the matter (*Páramo*, 84). The woman's refusal to accept the offer, though, does not guarantee her justice. On the contrary, Pedro Páramo dismisses the claim on the grounds that he does not know the accuser and, therefore, that she simply does not exist. Having first seized control of human laws, he now grants life through his recognition of other individuals and takes it away through homicidal actions, both acts tantamount to displacing God himself. And because all social transactions have become financial, the cacique views Miguel's death not as retribution but as a down payment for his own sins: "I'm beginning to pay. The sooner I begin, the sooner I'll be through" (*PP*, 68). And he bribes Father Rentería to say prayers, attempting both to "buy" Miguel's salvation and to clear the debit column in his own moral ledger (26).

While overwhelmingly present in his capacity as cacique, Pedro Páramo is absent in his multiple roles of father. He deprives the town of a father figure in the capacity of head of the family, head of the community, and rector of spiritual life. He denies paternity of his illegitimate children and reneges on his obligations to his legitimate family; he refuses to honor his duties to his tenants; and, finally, he absorbs the Church's power, centered in a father figure who is but a figurehead for the cacique, leaving Comala's inhabitants without either spiritual or material support. An entire history of denied paternity in Mexico since the Conquest is condensed in his actions. In keeping with Paz's characterization of Mexican history as a form of orphanhood, a search for origins and parentage, Luis Harss and Barbara Dohmann analyze Rulfo's work as "a variant of the Mexican myth of the illegitimate child, born of rape, eternally in quest of his unknown father" (265). But the novel's explorations of themes of paternity may also be seen in light of its more immediate sociohistorical context. Multiple lines of descent characterize the plantation and *latifundio* systems, which I have discussed in previous chapters of this study, and are a recurrent topic in literature of the South and of Spanish America. Faulkner's Sutpen, as we have seen, had both an official family and miscegenated offspring, who lived in his house as slaves. He recognized neither the latter nor Charles Bon, who, like Juan Preciado, was born in wedlock but nevertheless bore his mother's surname. Isabel Allende's patriarch also has sexual relations with the women residing on his property but allows only the issue of his marriage to bear his name. Trueba's belief that those children whom he does not recognize simply do not exist holds true for all three patriarchs. The unrecognized offspring are both disinherited and exploited by the father's order. Finally, the dispossession is further compounded in the Mexican setting by the deracination wrought by the revolution and the Cristero War, which left countless children—including Rulfo himself—without one or both parents.

Self-orphaning, as we have seen, is necessary for Miranda's self-determination, but in Rulfo the dissolution of the family is never a choice, and never positive. In his works, male protagonists search for the father and affirm the family as a source of identity.[15] As the colonel in the story "Tell Them Not to Kill Me!" tells the man who had killed his father years before: "It's hard to grow up knowing that the thing we have to hang on to to take roots from is dead" (89). In *Pedro Páramo*, the root is absent from the very beginning, but the ramifications are the same, if not worse. Despite the cacique's abdication of paternity—or, perhaps, because of it—his law prevails. By denying the existence of individuals whom he does not know and by withholding sustenance from the entire town, Pedro Páramo's power to take life away voids his initial bestowal of life. The townspeople are dead as a result of his actions, direct and indirect, and damned by Rentería's complicity with his system. Literally and figuratively, Pedro Páramo orphans Comala.

The disintegration of the family structure and, on a wider level, the invalidation of a shared way of life underlie Comala's loss of autonomy. The townspeople accommodate Pedro Páramo's law, however, precisely because it is the only comprehensive order that is available to them. Additionally, they assist in the realization of his illicit intentions, and many even emulate his code of conduct. Dorotea, for example, arranges sexual liaisons for Miguel, and when Eduviges bears a child, none of the townsmen recognizes it as his. And ultimately the townspeople plead with Father Rentería to bless Miguel before he is buried. In the wake of Pedro's denial of assistance to Abundio and to the whole of Comala, charity goes into exile with those who leave. Dorotea is but one of many who dies because those who had given her alms turn their backs on what they leave behind. Chona, the only character in the novel to honor her filial obligations, refuses to elope because she knows that, despite her lover's claims, there are no "charitable souls" left in Comala to care for her father (*Páramo*, 60). Except for her, the few who remain do so, in fact, because the cacique has "bought" them, too, with the promise of remuneration. As Dorotea tells Juan Preciado, "Some stayed waiting for Pedro Páramo to die, because he'd promised to leave them his land and goods and they were living on that hope" (*PP*, 81). Without charity, the two other cardinal virtues cannot survive. And without faith or hope—virtues directed toward a future in which the individual is redeemed or compensated for suffering—the possibility of change is nonexistent. The townspeople's imprisonment in a past from which they cannot escape is a by-product of the disjunction that Pedro Páramo inserts between expectation and reward, between moral guidelines, individual behavior, and fate.

A few isolated instances of resistance to the new system may be found in the actions of several female characters who, as in *The House of the Spirits*, proffer their critiques from the margins. For the most part, the resistance takes the form of an affirmation of the family, coupled with a rejection of Pedro Páramo's economic valuation of human life. Eduviges's actions, for example, are in keeping with a gift economy in which she gives of herself without asking for payment. She refuses to allow the townsmen's denial of her child's paternity to undermine the family structure, as it does in the cacique's order and, instead, assumes the role of both parents, declaring to all that "I'll be the father as well, although fate chose me to be the mother" (30). Additionally, she undertakes the care of another child, Juan Preciado, who is not hers, but whom she considers her own. Pedro Páramo's mercantilization of memory is also resisted by the woman who refuses to accept a bribe as compensation for her husband's murder, and, most of all, by Dolores Preciado herself. Dolores, like Eulalia Bon, sends her repudiated son to seek restitution on her behalf. Juan's task is neither to make a request that would have to be repaid nor to exact revenge, but to collect on a debt long overdue: Pedro Páramo's expropriation of the Preciado's property and the exile of mother and son. Dolores, in fact, reappropriates Pedro Páramo's vocabulary and applies it to her own design: "Don't ask him for anything. Just [demand] what's ours," she entreats her son, "What he should have given me but never did. . . . Make him pay, son, for all those years he put us out of his mind" (3). As the only inhabitant to look back after she has left and the only one to have preserved the memory of the town as it was when it was alive, Dolores seeks a compensation for personal damages that is also a claim to restore Comala to memory, if not to life.

Where Dolores and Eduviges attempt to forestall Pedro Páramo's severing of family ties and his erasure of memory, Susana San Juan turns the cacique's strategies against him and the others who have adopted them. She rejects the three incarnations of the paternal figure who try to subsume her under their distorted authority: she is disrespectful toward her biological father, she ignores Pedro Páramo, and she derides Father Rentería with her eroticization of the Eucharist.[16] Also, at her mother's funeral, she rejects the commodification of human and spiritual values. In a community where people do not act on one another's behalf out of kindness, the labor involved in the burial is paid for, but she refuses to share her grief in a similar manner: "Death is not to be parceled out as if it were a [good]" (*PP*, 77; "bien" [*Páramo*, 99]). Susana also refutes the townspeople's claim that paying for masses is the only means of securing her mother's salvation. At this point and later, when she rejects Bartolomé's authority, Susana San Juan is deemed crazy, the traditional metaphor for marginalizing potentially subversive persons. She does not contest the designation, though, for it merely confirms her chosen deviance from and defiance of a shared code of conduct. Susana further casts aside shared memory in favor of highly personal and unconventional memories—of herself as an outsider, of her unabashed enjoyment of sensual pleasure—from which she builds her refuge and space of resistance. Here, then, her modes of resistance intersect with those of Porter's heroine: like Miranda, Susana orphans herself figuratively from the larger social structure.

The denial of family ties in both works may be further correlated with the experimentation with alternatives to chronological order in narrative that I will discuss in the following section. In *Time and the Novel: The Genealogical Imperative*, Patricia Drechsel Tobin discusses an implicit homology between linear time and causality, whereby links are established between events and purpose imputed to them on the basis of the sequence in which they took place. She argues that in the traditional realist novel, the parallel is extended: chronological succession is metaphorically equated with genealogical descent, conferring "ontological priority . . . upon mere temporal anteriority" (7). Tobin interprets the breakdown in chronological order in modernist fiction as a stylistic analogue to challenges to the family and its authority. Thus, identity and legitimacy cannot be established by tracing an individual's lineage back to the family's origin. I would like to suggest that the rejection of the genealogical line of descent—Miranda's denial of procession, of origins, and Pedro Páramo's of succession or progeny—complements the questioning of the concepts of temporal linearity and causal sequence conducted at the level of style.

The convergence of such critical issues as memory, self-orphaning, and the repudiation of a patriarchal cultural heritage in Miranda and Susana San Juan is intriguing, given the otherwise contrasting approaches taken by Porter and Rulfo. In the long run, however, Miranda's repudiation of her family bears a greater resemblance to Pedro Páramo's withholding of recognition and therefore of legitimacy from his offspring than it does to Susana's actions. Porter and Rulfo share a common focus on the transition between social orders, on the emergence of individual personalities out of the new orders, on the projects of self-definition and domination that set these characters apart from their communities, and on the breakdown of the family. In spite of this common focus, however, these authors have divergent views on communal identity and memory and on their role in configuring the future. This divergence reflects their own sympathy with the plight of individual or community, respectively.[17]

The Meaning of Revolution

During the Madero revolution I watched a street battle between Maderistas and Federal troops . . . a very old Indian woman stood near me, perfectly silent . . . Later she said to me, when the dead were being piled for burning in the public square, "It is all a great trouble now, but it is for the sake of happiness to come." She crossed herself, and I mistook her meaning.

"In heaven?" I asked. Her scorn was splendid.

"No, on earth. Happiness for men, not for angels!"

She seemed to me then to have caught the whole meaning of revolution.

—Katherine Anne Porter, "Why I Write About Mexico"

"I am the grandchild of a lost War, and I have blood-knowledge of what life can be in a defeated country on the bare bones of privation," Porter once declared (*CE*, 160). Rulfo, too, defined himself in generational and familial relationship to a war whose efficacy he called into question and whose devastating legacy he explored: "I am the son of wealthy people who lost everything in the Revolution" (quoted in Poniatowska, 44). The civil wars to which both authors refer established clear and irreversible boundaries between past and present in their respective regions. So, too, did the horrors committed by supposedly civilized nations in yet another war, the Great War—contemporaneous with the Mexican Revolution, and during which Porter began her career as a writer—cast doubts on shared norms and beliefs that had been taken for granted. We have seen how Porter and Rulfo address the (non)viability of communities still guided by old codes in new orders. I would now like to explore how setting their narratives in periods marked by change, disorder, and violent conflict has both regional and universal implications—how the context of war underscores the urgency of the problems arising out of the crossing of ways, and at the same time broadens their ramifications.

The visions of reality offered by Porter and Rulfo respond to the revisions of reality, as it were, the renovations and innovations of literary modernism that were discussed in the introduction. Both authors were attracted to the technical virtuosity of modern writers and, in particular, to their replacement of chronological order with alternative means of representing time. In general in Rulfo's novel, for example, techniques such as polyphonic narration, limited perspectives, the subjectivization of experience, the lack of consensus, and the refusal to resolve ambiguities, offer a stylistic correlative to the atomism of Comala; in effect, they express the lack of a collective reality other than the driving force of the cacique's will. More specifically, Porter and Rulfo found in the new approaches to representing time a style concordant with their concern with troubled pasts that continue to haunt and hinder the present. As we shall see, both authors intersperse chronologically ordered segments with others structured around visions, dreams, and explorations of memory wherein past and present or present and future are conflated. Or they present scenes that obviate time altogether.

During the 1930s and 1940s, as southern regionalism came under attack for antidemocratic tendencies, many southern writers, including Porter herself, moved away from a South-centered interpretation of history and reconceptualized their past as a microcosm of a more widespread process, a variant, albeit deviant, of the myth of modern history as progress. In addition to regional issues, problems of the individual subject were also addressed within national and international contexts. In "Pale Horse, Pale Rider," a short novel of the New Order published in 1939, Porter dramatizes the relationship between the self and her world in a setting that is not regionally delimited, deliberately broadening the implications of Miranda's experiences. The place is Denver; the time, the final days of the First World War, which Porter has described as "a period of grotesque dislocations in a whole society when the world was heaving in the sickness of a millennial change," a period that heralded the "majestic and terrible failure of the life of man in the Western world" (*CE*, 457). For Porter as well as many other southern writers, the Great War represented the culmination of a process of social deterioration that had been a reality in the South since the fall of the Old Order. "Pale Horse, Pale Rider" establishes its continuity with the stories of the Old

Order in the opening dream, which depicts Miranda's flight from the decadent South and its oppressive entanglements. She awakens to find that all of Western civilization has been stricken by spiritual malaise, symbolized in the epidemic raging through the city (the classical motif of the plague, with its attendant connotations of a world turned upside-down) and in the war wreaking havoc internationally. It is no accident that Miranda's recovery from the flu coincides with the Armistice nor that her lover, Adam, American innocence incarnate, perishes during the war. He is the "sacrificial lamb," the old world values slaughtered on the altar of modern social evil (*CS*, 295).

The stories of the Old Order's dismantling of the social construction of reality is recast in "Pale Horse, Pale Rider" as a study of public distortions of truth. To find out the "truth about what happens to me," Miranda has rejected the South's restrictions on women and the lies upon which her family predicates its identity, only to fall victim to modernity's collective self-deception and to the widespread manipulation of women and humankind (221). In the New Order, no correspondence exists between the language used to arouse support for the war and individual belief. Newspapers print stories that echo the government's position and curry favor with the nation's financial powers. Professional patriots urge their audiences to buy war bonds that they cannot afford, and refusal to comply is severely punished. To avoid the appearance of nonconformity, considered synonymous with treason, people parrot the information that they are fed and suppress their beliefs. Miranda's co-worker, for example, hides her rebelliousness and anger behind a self-sacrificing, patriotic exterior. Miranda sees through the social rhetoric and tries to act upon and write what she believes, but the honesty and integrity toward which she strives have no place in the public sphere and, in fact, have unpleasant consequences. She will only be able to avoid these, it seems, by writing what her superiors want to read. "Please them," a colleague tells her, "and you'll get a raise. Hand-in-glove, my poor dumb child, will you never learn?" (*CS*, 289). And with a raise, of course, Miranda would be able to buy a bond and do the "patriotic duty" that she has thus far avoided.[18]

Punishment for refusing to capitulate in her professional activities teaches Miranda that she must be especially cautious about speaking the truth on a much more sensitive issue, the war, for this would expose her to the risk of losing her job and being branded a traitor. As a result, she bows to pressure to conform to public values; she "pull[s] down the shutters" over the private world of her heart and conscience and gradually becomes one in appearance with the other "speechless animals" that tacitly consent to their own destruction (294, 291). She writes articles encouraging women to support the war effort, sings patriotic tunes, and, when a bond salesman claims that the war is being waged to protect democracy and civilization, wants to cry out, "Coal, oil, iron, gold, international finance, why don't you tell us about them, you little liar?" but can only ask her question silently (293). Thus she does not go visit the soldiers at the hospital again, for she would be unable to face the hostile young man who embodies her own feelings toward the war and who reminds her of the harmony between belief and action that she has forsaken. Ultimately, the distance between appearance and reality becomes so great that Miranda can only find her truth involuntarily, in dreams and visions and in the "new language" of silence that she shares with Adam (296).

In a discussion of the intersection of gender issues, the southern patriarchal aristocracy, and social change, Anne Goodwyn Jones claims that war represented the fullest actualization of patriarchal values for Porter and that "two fundamental truths about war and women have produced the necessity for the patriarchy to fabricate patriotism and femininity" ("Gender and the Great War," 144). In the case of patriotism, the Great War was not just a battle between countries and ideologies, but also between generations: fathers, or "tom-cats," want to kill their sons, thus sacrificing the "tom-kittens" to protect their own interests (*CS*, 294). And in the second case, where the wartime absence of men helps to expand women's options, menial, unproductive tasks are couched as patriotic duties in order to reinforce traditional gender roles and minimize the opportunities for independent thought and action:

> Work will win, sugar will win, peach pits will win the war. . . . So all the happy housewives hurry . . . to lay their baskets of peach pits on the altar of their country. It keeps them busy and makes them feel useful, and all these women running wild with the men away are dangerous, if they aren't given something to keep their little minds out of mischief. So rows of young girls, the intact cradles of the future . . . roll cockeyed bandages that will never reach a base hospital, and knit sweaters that will never warm a manly chest, their minds dwelling lovingly on all the blood and mud and the next dance. . . . Keeping still and quiet will win the war. (290)

Patriotism thus acts as an agent of ideology and the power relations that it sanctions. Undeceived by the fictions that sustain both the war and traditional gender arrangements, Miranda nevertheless perpetuates them in the articles she writes for her own "routine female job" (275). Not only has progress in options for women been slow, but the social restrictions that Miranda ran away from are clearly not limited to the South.

Miranda's illness indicates that her outward conformity to public demands has broken down the barriers protecting the private domain where she had tried to maintain her integrity. That her body and subconscious alike have been infected—that is, that she has internalized the rhetoric garnering support for the war—is evidenced when in her delirium she calls her doctor (Dr. Hildesheim) the anti-German epithets which had disgusted her earlier and which, even at that moment, her "reasoning coherent self" acknowledges to be "wrong" (309). Upon her recovery, Miranda decides to give up resisting altogether: she finally stops "learning all the wrong things" and does instead as she is told (289). She suppresses her despair at having survived and agrees with her friends that it was "a pleasant surprise . . . to find herself alive. For it will not do to betray the conspiracy and tamper with the courage of the living; there is nothing better than to be alive, everyone has agreed on that; it is past argument" (315). Acquiescence marks the final collapse of her determination to act upon her beliefs. Significantly, her capitulation is manifest as an espousal of traditional femininity: she adorns herself with makeup and accessories, of her own accord reviving the superficial image of womanhood and the anachronistic "law of female decorum" of which she had been disabused in "The Grave" (364). Thus when her dead lover appears to her in a vision, he is still "more alive than she was"; though "false" and a "lie," he symbolizes the truth that she has forsaken (317). The epidemic and the war have ended, but Miranda's surrender indicates the triumph of social hypocrisy and offers little hope of regeneration. Porter foreshadows in Miranda her own knowledge that the end of the Great War did not herald a new beginning—for women or men. Women gained the right to vote, but failed to impact upon the nation's economy or politics. Hope waned as the awaited reconstitution of American culture failed to materialize.

The relationship between the regional and the universal, the question of whether Comala's desolation emblematizes the fate of Mexico or the condition of man in general, has also been a prominent topic of criticism on *Pedro Páramo*. Donald Shaw avers that *caciquismo* and related problems of *latifundismo*, including the abuse of authority and the corruption of the clergy, serve Rulfo—to paraphrase Faulkner—as the terms he knows best. He concludes that the novel is an allegory not just of Mexican life but of man's wanderings on this earth and of the spiritual (dis)orientation of modern man (*Nueva narrativa*, 134). Thus, Juan Preciado searches for his origins, for his father and a lost paradise, but finds only disillusion and rejection. Carlos Fuentes and Julio Ortega focus on the resonances of Greek and Roman myths in Juan's quest, while Joseph Sommers suggests that the novel has a mythical dimension because it draws on universal motifs and archetypes: a descent into hell; the search for power; the search for the father; unrequited love; sin, failure, and fatalism; violence and cruelty, to name but a few (*After the Storm*).[19] There is no question that Rulfo's novel fuses international and national literary currents. As I have already noted, James Irby's prescient landmark study details how Rulfo and many of his successors in Spanish American letters were attracted to Faulkner precisely because he was both modernist and regional writer and because he depicted a reality that they perceived as kindred to their own.

Perhaps Rulfo himself encouraged the universalizing interpretations of his novel with comments that suggest the inevitability of Comala's demise, and by declaring that his works revolve around three basic themes: love, life, and death ("El desafío," 384). At the same time, however, he left no doubt that his works referred to a specific set of circumstances, that he tried "to show a reality that I know and that I want others to know. To say: 'This is what has happened and what is happening'" (quoted in Harss and Dohmann, 275). He further emphasized that the novel's setting was reminiscent of his native province and also representative of Mexico as a whole, while the cacique, too, was grounded in a regional reality: he was the "prototype of the medium-sized landowner there used to be in Jalisco, a man who lives on his lands and works them himself" (267). It is my belief that Rulfo's recourse to universal and mythical motifs complements the specific regional predicament that he depicts, deliberately enhancing its removal from the passage of time. The novel's significance is not circumscribed within, but is certainly of particular importance to, the nation itself. After all, Rulfo spent years working at Mexico's Instituto Nacional Indigenista, addressing the problems plaguing his homeland, many of which are graphically depicted in his earlier short stories. Yes, *Pedro Páramo* incorporates modernist innovations, but at the same time it draws upon the tradition of the novel of the Mexican Revolution. Similarly, the world of Pedro Páramo—with its inverted values, collapsed religious structures, poverty and injustice—may be ascribed to the aftermath of the Great War, but it is also comprehensible in light of the civil war which decimated the nation and the ensuing upheaval.

While World War I raged internationally, the fall of modern civilization's deities of reason, progress, and order was taking place independently in Mexico, in the revolution's demonstration of the extremes to which "progreso y orden," Porfirio Díaz's motto, could be taken.

Juan Rulfo's works question the legitimacy of the revolution and criticize the consolidation of its power. His narratives of injustice, poverty, exploitation, and the shortcomings of land reform dramatize various aspects of the revolution's failure. Its promises went unkept. Or, as "They Gave Us the Land" so clearly attests, many reforms were, in the end, pro forma, implemented in such a manner as to reinforce prevailing (im)balances of power. In *Pedro Páramo*, the war is far from occupying the center stage that it is afforded in the novel of the revolution. Like *The Edge of the Storm* (1947), another late exemplar of the tradition, Rulfo's novel depicts a hermetic town dominated by all-powerful, repressive institutions. However, where the "storm" eventually irrupts in Agustín Yáñez's unnamed town and breaks down its stifling atmosphere, Comala remains forever on its edge. Even the revolution falls prey to the cacique: by supplying the local revolutionaries with funds, weapons, and men, he essentially purchases it and accommodates it, too, to his system. By arming, he disarms: he guarantees the men's loyalty, neutralizing their—and the revolution's—disruptive potential and, by extension, ensures the continuity of his regime. Perhaps fifteen years are collapsed into the brief scene that traces the revolutionaries' shifts in allegiance from Venustiano Carranza to Alvaro Obregón and, finally, to Father Rentería.[20] The scene conveys a sense of intense activity and of the rapid passage of time. And yet, rather than undermining the sense of paralysis that pervades Comala, it paradoxically underscores the fact that nothing ever happens there. Time goes by but nothing changes. Loyalty might be switched from one party to another, but the violence remains constant, fueling a war that provides no constructive solutions to the nation's difficulties. The majority of the revolutionaries never even know why they are fighting. Those who originally rebel "because others have done the same" fight on the side of the clergy in the Cristero War because "I like how they yell" (97, 117).

This stagnation openly challenges the revolution's claims to have effected change. In the same way that Sutpen's pursuit of his design spans the greater part of the heyday and decline of the southern plantation system, Pedro Páramo's centralization of landownership dates to the years of Porfirio Díaz's regime (1876–1910), which was notorious for facilitating the expansion of large estates, and his downfall takes place in the years following the revolution but is not a product of its reforms. Structurally peripheral to the story of Pedro Páramo's ascendancy and the town's death, the revolution is nevertheless thematically central. The very fact of its marginalization attests to the cacique's power and to the ability of landowners to defuse potential threats. In Comala and at the macro-level of the nation, the revolution passes through without altering prevailing relations of power or redistributing land or wealth. After breaking down the collective supports of family, charity, and religion and depriving Comala's inhabitants of the possibilities both of life and of life after death, Pedro Páramo completes the job by absorbing the energy of the revolution. The townspeople's hopes for redemption—whether through religion or social change, in heaven as angels or on earth as men—are in vain. The meaning of revolution has proven intranscendent.

Like many other artists in the 1920s, Katherine Anne Porter looked to so-called "primitive" cultures for affirmation of the values that had been shaken by the First World War. She spent several years living, studying, and traveling in Mexico, and, along with Diego Rivera, Alí Chumacero, and Adolfo Best-Maugard, among others, participated in the cultural renaissance of the early years after the revolution. Many of her early stories are set in the country, and she wrote extensively about her hopes for the nation's progress and, later, about the revolution's unfulfilled promise(s). On the one hand, she found the permanence that she sought and praised Mexican folk art for being a "profound and touching expression of a very old race, surviving and persisting in its devotion to ancient laws with a steadfastness that is anachronism in this fluctuating age" (*Outline,* 187). At the same time, though, she was keenly attuned to the nation's troubles and to the suffering of its people. In 1920, she hailed Obregón as a "New Man" and his presidency as the beginning of a "New Order." She optimistically predicted that "[w]ith a nation granting complete recognition of all rights legitimately acquired, [Mexico] will soon be right with the other nations at issue. . . . With order, cleanliness, industry and labor established, Mexico with its riches would bound to the front" ("The New Man," 58). No such "New Order" arrived, however. There was no radical change of government, and necessary social and financial services did not materialize to the degree that they were needed. Later, Porter ascribed the difficulties in implementing the revolution's programs to what she called "the Mexican Trinity" of land, the Church, and oil, which had conspired to become "the powers that hold this country securely in their grip" (*CE,* 403). Pedro Páramo's control over Comala's land and spiritual life allows him to command the same power as Porter's unholy trinity to block any movement toward change, including—especially—the revolution itself.

Et in Arcadia Ego:
Keeping the Past Alive in the Present

The reason I am so long in finding the meaning and seeing the end of something I know I must tell, is that I have stubbornly refused to accept the shock and the suffering, I *will* not reconcile myself; the memory, instead of staying fluid and going on and changing and living, sets itself and fixes upon that point in time where the shock occurred and cannot be persuaded away from it, and slowly turns to stone.

—Katherine Anne Porter, letter to William Goyen, 8 April 1951

In Mexico, as in many countries, the recreation of the agrarian past is
an essential ingredient in the configuration of national culture. . . . A
mythical Eden is *invented* . . . which is indispensable for establishing
order in a society convulsed by the rapid arrival of modernity and
shaken by the contradictions of the new industrial way of life. . . . It is
an evocation, in the present, of a prior, ancient place in which
happiness reigns; but it is a past and withered happiness that rests in
a deep, mythical stratum, buried by the avalanche of the Mexican
Revolution . . . [i]n a place where past and present merge, and
exclude the future.

 —Roger Bartra, translated from "El edén subvertido"

In the stories of the Old Order and *Pedro Páramo*, collective memory performs a function similar to the structuralist definition of myth:
it explains the past to a community in the present and transmits the
group's sense of identity, as well as the rules, roles, and relationships that
it authorizes. This is of great importance when the advent of a newer
form of society makes past and present appear discontinuous and threatens the way of life being displaced. And yet, shared memory is excised
in Porter's stories and destroyed in *Pedro Páramo*, stifled in either case
by the agency of a single individual. As we have seen, Miranda's individualism constitutes an implicit rejection of a society that exists only
in her family's memory; it also reflects Porter's own challenge to the
Agrarians' nostalgic championing of the antebellum South as a community whose cohesion buttressed it against modernity at the price of
women's continued subordination (Fox-Genovese, 21). Accordingly, her
heroine's self-definition as an Inquirer and an independent woman
results in the denial of both memory and heritage. Pedro Páramo destroys
Comala's memory, codes of conduct, and the town itself in the pursuit
of his own ambitions. By vindicating Dolores, Juan Preciado hopes to
restore them. That is, the object of his quest is the past itself, a dead father
and a lost paradise known to him only through his mother's eyes and

memories. He seeks satisfaction and his identity within traditional social structures; where Miranda repudiates, Juan hopes to recuperate. Success would entail resurrecting the past, a task doomed to fail in a town denied salvation, forever condemned to the spiritual and geographical purgatory that is the final stop in Juan's journey. Hence the rejection or, conversely, valorization of memory in the two works seems to be correlated with the questing subject's relationship to community, and whether she or he pursues independence from or integration into it.

The power of memory has another side, however. "They carry their dead on their shoulders," is how Rulfo once described the ties that bind the villagers of his native Jalisco to their past (quoted in Harss and Dohmann, 250). It is an image that rings true literally and figuratively for Porter and Rulfo alike, for whom the inability or unwillingness of their communities to leave their dead behind and overcome the past is a fundamental concern. The centrality of physical monuments memorializing the past—whether tombstones, graves, or cemeteries—to the Rhea family and to *Pedro Páramo* reifies the cult of a past which *is*, is *in*, and overwhelms the present. Miranda's family forfeits the present to worship the memories that they have themselves constructed of their dead. Sophia Jane moves from one state to another, transporting her husband's remains with her. Her unwillingness to turn back is geographic alone: until she dies, she worships the memory of the man whom she had held in contempt while he lived. Gabriel likewise consecrates Amy's memory in the verses that he writes for her tombstone and continually holds her up to his second wife as a paragon. Even in death he is unfaithful, asking to be buried at his first wife's side. Similarly, in Rulfo's story "Luvina," the inhabitants of the town—which critics have considered a preliminary model for Comala—refuse to leave in search of better prospects, precisely because they cannot take their dead with them: "They live here and we can't leave them alone" (119). The "shadows" ("sombras") that haunt Luvina in life, living only in anticipation of their death, become in the novel *ánimas en pena* [suffering souls] who roam the streets of Comala in death (117). They literalize Rulfo's description of the villages in Jalisco as graveyards, "dedicated to the cult of death" (quoted in Harss and Dohmann, 266).

The role of memory and of the breakdown of linear time in keeping the past alive, making it responsible for condemning the present to death, is a prominent concern for Porter and Rulfo. Time and again, their characters strive to counter the effects of time by engaging in acts of remembering aimed at resurrecting a lost state of plenitude. The desire to extricate the self (or the community) from the flow of time may be a product of the despair that seeks remnants of past contentment in the present, in which case a perpetual present (or a perpetuated past) is the only source of comfort. Memory is granted this power since by nature it subverts linear time and transports the past to the present.

In "Pale Horse, Pale Rider," Porter complements memory's breakdown of temporal boundaries with various tropes that extend the present or superimpose the future or past on the present. Premonitions of Adam's death induce Miranda to attempt to thwart time and the ubiquitous deadlines, clocks, and tolling of bells that mark its passage: she strives to prolong the present by keeping "unnatural" hours and by filling the few days and nights of his leave with countless activities (280). Her illness-induced delirium is also an exercise in obliterating time: "There were no longer any . . . tough filaments of memory and hope pulling taut backwards and forwards holding her upright between them. There was only this one moment and it was a dream of time . . . and there was to be nothing more" (304). This redemptive condensation of time foreshadows her final dream's distillation of the self into its very essence, the will to survive. Adam's death, however, makes her "dream of time" a waking nightmare of timelessness, an endless state in which there is nothing to hope for, tantamount to a living death. Memories of Adam, and of a lost paradise of happiness and communion, usurp the present and future. The grammar and tropes of the final pages of the novel reflect Miranda's stagnation: anaphora, gerundives, and the imperfect tense express the repetition of actions and time that does not advance.[21] This is, in fact, a period in which Miranda loses track of time. And although the final paragraph suggests movement, it lacks verbs, other than in adjectival clauses and the "would be" of the last sentence, which only underscores the fact that all that awaits her is a perpetuation of her current state: if at first there was no time for her and Adam, "[n]ow there would be time for everything" (317). As Robert Brinkmeyer observes, Miranda succumbs to the disorder from which she has fled in her family, the fact that "there was always a voice recalling other and greater occasions" in the past, occasions that are the standard by which all later experiences are measured and of which the latter will always fall short (*Artistic Development*, 174; *CS*, 179). To escape the despair promised by this extension of a bleak present, Miranda surrenders to oblivion, the lack of memory which, like the eternity that it is to counteract, is a curtain "hung before nothing at all" (309). Miranda thus renews the vow that she made in "Old Mortality" to excise her memories of the past, but here it does not constitute an act of self-empowerment. Instead, the renunciation has become a search for deliverance from the individuality that compels her to seek out truths and an espousal of conformity.

In *Pedro Páramo*, Rulfo similarly frees himself from the constraints of time. The nonlinear narration and the juxtaposition of scenes without temporal indicators correspond to the author's perception of a chaotic world where events do not unfold in an orderly, sequential manner, and in which there is no transcendent authority who guides or makes sense of experience. Multiple temporal planes and scenes are interwoven seamlessly through conversations in the grave and the presentation of the only realities still of importance to the dead: memories, the recollected experience of reality, and emotions. As in "Pale Horse, Pale Rider," deterministic techniques offer glimpses of the future in the present which alert the reader beforehand that any effort to avert the premonitions or to effect change will prove futile. As in Ellison's *Invisible Man*, then, "the end is in the beginning" (9). Rulfo's novel is a series of flashbacks. Actions and conversations are interrupted by other sequences of events and later resume where they had left off. Eduviges's narration of Miguel Páramo's death, for example, is interrupted by several other versions of the event in the pause between her repetition of the phrase "You're lucky" (*PP*, 23, 32; "[m]ás te vale" [*Páramo*, 32, 43]), while the arrangement of the cacique's marriage to Dolores Preciado is narrated retrospectively in the interval between knocks on the door to Páramo's house as Sedano awaits a meeting (*PP*, 34, 41). On a larger scale, Dorotea and Juan's conversation at the novel's midpoint echoes the latter's opening statement and returns the reader to the beginning of the text: "I came to Comala because I had been told that my father . . . lived there" (3) becomes "I told you that at the very beginning. I came to find Pedro Páramo, who they say was my father" (60). This retrospectively recasts the action up to this point as a flashback, the duration of which is compressed into that of Juan and Dorotea's dialogue. The entire first half of the novel is thus shown to be a "wrinkle" in time containing multiple internal regressions of its own. Rather than advance the narrative action, these wrinkles retrace steps only to return, fatalistically, to the present, to the denouement whose disclosure preceded and precipitated the retrospective narration; like anaphora, they are structural restraints on the flow of time. Pedro Páramo's death is announced in the first pages of the novel, condemning to failure Juan Preciado's search and foretelling the novel's outcome from its very outset. In many respects, the novel is itself a wrinkle in time whose structure reduplicates the dead town's paralysis, as well as the revolution's failure to effect change. Through the endless retelling of prior events, gradually, the lived and recalled past fuses with the "present" of posthumous remembrance. In any event, with characters who are dead, all action can only be in the past, while the present and future as spaces of choice no longer exist.

Life and death form a continuum in Comala. The dead live side-by-side with the living, while a rememberer such as Susana San Juan is considered dead long before she dies. Rulfo drew on Mexican beliefs about the dead, including the *ánimas en pena* and the dead's ability to communicate with each other and with the living, to enhance the effect of timelessness in the town. He once claimed to have peopled his novel with dead characters precisely because they "live outside space and time" (quoted in Harss and Dohmann, 270). Where novels-in-a-day such as James Joyce's *Ulysses* and Virginia Woolf's *Mrs. Dalloway* condense past, present, and future within the temporal frame of a single day by plumbing the depths of consciousness in which all reside, Rulfo eschews time altogether by situating his tale in the realm of the dead, "where everything takes place in a simultaneous time that is a not-time" (quoted in Benítez, 6). Comala's inhabitants are exempt from time and are, paradoxically, its prisoners, for they will remain as they are, condemned by death to the past, until the end of time. The novel would appear to dramatize the aforementioned claim by Paz that Mexicans' conception of death has become as intranscendent as their lives have become unproductive. At the same time, though, Rulfo, however inadvertently, appropriates and inverts Paz's conception of time—or timelessness. Whereas the latter valorizes a mythical understanding of time not as "succession and transition but the perpetual source of a fixed present in which all times, past and future, were contained," *Pedro Páramo*'s characters have not been "exiled from that eternity in which all times were one" but, rather, condemned to it, sentenced to wander the earth forever without the possibility of redemption (*Labyrinth,* 208). "You'll feel that one would like to live there for all eternity," Dolores Preciado tells her son (*Páramo,* 75). Apart from the element of volition, her statement contains more than a grain of truth. Timelessness for Rulfo is the endless perpetuation of the past, emblematic of the permanence of Pedro Páramo's reign. Time is obviated and, with it—as with Miranda at the end of "Pale Horse, Pale Rider"—hope.

Whereas Miranda can only escape her memories by relinquishing them and surrendering to the nothingness of oblivion, Rulfo's characters actively seek shelter from their solitary isolation in the only action allowed them: the remembrance of things past, the nostalgic evocation of life and other times. Susana San Juan, Dolores Preciado, and Pedro Páramo in particular apotheosize the past in their efforts to recover or avenge what no longer exists. Susana derives comfort from a visceral sense of her mother's presence and from erotic memories of Florencio. While she lives she denies the present and thus withstands the cacique's desire to own her soul, if not her body. Dolores preserves the memory of a fertile and vital Comala, redolent in imagery of the promised land: "Green pastures . . . the smell of alfalfa and bread. A town that smelled like spilled honey . . . Not to know any taste but the savor of orange blossoms in the warmth of summer" (*PP,* 18–19). And yet, her dreams delude: she was, after all, exiled from the town for wanting to leave, by a husband whom she despised. The images that she bequeaths to Juan to guide him in his journey—of a land of milk and honey, a father who will be pleased to meet his son, and the hope offered by the reunion— are, in the final analysis, but illusions that "cost" him dearly (*Páramo,* 77). In the spirit of Ramón López Velarde's "Retorno maléfico" (Evil Return), the quester arrives at the town only to find a "subverted Eden": Dolores's directions have led him to "the wrong place . . . to an abandoned village. Looking for someone who's no longer alive" (*PP,* 8). Like the incestuous couple for whom obedience of the divine commandment to "be fruitful and multiply" results in damnation, Juan follows his mother's idyllic memories to a town situated at the mouth of hell, an upsidedown world where values have been inverted and even life has become a commodity.

Pedro Páramo alone amongst the dreamers projects his world toward the outside, but he, too, is unable to exorcise the demons that pursue him. He instates a new order over which he wields absolute control, a kingdom of this world that is nevertheless its inhabitants' final resting place. All action, all change is subject to his machinations. He provides structural cohesion to the novel and Comala's life—insofar as it can be said to exist in either case—but in the final analysis his control does not extend to the private lives of the townspeople. He erases the past as a way of life, but he simply cannot touch it as internal reality. He cannot buy the memory of the woman whose husband was murdered by Miguel, nor, more importantly, that of Susana San Juan. "Nothing can last forever," he tells himself; "there is no memory, however intense, that does not fade" (*PP*, 95). But there is: that of Susana San Juan's love for Florencio, and his own love for her, and he is powerless to change either.

If, on the one hand, Pedro Páramo sought to possess Susana for fulfillment in his lifetime, he further looked to her to deliver him from the memories that tormented him. "Because of her," he hoped, "he would leave this earth illuminated by the image that erased all other memories" (*PP*, 95). In particular, she was to release him from the death of his father, a memory which haunted him and "brought others with it, as if a bulging sack of grain had burst and he was trying to keep the kernels from spilling out. The death of his father dragged other deaths with it, and in each of them was always the image of that shattered face" (67). After Susana dies without freeing him from his memories, Pedro Páramo spends his last years staring at the path that had led her body and soul out of Comala and at the paradise tree[22] whose last leaves had, appropriately, fallen as she passed by. The novel reduplicates the cacique's efforts to freeze time at this moment by returning repeatedly to the scene: Dorotea and, later, the third-person narrator describe it.[23] The novel's last fragment, which narrates Pedro Páramo's death, offers the final version of the scene and suggests that his wish to have his beloved, like Dante's Beatrice, guide him to the next world, might perhaps have been granted. His final sight is, after all, that of the paradise associated with Susana San Juan's death:

> Behind them, still in his chair, Pedro Páramo watched the procession making its way back to the village. . . . He watched the leaves falling from the Paradise tree. 'They all follow the same road. They all go away . . . Susana . . . I begged you to come back.' . . . The sun was tumbling over things,

giving them form once again. The ruined, sterile earth lay before him. . . . His eyes scarcely moved; they leapt from memory to memory, blotting out the present. Suddenly his heart stopped, and it seemed as if time and the breath of life stopped with it. (123–24)

While the details and explanations offered by the different perspectives vary, all coincide in the paradigmatic features of the scene: Pedro Páramo sitting in his leather chair by the doorway, facing the road leaving Comala and leading to death, following the same train of thoughts, watching the tree of paradise that had died with Susana's departure, and trying to freeze the passage of time into an eternal present. But if time has, for his intents and purposes, stopped, evidence of its progression is nevertheless apparent in the fact of the destruction of the land, the direct and deliberate consequence of his actions, regardless of whether these were motivated by disillusion or by his vow to exact vengeance from the town for having had a celebration at the time of Susana's death. "And all of it was don Pedro's doing," Dorotea tells Juan, "because of the turmoil of his soul" (81).

The image of Susana's death overshadows his own memories and thus becomes, during his lifetime, the death that he wishes for himself; he lives with her even as she had lived with Florencio after the latter's death. Like Eduviges when she commits suicide, Pedro Páramo, too, tries to force the divinity's hand by immersing himself in a state of death in life. And yet, despite the cacique's successful achievement of absolute power over Comala, his self-making project is a subjective failure. In the final analysis, he is unable to recapture what he most wants, the trinity taken from him by actions beyond his control: his father, his son, and his beloved, a woman who, spirit-like, was "not of this world" (108).

Virginia Woolf once described Joyce's work as conveying a "sense of being in a bright yet narrow room, confined and shut in . . . centered in a self which . . . never embraces or creates what is outside itself and beyond" (2035). Except for the aspect of brightness, her words also, eerily, capture the plight of Rulfo's characters, each of whom is trapped in a private world, in a paradise long lost. Each, that is, is "centered in a self" that has foregone contact with others and, instead, embraces what is inside itself as the only escape from a world that it cannot control. Change, action, and interaction belong to the public world which, in turn, belongs to Pedro Páramo. Only memory and consciousness cannot be purchased, and here alone it is given to a select few to recapture, briefly, what has been lost. Otherwise, denial of passage out of Comala is absolute. The light, or paradise, at the end of the tunnel is not the divine realm but, rather, a mere object, a dying tree as unlikely to achieve transcendence as the human inhabitants of the town that Pedro Páramo bought.

In one instance in Porter's fiction, the same mechanism that underscores the entrapment within the past or a present of despair uncharacteristically grants release from these burdens. In the remembered conjunction of tomb and womb, and of literal and figurative "burial places" in "The Grave," Miranda finds lessons in mortality and reproduction and a revelation that returns her past to her and, possibly, reopens the future. This story is the only one in the cycle successfully bridging past and present, death and life. It presents two distinct physical manifestations of grave imagery: the empty plots in the family cemetery and the exposed womb of the pregnant rabbit killed by Miranda's brother. As we have seen, the latter's symbiosis of birth, life, and death discomforts the young girl. It shows her what death is at the same time that it precipitates her understanding of her own sexuality. The end of the story is the final installment of the tales of Old and New Order alike, and it takes place outside of both, twenty years later, in a market in a "strange country," which is unnamed but recognizable as Mexico (*CS*, 367). Here, two moments in time are conflated, and the resulting re-vision of the past restores transcendence to the present. Upon seeing the candy figures shaped like animals that a street vendor places before her, Miranda sees again the dead baby rabbits from long before: "as if she looked through a frame upon a scene that had not stirred nor changed since the moment it happened, the episode of that far-off day leaped from its burial place before her mind's eye ... the scene before her eyes dimmed by the vision back of them" (67). She experiences anew her horror at learning about death and the procreative dimension of womanhood. However, the image of the rabbits fades, replaced by that of the empty graves where she and her brother had been playing, and Miranda remembers that she had found treasure that day as well as bittersweet knowledge. The wedding ring that had fascinated her, along with the attendant images of the belle, conventional womanhood, and the South's myths of its past, are absent from the second flashback. What remains is the memory of the silver dove found by the children, which Porter recognizes as a symbol of sensuality and the Holy Ghost, each in their own way affirmations of life (Porter, O'Connor, et al., 13).

Like the rabbit, then, the dove embodies the interrelatedness of life and death but additionally offers hope of a spiritual permanence that transcends death. In a mirror image of the scene in "Pale Horse, Pale Rider" in which Miranda catches a glimpse of Adam in the future, "when he would have been older, the face of the man he would not live to be" (*CS*, 295), she looks into the past and again sees her brother, "whose childhood face she had forgotten," as he once was (368). Paul and the dove alike are resurrected and immortalized by memory's power to arrest its objects in time. This power also belonged, Porter believed, to the arts as well. These, she once wrote, "live continuously ... their basic meanings survive unchanged ... through times of interruption, diminishment, neglect; they outlive governments and creeds and the societies ... that produced them. They cannot be destroyed altogether because they represent the substance of faith and the only reality. They are what we find again when the ruins are cleared away" (*CE*, 457). In this work of art, written during years of political and spiritual crises, it is an act of memory that survives the ruins and defeats the power of time, reversing "Pale Horse, Pale Rider"'s equation of timelessness with death and nothingness. As Rosemary Hennessy observes, the conclusion expands Porter's metaphor of the "burial place" to include consciousness, which becomes "a grave of memory, of collective and individual experience, offering treasure to those willing to seek it" (314). Miranda's dismay is dispelled as the perspective afforded her by the intervening years helps her to understand that with death she had also found the promise of life and to realize that she had already come to terms with the new dimension of womanhood.

This final glimpse of Miranda offers no conclusions, no closure. Instead, it shows her doing as the author herself had at the same age, traveling through Mexico in flight from her past, having first repudiated her southern home and subsequently turned away from Denver, too. The disillusionment and pessimism that characterized Porter's later Mexican stories and journalism are absent here. Miranda finds new meaning in her heritage and, at least temporarily, comes to terms with it in the culture that Porter had once praised as a site where "the past is interwoven visibly with the present, living and potent" (*Outline,* 140). Here, Miranda finds a way to lay her family to rest in the same mental "burial place" from which she exhumes it. If her uneasy relationship with her home state reflects that of her creator, so, too, does this reconciliation. As Porter herself once wrote, "My time in Mexico and Europe served me in a way I had not dreamed of. . . . It gave me back my past and my own house and my own people—the native land of my heart. This summer country of my childhood, this place of memory" (*CE,* 470).

The possibility of deliverance that Miranda finds here is an exception. In Porter's stories and in *Pedro Páramo*, graves as space and metaphor for reliving the past are significantly lacking in any promise of redemption. Memory might offer some consolation, but ultimately it is a "burial place" in life (and death) for Rulfo's characters. It is the antithesis of Miranda's revelation, for it encloses and paralyzes. On a larger scale, the attempts to eternalize the past that I have discussed in this chapter emblematize the paralysis and stagnation of the South's Old Order, as well as of the new but sterile orders of "Pale Horse, Pale Rider" and *Pedro Páramo*. The inhabitants of war-torn worlds desperately hearken back to times gone by for the stability lacking in their own. In Porter, the antebellum southern past haunts the present because the community has called it back and held it up as a Golden Age to be emulated; similarly, memory is all that is left to Rulfo's characters, and, as we have seen, it is neither sacred nor trustworthy.

The prelapsarian states that Porter and Rulfo's characters evoke and strive to resurrect are impossible refuges, mirages that never existed. Porter has written that the artist's task is one of "endless remembering," forever changing, reshaping, and reinterpreting one's experiences in order to transform them into fiction (*CE*, 468). This "healthy" memory, as it were, stands in direct contrast to that which, as in the epigraph to this section, "sets itself and fixes upon a point in time where the shock occurred . . . and slowly turns to stone" (Letter to William Goyen). Memory petrifies those who cling too tightly to it. In the Miranda stories— and in the author's personal experience—and in *Pedro Páramo*, both self and community are immobilized in the past, but the comfort that they seek there cannot materialize. Torn from the myths that make sense of the past, the communities can no longer function as a whole, and they fissure. Critics speak of a modernist project of creating new world orders, geographies of the imagination that endeavor to break with a dead past but paradoxically only succeed in replicating it. Porter's heroine strives to create not a world but a self apart from her family's futureless present; that is, she seeks to find her own time and people, and her own truths. Pedro Páramo does form a new order even as he condemns Comala's inhabitants to the past that he has overridden. Ultimately, deprived of what they hold most dear, even the most active subjects surrender to their memories in the hope of recovering a lost paradise, even as they despair at knowing that their task is condemned to fail.

In the Miranda stories, we follow Porter's efforts to work through her own ambivalence toward the South. She was never able to resolve her longing for the security of its traditions and her need to reject its confining way of life. Briefly, she found what she sought in Mexico, "my much-loved second country," but reality failed to live up to her hopes for it (*CS*, v). In the long run, she found a sense of home only in the nostalgic backward glances of her imagination: with time, distance, and the palliative effect of memory, the South became, in the words of one of her characters, "my loved and never-forgotten country" (414). For Rulfo, Mexico could never be Porter's prelapsarian paradise. Experience repeatedly denied him optimism about his country's prospects and hope for the possibility of a future different from the present or past. Perhaps he might have agreed with Porter that in Mexico, "the past is interwoven visibly with the present." However, the author who once declared that "the great novel from here would not be able to speak of anything other than misery and ignorance" would have been quick to challenge the Texan's claim that this past was living and potent, as well as her romantic exaltation of the Mexicans for loving their past uncritically (*Autobiografía*, 48).

CHAPTER FIVE

Race and Place in Identity and History

The pursuit of an endogenous identity—whether gendered, racial, regional, or national—through the destruction of stereotypes, imposed codes and ways of life, and fossilized roles, is a central part of the texts that I have examined in this study. The clustering of these issues around questions of race and national heritage is also a recurrent phenomenon. In *Absalom, Absalom!* as we saw in chapter 2, Faulkner described the West Indies as

> a little island . . . which was the halfway point between what we call the jungle and what we call civilization, halfway between the dark inscrutable continent from which the black blood, the black bones and flesh and thinking and remembering and hopes and desires, was ravished by violence, and the cold known land to which it was doomed . . . a soil manured with black

blood from two hundred years of oppression and exploitation until it sprang with an incredible paradox of peaceful greenery . . . and sugar cane sapling size and three times the height of a man . . . but valuable pound for pound almost with silver ore, as if nature held a balance and kept a book and offered a recompense for the torn limbs and outraged hearts even if man did not, the planting of nature . . . the planting of men too. (250–51)

In Fuentes's *Constancia*, the protagonist, a southerner of the old, genteel tradition, has recourse to similar images to describe his hometown. "Savannah's domestic architecture," he writes,

dates from a period between the end of the eighteenth century and the third quarter of the nineteenth century; that is, the years between the independence of the Union and its severing in the Civil War, when our pride was greater than our sense of reality. The noble edifices of our city are symbols of two commerces, one famous, the other infamous. Cotton and slaves; blacks imported, white fibers exported. As an old southerner, I appreciate the chromatic irony of this exchange. We sent our messengers as fresh and ethereal as clouds to the world, and in exchange we received flesh charred on the coals of hell. (4)

And Fernando Ortiz in *Cuban Counterpoint*, his essay on the role of the sugar and tobacco industries in Cuba's social, political, and economic history, similarly observes that

Tobacco and sugar each have racial connections. Tobacco is an inheritance received from the Indian, which was immediately used and esteemed by the Negro, but cultivated and commercialized by the white man . . . Negro labor and sugar cane have been two factors in the same economic binomial of the social equation of our country. . . . Tobacco goes out and comes in; sugar comes in and goes out—and stays out. The whole process of tobacco's development in Cuba, by reason of its native origin . . . is one of economic centripetalism. . . . The sugar industry, on the other hand, because of its exotic origin, its European antecedents, and the foreign capital invested in it, is economically centrifugal. . . . And for this sugar has exercised an almost tyrannical pressure throughout our history, introducing a constant note of oppression and force, without contributing toward the creation of robust institutions. . . . The history of Cuba, from the days of the conquest to the present moment, has been essentially dominated by foreign controls over sugar. . . . (57, 58, 69, 70)

Sugar, cotton, tobacco, and slaves. White and black, white for black. A chromatic exchange that is financial and political as well: the import and export of goods, labor, people, and power. Silver for flesh and blood and pain. As described by Faulkner, Fuentes, and Ortiz, the commerce by means of which the South, the Caribbean, and Spanish America as a whole have gained access to the world system is inextricably bound up with the regions' racial dynamics. Blacks have sown, but they have reaped little benefit for themselves from a nature which cannot balance the social equations governing their lives and their homelands' economies. In *Absalom, Absalom!* the shifting sand on which Thomas Sutpen's design was erected is the wealth that he earned in Haiti, model and precursor of the South's own racial system, of its own moral and economic edifice. Faulkner's evocation of this Caribbean connection lays a foundation for elucidating further parallels in the regions, determined by the presence of the plantation system and by its power as a primary paradigm. Antonio Benítez-Rojo has characterized the plantation as a machine that "suit[s] to its own convenience, the political, economic, social and cultural spheres of the country that nourishes it until that country is changed into a *sugar island*" (72; italics in original). The plantation has left an indelible mark on the social organization of the South, the Caribbean, and elsewhere in Spanish America, as well as giving rise to many of the other literary and historical correspondences that I have discussed in this study. Racial tensions and exploitation have been powerful forces in the orders that the system has shaped. Perhaps recognition of this fundamental commonality of heritage, and the analogous sets of issues to which it has given rise, lies behind Faulkner's and Fuentes's literary excursions into foreign yet not unfamiliar territories. I would like to conclude now with a brief discussion of the coalescence of these issues in moments and movements in the South and Spanish America that have explored regional and national identity in terms of race.

In one of the more interesting twists of history, the paths of the South and Spanish America briefly crossed during the late nineteenth century. For a short while, the regions' destinies were bound up with one another. Cuba's struggle for social, political, and economic independence from Spain bore more than a passing resemblance to the South's embattled relationship with the North. It is an intriguing coincidence that Cuba tried unsuccessfully to gain its independence during the years of Reconstruction in the South.[1] Two decades later, when fighting broke out anew, the South saw an opportunity for deliverance from its own neocolonial status, and for reestablishment of its sovereignty. Removed from Spanish domination, Cuba would be an overseas market potentially offering the South a chance to increase its revenues dramatically and, by extension, attain self-sufficiency. At the same time, the U.S.'s military involvement in the Spanish-American War brought about a temporary sectional reconciliation between the North and the South, quickly defusing domestic tensions. Proverbially, nothing succeeds like a common enemy in overcoming differences and uniting warring parties. And the U.S.'s first casualty hailed from the South, which moved the region further back into alignment with national values. "The South furnishes the first sacrifice of this war," the New York *Tribune* proclaimed. "There is no north and south after that, we are all Worth Bagley's countrymen" (quoted in Ayers, 332).

There was, however, another side to this reintegration. For years before the sinking of the *Maine*, black spokesmen had spoken out in favor of U.S. intervention in the Cuban conflict. They understood the

Cubans to be, like themselves, fighting for the freedom of an oppressed, colored people. African Americans further thought that involvement in the war would ultimately result in improved race relations in the U.S. Their expectations were disappointed. The regions' putting aside of old boundaries and hatreds contributed instead to greater tensions and, additionally, to the North's increased oppression of blacks. Many blacks claimed, in fact, that the war offered whites an excuse to ignore the injustice in their own backyards. They wanted to secure the freedom of black southerners before committing to fight for that of the Cubans. Thus did John Mitchell, an editor from Richmond, Virginia, denounce the U.S.'s involvement in the war, crying out that "in the South today [there] exists a system of oppression as barbarous as that which is alleged to exist in Cuba" (quoted in Ayers, 328).[2]

One prominent figure in the Spanish American literature and politics of this period crossed the ocean from the direction opposite President McKinley's army. José Martí, the revolutionary poet who later lost his life in the war against Spain, spent several years living in exile in New York. While visiting South Carolina in 1886, the outspoken anti–North Americanist was captivated by the scent of magnolias—that is, by the image that the South projected of its aristocratic civilization, its foundations of beauty, nobility, decorum, and poetry. His admiration for the Lost Cause, however, did not obscure his view or temper his denunciation of the evil of racial exploitation which had sustained it. Slavery, he wrote, "was capable of putting out the sun itself." "Whoever foments and spreads antagonism and hate between the races," he declared, "sins against humanity." And yet elsewhere: "Always to dwell on the divisions or differences between the races, in people who are sufficiently divided already, is to raise barriers to the attainment of both national and individual well-being, for these two goals are reached by bringing together as closely as possible the various components that form the nation."[3] His position was clear: hierarchies and hatreds established on the basis of race constitute a sin against humanity and the public good alike. It must be noted, though, that the latter two statements were directed at Cuba, not the South.

Martí also argued that race was a category that did not truly exist, for man's identity is universal and the soul is the same in all of us, regardless of appearance. More concretely, though, he saw race as a fraudulent division because the "black blood . . . and thinking and remembering and hopes and desires" brought over to Cuba had commingled with other elements and become an integral part of (if not always integrated in) the culture and lives of all of the nation's inhabitants (*Absalom,* 1972, 250). The notion of race, and of the role of blacks in Cuba's past and present, has been reexamined and reformulated many times during this century. In particular, the recognition of African heritage was a cornerstone of many attempts to define national identity in the years preceding the Cuban Revolution. In 1931, Nicolás Guillén designated his poems "versos mulatos" (mulatto verses) because the heterogeneity of their constituent elements reflected that of Cuba's ethnic composition. "I believe," he declared, "that amongst ourselves, there simply cannot be a creole poetry without taking into account the black. In my opinion, the black contributes very strong essences to our cocktail. For the time being, Cuba's spirit is *mestizo*. And the definite color will move from the spirit to the skin. Some day, people will say 'Cuban color'" (114). Fernando Ortiz also foregrounded the integration of the island's economic, political, and racial histories: "tobacco and sugar each have racial connections" (57). The cultivation of both products has been dependent on black labor and the dispossession that it entails. Tobacco—originally "a thing for savages . . . a thing for Indians and Negroes," later expropriated by the white elite and transformed into a status symbol (57)—has nevertheless benefited the nation, strengthening its economy and political institutions. In contrast, Ortiz depicts the sugar industry as both microcosm and handmaiden of Cuba's subordination to foreign powers.[4] Since the Conquest, he wrote in 1940, the nation's history "has been essentially dominated by foreign controls over sugar" (70). And, in 1949, Alejo Carpentier ascribed to Haitian blacks' supernatural belief the power to bring about revolutionary change in the nation's struggle for independence. Many years before, their collective faith had endowed Mackandal with his magical powers, giving rise to nothing less than a miracle in one of history's most dramatic uprisings. In this act, and in the vibrant treasure trove of belief that it presupposed, Carpentier identified the force from which the renewal not just of Haiti but of all Spanish America would eventually derive ("On the Marvelous Real").

Blacks in the U.S. as well have long struggled with the problems of their identity and their place in (more frequently, on the outskirts of) society. The "peculiar institutions" of slavery and segregation have deprived African Americans of their cultural heritage, silenced their voices, and rendered their history invisible. Their identity has been largely exogenous: they have been constructed as Other, cast as Outsider, and further alienated from their origins by being forced to follow the strictures of white society, without being able to enter into it. Despite differences in race and social status, though, Ralph Ellison writes in his essay "What America Would Be Like Without Blacks," that

> something indisputably American about Negroes not only raised doubts about the white man's value system but arouses the troubling suspicion that whatever else the true American is, he is also somehow black ... [P]art of the nation's heritage is Negro American, and whatever it becomes will be shaped in part by the Negro's presence. Which is fortunate, for today it is the black American who puts pressure upon the nation to live up to its ideals. (*Going,* 110)

The passage is a striking, if unknowing, echo of Guillén. The invisible man spends much of his life attempting to ascertain his relationship to a country in which he and "all the others in the loud clamoring semi-visible world ... [were] seen only as a fertile field for exploitation ... [and] were tired of being the mere pawns in the futile game of 'making history.'" His struggle is temporarily resolved with his decision to take action within his community and thereby "mak[e] history" (*IM*, 496). In the "semi-visible world" outside of the novel, though, his questions resonate to this day, as, significantly, do his answers of responsibility and identification with a shared past. As I have previously noted, several authors and critics have identified a growing tendency in black writers—outsiders to the South and natives alike—to turn to history and, especially, to southern history, for their subject matter. For Toni Morrison, this move represents an assumption of responsibility for refusing to allow the violence and injustices of the past to be glossed over or erased. Those who do not remember the past, Santayana reminds us, are condemned to repeat it. Thadious Davis views the trend as a revision of communal and public history, and tantamount to an act of reappropriation. Central to the process is the recognition of the South and its multiple meanings as a cornerstone of black identity (6). Significantly, C. Vann Woodward wrote in the 1950s that expression of the African American's tragic past would presuppose the "acknowledgment that he is also a Southerner as well as an American" (22). Davis describes how many African American authors—including the midwestern Morrison—have drawn on the southern tradition in their writing, looking to the South "to claim a history, to explain a legacy, and to understand the regionality of the black self" (7). At the same time, race must be acknowledged as an important component of any definition of the South and its culture; it must be reinscribed into the region's past and present, rather than dismissed as relevant to African Americans alone. In the same manner that the South is a formative part of black identity, racial injustice and oppression constitutes one of the heaviest burdens of southern history, and one of its more significant components. As in the case of Cuba, the redefinition of race and place is seen to center on the intersection and integration of these two elements. Both are necessary to the construction of individual and collective identity. Davis's observation that black authors are, in word and deed, self-consciously reconfiguring history and identity through the inversion of traditional power structures applies to writers in Cuba and elsewhere in Spanish America as well (9). The cathartic and healing powers of narrating the regions' histories and stories, and forging from shared experiences a sense of communal solidarity, hold here, too. By remembering the past, these authors endeavor to shape a future less marked by the hardships that have plagued them.

Time and again, voices from the South and Spanish America have cried out against historical discourse's manipulation and censorship of their experiences. As literature has frequently served as a space for redressing the failure of official channels to address social and political issues, writers have often sought to restore untold tales to the record, rewrite their history, and participate in the construction of a collective identity. Two of the novels studied in the preceding chapters render this dialogue of point and counterpoint, official and unofficial stories, call and response, in genealogical terms. In *Absalom, Absalom!* the would-be patriarch's white and black daughters both bear the "Sutpen face." Judith tries to weave her pattern into the rug of history by passing on a document that is not only written, and thus endowed with social and historical validity, but written with paper and ink that represent "the best of the old South which is dead, and . . . the best . . . of the new North which has conquered" (132). And yet, Clytie, too, leaves her mark with an alternative but equally (if not more) expressive gesture. She sets the fire that destroys both herself and the last concrete and socially visible remnants of Sutpen's design—that is, the last to bear his name: Sutpen's Hundred and Henry Sutpen, the patriarch's only legitimate male heir, perish in the blaze. In *The House of the Spirits*, both Alba and Esteban García trace their origins to Esteban Trueba. Alba (like her female fore-bears) struggles to renegotiate the code established by the senator, but her line is legitimate, and thus, despite other limitations, she is entitled to numerous privileges. In contrast, García's existence goes unacknowledged. Inhuman, inexcusable, and horrendous, the vengeance that he exacts on Alba for having received what he claims as his birthright is an act for which Trueba's refusal to recognize other branches of the family tree—and other versions of the past—bears some responsibility. García's is a brutality engendered by dispossession. In their own ways, through acts of destruction, he and Clytie resist being silenced, and reinscribe their presence into the story that is visible to the empowered. It is, however, only in Alba's words and projected actions, which deliberately subvert society's dominant voice and forge a link between individual and collective experience and goals, that I find hope of transcendence.

Many of these issues are revisited and synthesized in a work that I have not included in this study, Puerto Rican writer Rosario Ferré's *Sweet Diamond Dust* (a significantly modified translation, done by the author herself, of *Maldito Amor*). As in many of her other works, there are numerous deliberate nods to Faulkner's novel, at the level of motifs, historical backdrop, and, of course, structure. *Sweet Diamond Dust*, like *Absalom, Absalom!* and *The House of the Spirits*, condenses a significant period in a region's history—in this case, all of the island's twentieth-century racial and political tensions as well as the decline of the creole plantation industries—into the saga of a house divided. As in *Absalom,* the story of the heroism and patriotism of the patriarch, Ubaldino De La Valle, of the rebuilding of his heritage and his denial of black blood in his family, is presented in several contradictory versions. Each of Ferré's narrators similarly explains De La Valle's life in terms of a single cause, whether this is the changing of orders precipitated by the arrival of the U.S., the racism that erases all evidence of miscegenation from the family tree, or the quest to resolve Puerto Rico's political status in a manner that would also bring reform to the island's poorest inhabitants. In Ferré's novel, however, the fourteenth blackbird of truth is clearly to be found in those versions which are farthest—in terms of both textual space and content—from those offered by the rich, "white" male creoles and the power structure that they represent.[5] The novel closes with Gloria, Ubaldino's daughter-in-law (who is variously described as a mulatta, a crazy woman, and the town whore), burning down the house on the island's last independent sugar plantation, the house that was a microcosm of the system and its racial and political dynamics and that had been left to her in a secret will that the powers-that-be would no doubt have prevented from being carried out.

Despite the obvious parallel with Clytie's final actions, I am even more interested in Ferré's reworking of *Absalom*'s treatment of the twinned issues of incest and miscegenation.[6] Two divergent explanations are offered of Gloria's son's paternity in *Sweet Diamond Dust*. Arístides, the only living son of the patriarch, and the one who stands to inherit if the official will is honored, tries to discredit Gloria by accusing her of having had relations with his father, brother, and himself and characterizes her offspring as a "monster . . . be it reptile, fish, or fowl" (49). In contrast, Laura, Ubaldino's wife, says that the child was the product of relations that Gloria had had as a prostitute with northerners and Puerto Ricans, foreigners and islanders, the rich and the poor. As in Faulkner's novel, then, the primal taboo is swept away and revealed to be a smoke screen behind which an even more explosive motive lurks. However, where both the fact and issue of incest had horrified Arístides, Laura takes great pride in the fact that Nicolasito is "the child of all. In her body . . . both races, both languages, English and Spanish, grew into one soul" (76). The would-be accusation of miscegenation is thus defused by Laura's explicit positing of the mestizo child as a source of renewal and the true direction of the island's future. Faulkner's Clytie, "who in the very pigmentation of her flesh represented that debacle which had brought Judith and me [Miss Rosa] to what we were and which had made of her (Clytie) that which she declined to be just as she had declined to be that from which its purpose had been to emancipate her, as though presiding aloof upon the new, she deliberately remained to represent to us the threatful portent of the old," was a living refutation of racial categories and, as such, a bridge between past and future (*Absalom*, 1972, 156–57). By destroying the family mansion, she, like Gloria after her, casts off the past. However, where both Clytie and Henry Sutpen perish in the blaze and thereby forfeit the future as well, the readers of Ferré's novel never learn definitively the fate of the scion of the De La Valle family. We are simply left to hope that he does survive to preside over the new.

The marginalization of the South and Spanish America has been internal as well as external. On the one hand, both regions have fought the political, economic, and cultural expansionism of a northern neighbor, whether the northern U.S. or the nation in its entirety. On the other, they reduplicate their own subordination in the dispossession by race, ethnicity, gender, and class that has created "fourth world" populations within their perimeters. Each of these communities has experienced the past subject to different constraints, and each has filtered its trials through a different perspective or world view. Their versions of history represent the pieces of a puzzle that may approach, but never reach, completion, and from which the seams will never quite disappear. All of the texts that I have discussed in this study attempt to restore dissenting voices that have been repressed to audibility, and their marginalized experiences to visibility. At the same time, they elucidate the mechanisms through which one tale comes to prevail. Against the backdrop of a composite picture that accommodates many histories and genealogies, then, the claim by any single voice to authority or truth is automatically called into question, giving condemned races and regions another opportunity in life, literature, and history.

NOTES

(For full bibliographic information on cited titles, see the list of works cited.)

Chapter 1: The U.S. South and Spanish America: Neighboring Spaces and the Search for Meaning in Difficult Pasts

1. To include those readers who only speak English as well as those who speak both English and Spanish, quotations from works by Spanish-speaking authors will be taken from the published English translations, as indicated; when these are not available, the translations are my own. Also, when published versions differ markedly from the original, and when the difference (in phrasing, in lexicon) is crucial to the points that I am trying to establish, I use my own translations, as noted.

2. Extending the comparison to Brazil would render my task even more unwieldy, given that nation's significant differences vis-à-vis Spanish America: a distinct cultural and linguistic heritage, the differing set of policies (economic, political, and administrative) that governed it during its colonial period, and the unique path it followed after independence (an imported independent monarchy that lasted from 1822 until 1889, when the Republic was established). Hence, with few exceptions, I will not be including Brazil in this study. As a result, I use the term *Latin America* solely to refer to the region including both Spanish America and Brazil; however, because that term is used interchangeably with *Spanish America* by numerous authors and critics, when quoting and translating I follow the usage in the original texts.

3. See Barbara Ladd's "'The Direction of the Howling': Nationalism and the Color Line in *Absalom, Absalom!*" for a discussion of these differences within the context of *Absalom, Absalom!*

4. Plantation society will be addressed in greater detail in my comparison of Porter's stories of the Old Order and Rulfo's *Pedro Páramo* in chapter 4, while official and unofficial genealogies figure prominently in my discussions of the novels of Faulkner, Allende, and Rulfo.

5. Faulkner's influence had a different trajectory in Brazil from that which it followed in Spanish America and, unfortunately, lies outside the scope of this study. In general, however, the theme has attracted much less attention. In 1996, in fact, Luiz Valente noted that the MLA Bibliography listed only three comparative works on Faulkner and João Guimarães Rosa, one of Brazil's foremost twentieth-century authors, since 1963 ("Marriages," 150): Elizabeth Lowe's "Visions of Violence: From Faulkner to the Contemporary City Fiction of Brazil and Colombia"; Paulo Vizzioli's "Guimarães Rosa e William Faulkner"; and Valente's own dissertation, "The Reader in the Work: Fabulation and Affective

Response in João Guimarães Rosa and William Faulkner." Consult works by the following authors for further information on Faulkner's influence on Brazilian literature in general as well as on specific authors: Nelson Cerqueira, George Monteiro, Celso de Oliveira, Rosa Simas, and Arline Standley.

6. As a side note, this subject has been almost exclusively the domain of scholars in the field of Spanish American literature. The fact that an entire recent (double) issue of *The Faulkner Journal* (vol. 11, nos. 1 and 2 [Fall 1995 / Spring 1996]) was dedicated to the subject of "The Latin American Faulkner" indicates—happily, to this Latin Americanist—a growing reciprocal interest on the part of Faulknerists.

7. E.g., Arnold Chapman, *The Spanish American Reception of United States Fiction, 1920–1940* (see especially his chapter "William Faulkner: The Demonic Novel," 127–50); Mary Davis's "The Haunted Voice: Echoes of William Faulkner in García Márquez, Fuentes, and Vargas Llosa," and "William Faulkner and Mario Vargas Llosa: The Election of Failure"; Wendy Faris's "Marking Space, Charting Time: Text and Territory in Faulkner's 'The Bear' and Carpentier's *Los pasos perdidos*"; Katalin Kulin's "Razones y características de la influencia de Faulkner en la ficción latinoamericana moderna" and "Reasons and Characteristics of Faulkner's Influence on Juan Carlos Onetti, Juan Rulfo and Gabriel García Márquez"; Josefina Ludmer's "Onetti: 'La novia (carta) robada (a Faulkner)'"; Alfred MacAdam's "Carlos Fuentes: The Burden of History"; Nijole Rukas's dissertation, "A Comparison of Faulkner's and Rulfo's Treatment of the Interplay Between Reality and Illusion in *Absalom, Absalom!* and *Pedro Páramo*"; J. P. Shapiro's "'Une histoire contée par un idiot . . .' (W. Faulkner et J. Rulfo)"; and Luis Vargas Saavedra's "La afinidad de Onetti a Faulkner." In his broader study of the Lost Generation's literary legacy, "A Game of Shifting Mirrors: The New Latin American Narrative and the North American Novel," Emir Rodríguez Monegal offers several relevant observations on Faulkner's influence. In *Journeys Through the Labyrinth*, Gerald Martin proposes an extended analysis of Faulkner's legacy but ultimately arrives at a somewhat reductive division of modern Latin American fiction into two periods: the 1920s through the early 1960s, dominated by Faulkner and with a largely rural orientation, and the years following the publication of Julio Cortázar's *Rayuela* (1963), in which James Joyce was the dominant model and the fictional stage shifted to the urban realm. There are other related studies on this topic; however, I have found those listed here and in the following notes to be the most substantial.

8. See, for example, the following: John Christie, "Fathers and Virgins: García Márquez's Faulknerian *Chronicle of a Death Foretold*"; Florence Delay and Jacqueline de Labriolle, "Márquez: Est-il le Faulkner colombien?"; Wayne Fields, "*One Hundred Years of Solitude* and New World Storytelling"; J. L. Ramos Escobar, "Desde Yoknapatawpha a Macondo"; Susan Snell, "William Faulkner, un

guía sureño a la ficción de García Márquez"; Patricia Drechsel Tobin, *Time and the Novel: The Genealogical Imperative*; and Lois Parkinson Zamora, "The End of Innocence: Myth and Narrative Structure in Faulkner's *Absalom, Absalom!* and García Márquez's *Cien años de soledad*," and her chapter on García Márquez in *Writing the Apocalypse*; and the many works by Harley Oberhelman.

9. In fact, the formalization of the Southern Renaissance may be partially attributed to a crossover between fiction writers and theorists, for many of those who forged and publicized the movement's now-traditional definitions were participants as well or had close ties to its early writers (e.g., Allen Tate and Cleanth Brooks, respectively).

10. Many of these authors likewise also contributed to the process of canon formation, writing critical works that complemented, supplemented, and promoted their literary projects. For example, Fuentes's study *La nueva novela hispanoamericana* (The New Spanish American Novel) is widely considered a classic, while Donoso has written his own "personal history" of the period, *The Boom in Spanish American Literature*.

11. Fuentes similarly observed in the late 1960s that "[b]ecause Latin America is caught in a perpetual cultural lag of at least forty or fifty years, forms reach it with delay. The substance of Latin American experience itself is in perpetual delay. Now the moment has arrived when it finds a very adequate form of expression in the kind of literature John Dos Passos was producing forty years ago" (quoted in Harss and Dohmann, 295).

12. Fuentes has often reclaimed Cleanth Brooks's derogatory labeling of Faulkner as a "Dixie Gongorist" precisely because the quality that links the two authors, that is, their baroque style, is one that he values in its literary manifestations and also as a constitutive element of Spanish American identity. Recently, he stated that "Góngora . . . was the greatest crafter of the baroque in poetry, and it was the relationship Góngora-baroque-Faulkner-baroque that showed me the 'Latin American' dimension of William Faulkner. After all, the baroque, transferred to the Americas, is the aesthetics of the New World that allows the conquered world of the Indians and the enslaved world of the blacks to make themselves heard" ("Clinton y Faulkner," 2).

13. In 1972, in his review of García Márquez's newly translated *Leaf Storm*, Alfred Kazin came to a similar conclusion. He remarked that "I am guessing but I wonder if the outbreak of creative originality in Latin America today, coming after so many years of dutifulness to Spanish and French models, doesn't resemble our sudden onrush of originality after we had decided really to break away from the spell of England" (27).

14. Edwards's singling out of the latter for his incompatibility with Spanish American reality is also particularly ironic when one considers that in 1926

Valle Inclán published *Tirano Banderas,* which launched the specifically Spanish American literary tradition of the *novela del dictador* (novel of the dictator) and which subverted realism, relying on exaggeration, deformation, and the grotesque to portray an integral and recurrent figure in the region's politics.

15. Donoso is the most strident in his censure. He continues: "The gentlemen who wrote the basic Spanish American novels . . . looked to us like statues in a park . . . all essentially indistinguishable and none with any power over us. Neither d'Halmar nor Barrios, neither Mallea nor Alegría offered temptations even remotely like those of Lawrence, Faulkner, Pavese, Camus, Joyce, and Kafka. In the Spanish novel that teachers liked to offer us as an example and, to a certain degree, as something we also might call 'our own'—in Azorín, Miró, Baroja, Pérez de Ayala—we discovered stagnancy and poverty when we compared them to their contemporaries in other languages . . . [T]oday's Spanish American novel was from the very beginning a *mestizaje* . . . a disregarding of Hispanic-American tradition . . . and draws itself almost totally from other literary sources, because . . . our orphaned sensibility let itself be infected by the North Americans, the French, the English, and the Italians, all of whom seemed to us more 'ours,' much more 'our own' than a Gallegos or a Güiraldes, for example, or a Baroja" (13–14).

16. Given García Márquez's many homages to modern European writers and his insistence that the Virginia Woolf of *Mrs. Dalloway* as well as Faulkner had provided him with "a method and a manner to go with it," the European method to which he refers should be understood as realism rather than modernism (quoted in Harss and Dohmann, 322).

17. In his memoirs, *El arte de la fuga* (The Art of the Fugue), as well as in a recent talk at Columbia University (25 October 1996), Mexican novelist Sergio Pitol similarly acknowledged that Faulkner had been a primary influence on him because the land and people described by the southerner had resonated with his own experiences. The destroyed world, the subverted Eden, the nostalgia for the antebellum period and the concomitant belief that "the time that was worth living had been left behind," the sense of enclosure and frustration, the racial tensions, the conflicts between victors and vanquished, the rise of a new class, and the paralytic interweaving of past and present, he claimed, all reminded him of the world in which he had grown up (*El arte,* 113–14).

18. In a 1965 essay, "On Modern Fiction," Katherine Anne Porter reiterated her friend's assessment: "Gordon's *None Shall Look Back* is a masterpiece, out of print now, probably because her scene is the South during the Civil War, and she knows and tells things that are not acceptable now when Southern history is being rewritten or reconstructed to the fancy of those who took no part in it" (*Collected Essays,* 87).

Chapter 2: The Case of the Fabricated Facts: Invented Information and the Problems of Reconstructing the Past in *Absalom, Absalom!* and *The Real Life of Alejandro Mayta*

1. See Ermarth (27–28) for her discussion of the construct of "Narrator as Nobody."

2. Also, see articles by Matthews and Snead for further discussion of the novel's perspectivism.

3. E.g., "maybe," "no one knew," "seemed to," "must have."

4. I will discuss Quentin and Shreve's imaginative version of the events in greater detail in the following section.

5. *The Real Life of Alejandro Mayta* (also *RL*) 67. When my interpretation requires strict adherence to the Spanish phrasing or vocabulary, I use my own translations of the original; these references are cited as *HM* (*Historia de Mayta*, the Spanish title).

6. Revolutionary Workers' Party (Trotskyist).

7. The Spanish title anticipates the novel's central concern—that is, whether what is told is Mayta's history or his story—with a conceit that is impossible to translate. The English title suggested by Alfred MacAdam draws on the ironies implicit in the title of Vladimir Nabokov's *The Real Life of Sebastian Knight* (personal communication).

8. See James Snead and Charles Sherry for excellent discussions of these issues in *Absalom*.

9. Snead discusses this dynamic of storytelling in his *Figures of Division*.

10. E.g., "From the corner of his eye [Armstid] watches [Lena's] profile, thinking, *I dont know what Martha's going to say* thinking, 'I reckon I do know what Martha's going to say . . . ' thinking *Yes I do. I know exactly what Martha is going to say*" (*Light*, 13; italics in original).

11. E.g., "They did not know then that he was the man. He did not tell them so. All they knew was that a man who had resided for a short time in the town . . . appeared on the square in a state of excitement. . . . Then it began to piece together" (324); also, "That was what he told, because that was what he knew. He had departed immediately: he did not know that at the time he was telling it, the negro Roz was lying unconscious . . . " (357).

12. The Chronology lists Quentin and Miss Rosa's meetings as taking place in September and December of 1910, while the text itself indicates both 1909 and 1910. The Genealogy lists Quentin's death as 1910, which does not per se contradict the previous dates, although, if taken into consideration, *The Sound and the Fury*'s specification of June 2, 1910, as the date of his death would make them problematic. Charles Bon's birthplace appears as New Orleans on his tombstone and Haiti in the Chronology. All sources concur on the year of his death (1865), but the text claims that he was thirty-three, while the Chronology says

that he was born in 1829, which would make him thirty-six. The Genealogy and Chronology also list Ellen Sutpen's dates of birth and death as 1818 and 1862, while the omniscient narrator states that her tombstone reads 1817–1863; relative dates provided by Miss Rosa and Mr Compson support both death dates. In addition to this general confusion, the Genealogy simply refuses to offer certain facts, designating them as "unknown," "rumored," or not recorded. See Parker's "The Chronology and Genealogy of *Absalom, Absalom!*" for further elaboration of these discrepancies and their significance. Although numerous critics have acknowledged the discrepancies as a deliberate part of Faulkner's strategy for challenging the truth-value of historical discourse, the 1986 Vintage International edition took it upon itself to "correct" them, despite the editor's claim to reproduce the original transcript "faithfully, even to the point of preserving certain of Faulkner's inconsistencies and eccentricities" (311; this edition was published under the title of *Absalom, Absalom!: The Corrected Text*). Most of the typographical "regularizations" in the text were made in accordance with what appears in the holograph manuscript of the novel and the corrected galleys of the first edition; ironically, or perhaps appropriately, the sources of the corrected data from the Chronology and Genealogy are not identified, other than by the claim that they were made "to agree with the dates and facts of the novel" (305). Of course, the authority of the voice making these corrections may also be called into question on the grounds of incorrect knowledge of the high points of Faulkner's life: the blurb "About the Author" at the end of the novel identifies 1949 (rather than 1950) as the year in which Faulkner was awarded the Nobel Prize for Literature.

13. Vargas Llosa's terminology in this passage is inconsistent with his previously cited categorization of fictions: "literary" would appear to correspond to his definition of ideological fictions, rather than literary fictions.

Chapter 3: To See or Not to See: In*visibility*, Clairvoyance, and Re-*visions* of History in *Invisible Man* and *The House of the Spirits*

1. In fact, the novels' emphasis on an "otherly" experience of reality has invited comparisons to works by authors from other marginalized traditions: Michael Cooke, for example, has analyzed Ellison's novel and García Márquez's *One Hundred Years of Solitude* as examples of burgeoning "hyphenated-American" (African and Spanish, that is) literary traditions, while P. Gabrielle Foreman discusses the use of magical realism in Allende's novel and in Toni Morrison's *Song of Solomon*, as a feminist strategy for repossessing the past (369).

2. My use of the terms "magic(al) realism" and "the marvelous real" in this chapter draws on Walter Mignolo's definition of the discourse as an expression of "a shared aesthetic concern: the effort to grasp an American 'reality' that, deriving from traditional cultures and from folklore, eludes our understand-

ing of 'reality.' In the final analysis, it is a question of 'two realities': one which inserts itself in the myth of reason; the other, in 'mythical reason'" (40). His discussion of magic realism's endeavor to interpret American reality in terms of its syncretism of coexistent cultural realities is also important for my purposes (46).

3. *Invisible Man*, 379. Henceforth the novel will be cited parenthetically as *IM*.

4. Ellison's essay, "The World and the Jug" (in *Shadow and Act*), elaborates upon his views of social realism. I am indebted to Thomas Schaub's critical discussions of Ellison's use of realism and social realism for helping me to frame my approach to Ellison and Allende. I draw upon them throughout this section in particular.

5. *Shadow and Act*, 120 (henceforward *S&A* in references).

6. Cushing Strout associates Ras the Exhorter with the back-to-Africa and racial pride themes of Marcus Garvey's black nationalist movement of the 1920s (82); the Brotherhood, which is the first organization to offer the invisible man the opportunity to be "more than a member of a race," reflects the Communist Party's activities in Harlem in the 1930s (*IM*, 307). Susan Blake makes a more specific correlation between the institutions dominating each of the novel's episodes and a period of black history: the southern black college is associated with Reconstruction, and the narrator's departure with the Great Migration; Liberty Paints with northern industrialism in the 1920s; the Brotherhood with Communism during the Depression; and the end with disillusionment with the Party and the Harlem riot of 1943 (126–27). Russell Fischer focuses on the thwarted leadership roles that the narrator assumes in each of these stages: student and accommodationist, industrial worker in urban society, and political organizer. These correspondences are in keeping with Slemon's aforementioned identification of "transformational regionalism" and the "foreshortening of history" as characteristics of magic realism (411).

7. The Brotherhood's activities, rhetoric, and internal organization, of course, bear an undeniable resemblance to the Communist Party of the 1940s, even though Ellison has protested any absolute identification.

8. He further affirmed that the emergence of African American folklore within a culture that regarded it as inferior attested to "the Negro's willingness to trust his own experience, his own sensibilities as to the definition of reality, rather than allow his masters to define these crucial matters for him" (*S&A*, 172).

9. For a detailed discussion of the novel's relationship to *Notes from Underground* and other works by Dostoyevsky, as well as similarities in the authors' strategies for undermining hierarchical structures, see Joseph Frank's "Ralph Ellison and a Literary 'Ancestor': Dostoevski."

10. Works on this subject include Foreman's "Past-on Stories"; Robert Antoni, "Parody or Piracy: The Relationship of *The House of the Spirits* to *One Hundred Years of Solitude*"; René Jara, *Los límites de la representación*; Mario Rodríguez Fernández, "García Márquez/Isabel Allende: Relación textual"; Mario Rojas, "*La casa de los espíritus,* de Isabel Allende: Un caleidoscopio de espejos desordenados"; and Philip Swanson, "Conclusion: After the Boom." The obvious question of the relationship of *The House of the Spirits* and García Márquez's *One Hundred Years of Solitude* has also generated much discussion. While conscious stylistic and thematic modeling is clear in Allende's novel (in its textuality, its nonchalant tone for describing the extraordinary, and in its very assertion of difference, as when Clara refuses to repeat names so as not to cause confusion in her notebooks), the debate still rages as to whether the echoes are parody, parroting, or piracy; assessments tend to correlate with the critic's overall opinion of the book. While I agree with those who regard the novel as an example of Bakhtinian stylization, wherein Allende casts García Márquez's magic realism as a language to be appropriated for her own ends, my own analysis of *The House of the Spirits* will not specifically address the question of influence. Instead, it sets out from the authors' shared perception of Spanish American reality, summarized in the Colombian's comment that "[i]t always amuses me that the biggest praise for my work comes for the imagination while the truth is that there's not a single line in all my work that does not have a basis in reality. The problem is that Caribbean reality resembles the wildest imagination" (quoted in Meyer, *Lives,* 229).

11. *The House of the Spirits* (also *HS*), 177. When my interpretation requires strict adherence to the Spanish phrasing or vocabulary, I use my own translations of the original; these references are cited as *LCE.*

12. Rojas states that "Clara's magical world and her enchanted environment begin to break down when, following her death, the house opens its doors to the ominous world that surrounds it, where deeds of unbelievable fiction— which are at the same time terrible historical reality—take place" (918). Foreman claims that Clara's enchanted realm is gradually eclipsed by Alba's world of stark historical reality, her magic swept away by political cataclysm. Jara, in turn, suggests that "perhaps the Coup could not be narrated in any other way, perhaps it demands the stolid drama of the epic to describe its brutality. In the final analysis, the Coup entailed the collapse of everyday life; even the spirits stop speaking for a while. Within the epic mode that Isabel Allende's discourse adheres to, testimonial fiction seems to be the most appropriate form for narrating this traumatic event" (26). Rodríguez Fernández views "a gradual withdrawal of the marvelous, the fantastic and the strange, and their replacement by a social and political emphasis which prevails in the final chapter" (80). Antoni claims that the novel's focus changes from family saga and romance to love story, and on to political history, as the focalization shifts from Clara to

Alba: "The 'magic' begins to disappear, slowly displaced by the 'historical' narrative," until "finally there is no longer magic but only realism, and the novel becomes the tragic political history of Chile" (22, 20).

13. To criticism that the women's association with magic and the spirit world accentuates their passivity (see, for example, articles by Gabriela Mora), I would respond that Allende has judiciously contrived this impression in specific episodes. Clara's second pregnancy, that is, her fulfillment of the role of dutiful wife, returns her to the protected world of spirits and notebooks, causing her to lose interest in her charitable works. In this instance, then, her alternative spaces are subservient to the male order. However, Clara's tendency to find everything quite lovely, and the immersion in an enchanted realm of the imagination that this state entails, is far more insidious than the fact of the magic itself, precisely because it signals acceptance of the position allotted her within the patriarchal system. And this blindness to social injustice is the precursor to the willed ignorance of her compatriots, who later cover their eyes and ears to deny the horror surrounding their happy world.

14. The "rainbow poster" in the narrator's Brotherhood office offers a visual image of the letter's message: it is a photograph which depicts America's dispossessed but is not allowed to show an interracial couple.

15. Trueba's refusal to recognize his offspring is literal as well as legal, as is demonstrated by the fact that he does not realize that Esteban García is his grandson until after the latter's final vengeance. However, his descendants are not the only people who do not "count"—or are not recounted, as it were—in his narration. Trueba concedes that he would not have mentioned Tránsito Soto had her role in his story, her rescue of Alba, not made its recording possible in the first place.

16. When Clara stops speaking to Trueba, she reverts to her maiden name; Blanca accepts her husband's name to guarantee her daughter's legitimacy; and Alba uses this name in the university to dissociate herself from her grandfather's reputation. Jaime assumes his mother's maiden name for the same reason. As a result, Trueba's only namesakes are offspring whom he does not recognize: Nicolás, exiled for having ridiculed his father with their last name, and Esteban García, who views his surname as the symbol of his disenfranchisement. In the end, the latter fulfills one of the fates that Clara was trying to avoid when she refused to name her children after her husband, hoping not to pass on any of his traits to future generations (Glickman, 57).

17. Meyer ("Parenting," 362) and Campos (27) have made similar observations on the role of personal testimony in this novel as a bridge between public and private experience and histories.

18. "Here in the U.S.," Ellison once commented, "we have had a political system which wouldn't allow me to tell my story officially" ("Uses," 69). Allende similarly views her novels as "the history of Chile that is denied by the official

textbooks of the dictatorship—the forbidden and secret history that never-theless is still alive in the memories of most Chileans" ("Writing as an Act of Hope," 57). While these stands bring to mind social realism and its didactic ten-dencies, both Ellison and Allende are highly sensitive to the resonance, and have often declared their refusal to sacrifice aesthetic standards to social utility. Their artistic and social projects might be inextricably linked, but neither author lim-its the former to expressing an ideological platform or prescribed issues. Nevertheless, both have been taken to task precisely for not writing "effec-tive" novels of protest, and, instead, reinforcing dominant social, literary, and cultural traditions. That is, these criticisms claim that the authors' double vision is compromised by double-voiced discourse. Bernt Ostendorf questions Elli-son's use of black folklore as an emic expression of racial experience because it originated and was shaped within an oppressive symbolic universe (130). Michele Wallace accuses the author of harboring a unitary conception of the Other that posits an analogy between the oppressed position of black males and white women in American society, but still leaves the black woman without a voice (44). And still others perceive the suppression of differences entailed by the uni-versalization of the invisible man's plight, the extension of his identity to greater American society, as a betrayal of the race's goals that compromises the work's protest value. Similarly, there are qualifications of the effectiveness of women's resistance in *The House of the Spirits*, accusations that Allende has not ventured very far into the "wild zone" beyond male-generated and -dominated ideolo-gy. Mora, Marta Morello-Frosch, and Kavita Panjabi claim that her female char-acters never truly achieve greater independence, for their roles are adjusted—distorted, rather—to fit traditional male stereotypes. Morello-Frosch further accuses Allende of complicity with the patriarchal system on the grounds that the women's alternative paths do not empower them, but, rather, perpetuate their subordination. These condemnations, however, would seem to subject the authors to the critics' horizons of expectations and standards of exemplar-ity, reflecting their agendas more than the circumstances in which the authors wrote. They ignore the fact that both novels marked breakthroughs in their "otherly" strategies for representing marginalized groups. Allende has claimed that her protagonists are feminists "in their own way" (quoted in Agosín, 919). Like them, she and Ellison also "fight in keeping with what their charac-ters and the periods in which they lived allow" (Agosín, 919).

Chapter 4: Paradise Lost and Regained: The Old Order and Memory in the Miranda Stories and *Pedro Páramo*

1. In this study, I analyze the stories and short novel of the Old Order: "The Source," "The Old Order" (later republished as "The Journey"), "The Witness," "The Circus," "The Last Leaf," "The Fig Tree," "The Grave," and "Old Mortali-ty." I also examine her novella of the New Order, "Pale Horse, Pale Rider." All

works are included in Porter's *Collected Stories* (henceforth *CS*). I do not study works considered by some critics to be "implicit Miranda" stories because their protagonists (anonymous or named, as in "Holiday" and "Flowering Judas," respectively) bear some resemblance to Miranda (see, for example, DeMouy's study, *Katherine Anne Porter's Women*, and Stout's "Miranda's Guarded Speech"). These lack the intertextual continuities of the cycle and/or the references to the social milieu of Miranda's upbringing that are the focus of the present study.

2. Toni Morrison has similarly remarked that "We live in a land where the past is always erased and America is the innocent future in which immigrants can come and start over, where the slate is clean. The past is absent or it's romanticized. This culture doesn't encourage dwelling on, let alone coming to terms with, the truth about the past" (quoted in Gilroy, 222).

3. Although the order that Pedro Páramo instates is not slave based, Comala is indentured to the cacique, who expropriates the town's land and compromises its inhabitants with the promise of financial compensation after his death. While the absence of slavery in his system might raise objections to the terms of my comparison, I would argue that it allows for the identification of even greater similarities with the post-Emancipation South depicted by Porter, in which many blacks remained as servants in the households where they once had been slaves. While the communities depicted are on different scales (Porter focuses on a family whose social organization is representative of that found throughout the ante- and post-bellum South, while the system implemented by the cacique is a generalized phenomenon, encompassing the entire town), both are characterized by the economic dependence and social subordination of a collectivity to a dominant patriarchal figure.

4. *Collected Essays* (henceforth *CE*) 163, 161. As Joan Givner observes in her invaluable biography, *Katherine Anne Porter: A Life*, Porter "edited the story of her life as she might have shaped one of her short stories, rejecting certain experiences which she felt should not have happened and did not really belong to her and substituting others which seemed more appropriate" (20).

5. See her essay, "On a Criticism of Thomas Hardy" (*CE*, 3–13). She writes that Hardy's "mind led him out of the tradition of orthodoxy into another tradition of equal antiquity, equal importance . . . a body of opinion running parallel throughout history to the body of law in church and state: the great tradition of dissent. He went . . . with the Inquirers rather than the Believers" (6). We shall see how "Inquirer" is a category to which Porter herself subscribed, and also describes some of the characters in her stories, most notably Miranda.

6. These have been discussed in a collection of essays edited by Elizabeth Abel, Marianne Hirsch, and Elizabeth Langland, *The Voyage In: Fictions of Female Development*.

7. My analyses in this section are indebted to Jane Krause DeMouy's

insightful discussions of Miranda's observation of her role models and the lessons that she gathers from them.

8. In the same spirit of denying the passage of time, she gives all of her horses the same name throughout her life.

9. In "The Witness," Uncle Jimbilly tells of slaves who were whipped until they bled. In "Old Mortality," Miranda sees her uncle's horse bleed after the race and is pained to realize that this was a hidden cost of winning. Later, Eva tries to undercut the allure of the Amy myth by claiming that the latter's illness—induced, supposedly, by efforts to stop her menstruation—was not romantic precisely because she had coughed blood.

10. *Pedro Páramo*, 53 (Spanish version), translation mine. To avoid confusion, future references to the English translation (which has the same name as the original), will be cited parenthetically as *PP*, whereas references to the Spanish version will be cited as *Páramo*. Because my analysis relies heavily on lexical nuances that are not always easy to translate, I will be referring rather frequently to the Spanish version. When the most literal and accurate translations are simply too awkward, I provide the passage in Spanish as well as English.

11. "You'll pay dearly for that" (*Páramo*, 48).

12. Other important terms in this vocabulary are *bienes* (goods), *cobrar* (to charge), *comprar* (to buy), and *trabajo* (work or labor). Their meanings are expanded to include immaterial and emotional connotations that are also subsumed to Pedro Páramo's order.

13. "Dueño" is derived from the Latin *dominus*.

14. "[W]hat would it have cost him to grant pardon when it was so easy to say a word or two—or a hundred if a hundred were needed to save a soul?" (*PP*, 31).

15. Interestingly, in this identification of value with and in a stable family structure, *Pedro Páramo* resembles many texts written by men during the Southern Renaissance (Schulz, 89).

16. See Anthony Stanton's "Estructuras antropológicas en *Pedro Páramo*" for a similar observation and a different approach to discussing Susana San Juan's resistance to patriarchal authority (602).

17. In the aforementioned article, Zamora identifies a similar emphasis on individualism in Goyen, in contrast to Rulfo's and Garro's foregrounding of communal interests and destinies. She correlates the contrast with "the different relative importance placed on the individual and the community in U.S. and Mexican cultural ideology. Rulfo's and Garro's novels project a theory of the self as the *product* of the community, and hence tragically subject to it . . . whereas Goyen dramatizes the U.S. ideology of the self as *producer* . . . of community and hence able to transcend, or at least amend, its strictures" (68). While her analysis of Rulfo holds for my discussion as well, my argument about the

Miranda stories is that the heroine's individualism is a direct outgrowth not of a generalized U.S. ideology but, rather, of her (gendered) need to set herself apart from southern society, whose cultural ideology bears a much greater resemblance to that which Zamora associates with Mexico, and which, with its demands for adherence to traditional gender roles, stifles her.

18. The "square little mustache" worn by one of the government representatives suggests that the threat of totalitarianism (Porter's *bête noire*) is not limited to European Nazism, and warns that agents of patriotism—as well as the concept itself, as we shall see—may have their own insidious agenda (272).

19. It is interesting to note that many of these now-canonical critical works, all of which emphasize the universality of *Pedro Páramo*, were written during the 1960s and early 1970s, the years of the Boom in Spanish American literature. I would speculate that this foregrounding (favoring, even) of universal themes and the recourse to the technical and stylistic innovations of Euro-American modernism reflects the efforts—however unconscious—of critics of Spanish American narrative to complement in the critical sphere the authors' literary project by increasing their visibility and international resonance, and thereby enlarging their audience.

20. Carranza contested Victoriano Huerta's usurpation of the presidency in 1913. In 1915, Obregón, his army commander, defeated Pancho Villa; in 1919, Obregón led an uprising against Carranza and was inaugurated president in late 1920. In the novel, Father Rentería fights with the Catholic militants protesting, among other points, the revolutionaries' secularizing politics. This war, the Cristero War, was fought from 1926 to 1928.

21. E.g., "Breathing slowly, falling asleep and waking again, feeling the splash of water on her flesh, taking food, talking in bare phrases" (313); "Miranda looked about her with the covertly hostile eyes of an alien who does not like the country in which he finds himself, does not understand the language nor wish to learn it, does not mean to live there and yet is . . . unable to leave it at his will" (313); "'It is morning,' Miss Tanner would say . . . 'morning again . . . ,' showing Miranda the same monotonous landscape. . . . She would rustle about . . . saying, 'Look, my dear, what a heavenly morning. . . .' 'It's beautiful,' Miranda would answer. . . . Closing her eyes she would rest for a moment remembering that bliss . . . opening them again she saw . . . the dull world to which she was condemned" (313–14).

22. "El paraíso" is a Mexicanism for the sorrel tree.

23. Dorotea tells Juan that the cacique "spent the rest of his days slumped in a chair, staring down the road where they'd carried her to holy ground. He lost interest in everything. He let his lands lie fallow, and gave orders for the tools that worked it to be destroyed. Some say it was because he was worn out; others said it was despair. The one sure thing is that he threw everyone off his land and sat himself down in his chair to stare down that road" (80). The

omniscient narrator's presentation of the scene blends into the cacique's description of Susana's death: "Pedro Páramo was sitting in an old chair beside the main door of the Media Luna a little before the last shadow of night slipped away. He [was] there, alone. . . . He had forgotten what sleep was, or time. . . . 'You've been gone a long time, Susana. The light is the same now as it was then. . . . And it was just this hour. I was sitting here by the door, watching it dawn, watching as you went away following the path to Heaven. . . . As you went by, you brushed the branches of the Paradise tree beside the path, sweeping away its last leaves with your passing. . . . I called after you, "Come back, Susana!"'" (118–19). Many of the elements in this recurring image can also be found in the scene in "Luvina" which served as its prototype, in which the narrator describes his experiences in the town: "You must think I'm harping on the same idea. And I am, yes. . . . To be sitting at the threshold of the door, watching the rising and the setting of the sun, raising and lowering your head, until . . . everything gets still, timeless, as if you had always lived in eternity" (118). Additionally, in Luvina as well "Time is very long. . . . Nobody counts the hours and nobody cares how the years go mounting up. The days begin and end. Then night comes. Just day and night until the day of death, which for them is a hope" (118). For an elaboration of these points, and of the related issue of the relationship between the novel's stylistic treatment of time, memory, the revolution, and Mexican history, consult my article, "A Wrinkle in Time: Time as Structure and Meaning in *Pedro Páramo*."

Chapter 5: Race and Place in Identity and History

1. In 1868, Cuban nationalists rose up against Spanish rule and demanded their independence and the right to self-government. As part of the movement to expand both ranks and support, slavery was abolished. The war lasted until 1878 and failed in large measure because the creole elite felt that their economic interests and position atop the racial and social hierarchy were threatened. Interestingly enough, the latter had previously cherished dreams of annexation by the U.S. rather than strict independence from Spain. They believed that this would grant them greater political independence, democratic governance, and lay the foundation of a "great slave empire" comprising the South, Cuba, and Puerto Rico (Carr, 307)—a dream which was, of course, crushed with the South's defeat in the Civil War. The end of Cuba's "Ten-Year War" also saw the reinstitution of slavery, which was not abolished altogether until 1886.

2. For background information in this section, I have drawn on Edward Ayers's discussion of sectional reconciliation and of racial parallels between the U.S. and Cuba and their role in the Spanish-American War, in *The Promise of the New South* (328–34).

3. "The Charleston Earthquake" (103); "Our America" (94); "Passages on the Racial Question" (312).

4. This experience, as we know, is far from unique to Cuba. The designation of the Spanish American nations as "company-town countries" and "banana republics" expresses their orientation of production toward foreign powers, as well as the underdevelopment, economic dependency, and subjection to externally determined governments that this system entails (Fernández, 127). The Guatemalan coup d'état of 1954, orchestrated by the U.S. to protect the interests of the United Fruit Company, and the lengthy Somoza dictatorship in Nicaragua are but two of its more notorious manifestations.

5. It is, of course, no accident that don Hermenegildo, who is writing a novel about the town of Guamaní's great *independentista* senator (and having to falsify and invent numerous data as he proceeds) and whose voice frames *Sweet Diamond Dust*, is a lawyer: like the epic hero that he is trying to create for his community to rally around, Hermenegildo both represents and embodies the written code that was implemented by his class (and gender).

6. This reworking is only apparent in the translation, to which Ferré has added Laura's comments on the child's *mestizo* genealogy.

WORKS CITED

1. Primary Texts, Essays, and Interviews

Allende, Isabel. *La casa de los espíritus*. 1982. Barcelona: Plaza & Janes Editores, 1991.

———. *The House of the Spirits*. Trans. Magda Bogin. New York: Bantam, 1985.

———. Interview with Isabel Allende. In David Montenegro, *Points of Departure: International Writers on Writing and Politics*. Ann Arbor: University of Michigan Press, 1991. 114–26.

———. "La magia de las palabras." *Revista Iberoamericana* 51, nos. 132 and 133 (July, December 1985): 447–52.

———. "The Responsibility to Tell You: An Interview with Isabel Allende." John Rodden, *The Kenyon Review* 13, no. 1 (Winter 1991): 113–23.

———. "The World is Full of Stories: An Interview with Isabel Allende." Linda Levine and Jo Anne Engelbert, *Review* 34 (January, June 1985): 18–20.

———. "Writing as an Act of Hope." In *Paths of Resistance: The Art and Craft of the Political Novel*, edited by William Zinsser, 39–64. Boston: Houghton Mifflin, 1989.

Benítez, Fernando. "Conversaciones con Juan Rulfo." In *Inframundo: El México de Juan Rulfo*, edited by Fernando Benítez, 3–10. New York: Ediciones del Norte, 1980.

Benítez, Fernando, ed. *Inframundo: El México de Juan Rulfo*. New York: Ediciones del Norte, 1980.

———. *Inframundo: El México de Juan Rulfo*. 2d edition. New York: Ediciones del Norte, 1983.

Borges, Jorge Luis. "The Aleph." In *A Personal Anthology*, edited and translated by Anthony Kerrigan, 138–54. New York: Grove, 1967.

———. Review of *The Unvanquished*, by William Faulkner. *El hogar* 22 Jan. 1937. Reprinted in *Ficcionario*, edited by Emir Rodríguez Monegal, 123–24. Mexico City: Fondo de Cultura Económica, 1985.

Carpentier, Alejo. "On the Marvelous Real in America." In *Magical Realism: Theory, History, Community*, edited by Lois Parkinson Zamora and Wendy Faris, 75–88. Durham: Duke University Press, 1995.

Donoso, José. *The Boom in Spanish American Literature: A Personal History*. Trans. Gregory Kolovakos. New York: Columbia University Press, 1977.

Davidson, Donald. "A Mirror for Artists." In *I'll Take My Stand: The South and the Agrarian Tradition, by Twelve Southerners*, edited by Louis D. Rubin, Jr., 28–61. New York: Harper & Brothers, 1962.

DuBois, W. E. B. *The Souls of Black Folk*. [1903] 1953. Reprinted, Millwood, New York: Kraus-Thomson, 1973.

Durán, Armando. "Entrevista con García Márquez." In *Sobre García Márquez*, edited by Pedro Simón Martínez, 31–41. Montevideo: Biblioteca Marcha, 1971.

Edwards, Jorge. "Yoknapatawpha in Santiago de Chile." In *Faulkner: International Perspectives. Faulkner and Yoknapatawpha, 1982*, edited by Doreen Fowler and Ann Abadie, 60–71. Jackson: University Press of Mississippi, 1984.

Ellison, Ralph. *Going to the Territory*. New York: Vintage, 1986.

———. *Invisible Man*. New York: New American Library, 1952.

———. *Shadow and Act*. New York: Vintage, 1964.

Ellison, Ralph, William Styron, Robert Penn Warren, and C. Vann Woodward. "The Uses of History in Fiction: A Discussion." *Southern Literary Journal* 1, no. 2 (Spring 1969): 57–90.

Faulkner, William. *Absalom, Absalom!* 1936. Reprinted, New York: Vintage Books, 1972.

———. *Absalom, Absalom!: The Corrected Text*. 1936. Reprinted, New York: Vintage International, 1986.

———. *Faulkner in the University*. Edited by F. L. Gwynn and J. L. Blotner. Charlottesville: University of Virginia Press, 1959.

———. *Go Down, Moses*. 1940. Reprinted, New York: Vintage Books, 1973.

———. Interview, 1956. Jean Stein vanden Heuvel. Reprinted in William Faulkner, *Lion in the Garden*, edited by James Meriwether and Michael Millgate, 237–56. New York: Random House, 1968.

———. Interviews in Japan, 1955. Reprinted in William Faulkner, *Lion in the Garden*, edited by James Meriwether and Michael Millgate, 84–198. New York: Random House, 1968.

———. "An Introduction to *The Sound and the Fury*." *Mississippi Quarterly* 26 (Summer 1973): 410–15. Reprinted in William Faulkner, *The Sound and the Fury*, edited by David Minter, 220–24. New York: W. W. Norton, 1987.

———. *Light in August*. 1932. Reprinted, New York: Vintage Books, 1987.

———. *Lion in the Garden*. Edited by James Meriwether and Michael Millgate. New York: Random House, 1968.

———. *Requiem for a Nun*. New York: Random House, 1951.

———. *The Sound and the Fury*. [1928]. Edited by David Minter. New York: W. W. Norton, 1987.

———. *The Unvanquished*. 1934. Reprinted, New York: Vintage Books, 1966.

Fell, Claude, ed. *Juan Rulfo: Toda la obra*. Paris: UNESCO Colección Archivos, 1992.

Ferré, Rosario. *Sweet Diamond Dust and Other Stories*. Translated by Rosario Ferré. New York: Penguin, 1988.

Foner, Philip, ed. *Our America: Writings on Latin America and the Struggle for*

Cuban Independence. Translated by Elinor Randall. New York: Monthly Review, 1977. 84–94.

Freyre, Gilberto. *The Masters and the Slaves: A Study in the Development of Brazilian Civilization*. Trans. Samuel Putnam. 2nd rev. ed. Berkeley: University of California Press, 1986.

Fuentes, Carlos. *Casa con dos puertas*. Mexico City: Joaquín Mortiz, 1970.

———. "Central and Eccentric Writing." In *Lives on the Line: The Testimony of Contemporary Latin American Authors*, edited by Doris Meyer, 111–25. Berkeley: University of California Press, 1988.

———. "Clinton y Faulkner." *El País—Digital* (Cultura) 511 (26 Sept. 1997): 3 pp.: www.elpais.es/p/d/19970926/cultura/autorZ.HTM.

———. "Constancia." *Constancia and Other Stories for Virgins*. Translated by Thomas Christensen. New York: Farrar, Straus, Giroux, 1990. 3–64.

———. Interview. Jonathan Tittler, *Diacritics* 10, no. 3 (Fall, 1980): 46–56.

———. *La nueva novela hispanoamericana*. Mexico City: Mortiz, 1969.

———. "*Pedro Páramo*." *L'esprit des lettres* 6 (Nov.–Dec. 1955): 74–76. Translated by Joseph Sommers. Reprinted in *La narrativa de Juan Rulfo: Interpretaciones críticas*, edited by Joseph Sommers, 57–59. Mexico City: Sep/Setentas, 1974.

———. "Rulfo, el tiempo del mito." In *Inframundo: El México de Juan Rulfo*, 2d edition, edited by Fernando Benítez, 11–21. New York: Ediciones del Norte, 1983.

García Márquez, Gabriel. "Big Mama's Funeral." In *No One Writes to the Colonel and Other Stories*. Translated by J. S. Bernstein. New York: Harper & Row, 1968. 153–70.

———. *One Hundred Years of Solitude*. Translated by Gregory Rabassa. New York: Avon, 1970.

———. "Los problemas de la novela." *El Heraldo* (Barranquilla) 24 (April 1950). Reprinted in *Obra periodística. Vol. I: Textos costeños*, edited by Jacques Gilard, 269–70. Barcelona: Bruguera, 1980.

———. "The Solitude of Latin America." Nobel Prize Acceptance Speech, December 1982. Translated by Marina Castañeda. Reprinted in *Gabriel García Márquez and the Powers of Fiction*, edited by Julio Ortega, 87–91. Texas Pan American Series. Austin: University of Texas Press, 1988.

———. "William Faulkner 1897/1997." In *A Faulkner 100: The Centennial Exhibition. With a Contribution by Gabriel García Márquez*, edited by Thomas M. Verich. University: University of Mississippi Library Special Collections, 1997.

García Márquez, Gabriel, and Mario Vargas Llosa. *La novela en América Latina: Diálogo*. Lima: Carlos Millá Batres/Universidad Nacional de Ingeniería, 1968.

Guibert, Rita. *Seven Voices: Seven Latin American Writers Talk to Rita Guibert.* Translated by Frances Partridge. Introduction by Emir Rodríguez Monegal. New York: Vintage, 1972.

Guillén, Nicolás. Prologue to *Sóngoro Cosongo. Obra Poética 1920–1972: Tomo I.* Edited by Angel Augier, 113–14. La Habana: Editorial de arte y literatura, 1974.

Harss, Luis, and Barbara Dohmann. *Into the Mainstream: Conversations with Latin–American Writers.* New York: Harper & Row, 1967.

I'll Take My Stand: The South and the Agrarian Tradition, by Twelve Sourtherners. Edited by Louis D. Rubin, Jr. New York: Harper & Brothers, 1962.

———. Introduction. Pp. xix–xxx.

Martí, José. "The Charleston Earthquake." In *Martí on the U.S.A,* translated by Luis Baralt, 95–106. Carbondale: Southern Illinois University Press, 1966.

———. "Our America." In *Our America: Writings on Latin America and the Struggle for Cuban Independence,* translated by Elinor Randall, edited by Philip Foner, 84–94. New York: Monthly Review, 1977.

———. "Passages on the Racial Question." In *Our America: Writings on Latin America and the Struggle for Cuban Independence,* translated by Elinor Randall, edited by Philip Foner, 306–21. New York: Monthly Review, 1977.

Morrison, Toni. "Rootedness: The Ancestor as Foundation." In *Black Women Writers (1950–1980),* edited by Mari Evans, 339–45. Garden City, N.Y.: Anchor Press/Doubleday, 1984.

———. "The Site of Memory." In *Out There: Marginalization and Contemporary Cultures,* edited by Russell Ferguson et al., 299–305. New York: New Museum of Contemporary Art, 1990.

O'Connor, Flannery. "The Grotesque in Southern Fiction." In *Mystery and Manners,* edited by Sally and Robert Fitzgerald, 36–50. New York: Farrar, Straus & Giroux, 1961.

Ortiz, Fernando. *Cuban Counterpoint: Tobacco and Sugar.* Translated by Harriett de Onís. Durham, N.C.: Duke University Press, 1995.

Owsley, Frank L. "The Irrepressible Conflict." In *I'll Take My Stand: The South and the Agrarian Tradition, by Twelve Southerners,* edited by Louis D. Rubin, Jr., 61–91. New York: Harper & Brothers, 1962.

Paz, Octavio. *The Labyrinth of Solitude.* [1950/1959]. Translated by Lysander Kemp. London: A. Lane, 1969.

Pitol, Sergio. *El arte de la fuga.* Mexico: Ediciones Era, 1996.

Porter, Katherine Anne. *The Collected Essays and Occasional Writings of Katherine Anne Porter.* Boston: Houghton Mifflin, 1970.

———. *The Collected Stories of Katherine Anne Porter.* New York: Harcourt, Brace & World, 1965.

———. Letter to William Goyen. 8 April 1951. Papers of Katherine Anne Porter. Special Collections, University of Maryland Libraries, College Park, Maryland.

———. "The New Man and the New Order." In *Uncollected Early Prose of Katherine Anne Porter,* edited by Ruth Alvarez and Thomas Walsh, 51–61. Austin: University of Texas Press, 1993.

———. *Outline of American Popular Crafts.* Los Angeles: Young & McCallister, 1922. Reprinted in *Uncollected Early Prose of Katherine Anne Porter,* edited by Ruth Alvarez and Thomas Walsh, 136–87. Austin: University of Texas Press, 1993.

———. "The Portrait of an Artist (Interview)." Archer Winsten, *New York Post* 6 May 1937, 17.

Porter, Katherine Anne, Flannery O'Connor, Caroline Gordon, Madison Jones, and Louis D. Rubin. *Recent Southern Fiction: A Panel Discussion.* Macon, Ga.: Wesleyan College, 28 October 1960.

Ransom, John Crowe. "Reconstructed but Unregenerate." In *I'll Take My Stand: The South and the Agrarian Tradition, by Twelve Southerners,* edited by Louis D. Rubin, Jr., 1–27. New York: Harper & Brothers, 1962.

Rulfo, Juan. *Autobiografía Armada,* edited by Reina Roffé. Buenos Aires: Ediciones Corregidor, 1972.

———. "El desafío de la creación." In *Juan Rulfo: Toda la obra,* edited by Claude Fell, 380–82. Paris: UNESCO Colección Archivos, 1992.

———. Interview. Joseph Sommers, *Hispamérica* 11, nos. 4 and 5 (1973).

———. "Luvina." In *The Burning Plain and Other Stories.* Translated by George Schade. Austin: University of Texas Press, 1967. 111–21.

———. *Pedro Páramo.* 1955. Reprinted, Mexico City: Fondo de Cultura Económica, 1982.

———. *Pedro Páramo.* Translated by Margaret Sayers Peden. New York: Grove, 1994.

———. "*Pedro Páramo*: Treinta años después." *Cuadernos hispanoamericanos* 421–23 (July–September 1985): 5–7.

———. "Situación actual de la novela contemporánea." In *Juan Rulfo: Toda la obra,* edited by Claude Fell, 371–79. Paris: UNESCO Colección Archivos, 1992.

———. "Tell Them Not to Kill Me!" In *The Burning Plain and Other Stories,* translated by George Schade. Austin: University of Texas Press, 1967. 83–91.

Tate, Allen. "The New Provincialism." 1945. Reprinted in *Collected Essays.* Denver: Alan Swallow, 1959. 282–93.

Twelve Southerners. See *I'll Take My Stand: The South and the Agrarian Tradition.*

Vargas Llosa, Mario. "The Boom Twenty Years Later: An Interview with Mario

Vargas Llosa." Raymond Leslie Williams, *Latin American Literary Review* 15, no. 29 (Jan.–June 1987): 201–6.

———. "Faulkner en Laberinto." Reprinted in *Contra Viento y Marea II (1972–83)*. Barcelona: Seix Barral, 1986. 299–302.

———. "García Márquez: De Aracataca a Macondo." *Nueve asedios a García Márquez*. 3d ed. Santiago, Chile: Editorial Universitaria, S.A., 1972. 126–46.

———. *Historia de Mayta: Novela*. Barcelona: Seix Barral, 1984.

———. "Maestro de las voces (Interview)." By José Miguel Oviedo. In *Espejo de Escritores*, edited by Reina Roffé, 147–72. Hanover, N.H.: Ediciones del Norte, 1985.

———. "El papel del intelectual en los movimientos de liberación nacional." Reprinted in *Contra Viento y Marea I (1962–72)*. Barcelona: Seix Barral, 1986. 105–6.

———. *The Real Life of Alejandro Mayta*. Translated by Alfred MacAdam. New York: Aventura (Vintage), 1986.

———. "Social Commitment and the Latin American Writer." *World Literature Today* 52, no. 1 (Winter 1978). Reprinted in *Readings in Latin American History. Vol. II: The Modern Experience*, edited by John J. Johnson, Peter J. Bakewell, and Meredith D. Dodge, 455–64. Durham: Duke University Press, 1985.

———. "La Utopía Arcaica." Centre for Latin American Studies Working Papers Number 33, Cambridge University, Cambridge, U.K., 1978.

———. *A Writer's Reality*. Edited by M. Lichtblau. Syracuse: Syracuse University Press, 1991.

Warren, Robert Penn. *All the King's Men*. 1946. San Diego: Harcourt, Brace, Jovanovich, 1982.

2. Criticism, History, and Theory

Abel, Elizabeth, Marianne Hirsch, and Elizabeth Langland, eds. *The Voyage In: Fictions of Female Development*. Hanover, N.H.: University Press of New England, 1983.

Agosín, Marjorie. "Isabel Allende: *La casa de los espíritus.*" *Inter-American Review of Bibliography* 35, no.4 (1985): 448–58.

Alexis, Jacques Stéphen. "Du réalisme merveilleux des Haïtiens." *Présence Africaine* 8–10 (1956): 245–71.

———. "Of the Marvellous Realism of the Haitians." In *The Post-Colonial Studies Reader*, edited by Bill Ashcroft, Gareth Griffiths, and Helen Tiffin, 194–98. London: Routledge, 1995.

Antoni, Robert. "Parody or Piracy: The Relationship of *The House of the Spirits* to *One Hundred Years of Solitude.*" *Latin American Literary Review* 16, no.32 (July–December 1988): 16–28.

Ayers, Edward. *The Promise of the New South: Life After Reconstruction*. Oxford: Oxford University Press, 1992.

Bartra, Roger. "El edén subvertido." In *La jaula de la melancolía*, 33–38. Mexico City: Editorial Grihalbo, 1987.

Bassnett, Susan. "Coming Out of the Labyrinth: Women Writers in Contemporary Latin America." In *On Modern Latin American Fiction*, edited by John King, 247–67. New York: Noonday, 1987.

Benítez-Rojo, Antonio. *The Repeating Island: The Caribbean and the Postmodern Perspective*. Translated by James E. Maraniss. Durham: Duke University Press, 1992.

Berg, Mary. "Estructura narrativa y preocupación social en algunas obras de ficción hispanoamericana contemporánea." In *Actas del X Congreso de la Asociación Internacional de Hispanistas,* edited by Sebastian Neumeister, 463–68. Frankfurt: Vervuert Verlag, 1989.

Beverley, John, and Marc Zimmerman. *Literature and Politics in the Central American Revolutions*. Austin: University of Texas Press, 1990.

Blake, Susan. "Ritual and Rationalization: Black Folklore in the Works of Ralph Ellison." *PMLA* 94 (1979): 121–36.

Brenkman, John. "Multiculturalism and Criticism." In *English Inside and Out*, edited by Susan Gubar and Jonathan Kamholtz, 87–101. New York: Routledge, 1993.

Brinkmeyer, Robert H., Jr. "'Endless Remembering': The Artistic Vision of Katherine Anne Porter." *Mississippi Quarterly* 40, no. 1 (Winter 1986–87): 5–19.

———. *Katherine Anne Porter's Artistic Development: Primitivism, Traditionalism, and Totalitarianism*. Baton Rouge: Louisiana State University Press, 1993.

Brooks, Peter. *Reading for the Plot*. New York: Alfred A. Knopf, 1984.

Callahan, John. "Frequencies of Eloquence: The Performance and Composition of *Invisible Man*." In *New Essays on "Invisible Man,"* edited by Robert O'Meally, 55–94. Cambridge: Cambridge University Press, 1988.

Campos, René. "*La casa de los espíritus*: mirada, espacio, discurso de la otra historia." In *Los libros tienen sus propios espíritus*, edited by Marcelo Coddou, 21–28. Xalapa, México: Universidad Veracruzana, 1986.

Carr, Raymond. *Spain 1808–1975*. 2d ed. Oxford: Oxford University Press, 1982.

Castro-Klarén, Sara. *Mario Vargas Llosa: Análisis introductorio*. Lima: Latinoamericana Editores, 1988.

Cerqueira, Nelson. "Hermeneutics and Literature: A Study of William Faulkner's *As I Lay Dying* and Graciliano Ramos's *Vidas secas*." Ph.D. diss. University of Michigan, 1986.

Chapman, Arnold. "Pampas and Big Woods: Heroic Initiation in Güiraldes and Faulkner." *Comparative Literature* 11 (1959): 70–75.

————. *The Spanish American Reception of United States Fiction: 1920–1940.* University of California Publications in Modern Philology 77. Berkeley: University of California Press, 1966.

Chevigny, Bell Gale, and Gari Laguardia. "Introduction: History and the Literary Imagination." In *Reinventing the Americas: Comparative Studies of the Literature of the United States and Spanish America,* edited by Bell Gale Chevigny and Gari Laguardia, 3–33. Cambridge: Cambridge University Press, 1986.

Chevigny, Bell Gale, and Gari Laguardia, eds. *Reinventing the Americas: Comparative Studies of the Literature of the United States and Spanish America.* Cambridge: Cambridge University Press, 1986.

Christie, John. "Fathers and Virgins: García Márquez's Faulknerian *Chronicle of a Death Foretold.*" *Latin American Literary Review* 21, no. 41 (1993): 21–29.

Coddou, Marcelo. "*La casa de los espíritus:* De la historia a la Historia." In *Los libros tienen sus propios espíritus,* edited by Marcelo Coddou, 7–14. Xalapa, México: Universidad Veracruzana, 1986.

————. "Dimensión del feminismo en Isabel Allende." In *Los libros tienen sus propios espíritus,* edited by Marcelo Coddou, 29–53. Xalapa, México: Universidad Veracruzana, 1986.

Coddou, Marcelo, ed. *Los libros tienen sus propios espíritus.* Xalapa, México: Universidad Veracruzana, 1986.

Cohn, Deborah. "A Wrinkle in Time: Time as Structure and Meaning in *Pedro Páramo.*" *Revista Hispánica Moderna* 49, no. 2 (December 1996): 256–66.

Cooke, Michael. "Ellison and García Márquez: Nostalgia and the Destruction of 'Text.'" *Yale Journal of Criticism* 1, no. 1 (1987): 87–106.

Corvalán, Octavio. "Faulkner y García Márquez: Una aproximación." *Sur* 349 (July–December 1981): 71–88.

Cowley, Malcolm. *The Faulkner-Cowley File: Letters & Memories, 1944–62.* New York: The Viking Press, 1966.

————. Introduction. In William Faulkner, *The Portable Faulkner.* New York: Viking, 1951. 1–24.

Dale, Corinne. "*Absalom, Absalom!* and the Snopes Trilogy: Southern Patriarchy in Revision." *Mississippi Quarterly* 45 (Summer 1992): 323–37.

Davenport, F. Garvin., Jr. *The Myth of Southern History: Historical Consciousness in Twentieth-Century Southern Literature.* Nashville: Vanderbilt University Press, 1970.

Davis, Lisa. "An Invitation to Understanding among Poor Women of the Americas: *The Color Purple* and *Hasta no verte, Jesús Mío.*" In *Reinventing the Americas: Comparative Studies of the Literature of the United States and Spanish America,* edited by Bell Gale Chevigny and Gari Laguardia, 224–41. Cambridge: Cambridge University Press, 1986.

Davis, Mary E. "The Haunted Voice: Echoes of William Faulkner in García Márquez, Fuentes, and Vargas Llosa." *World Literature Today* (Autumn 1985): 531–35.

———. "William Faulkner and Mario Vargas Llosa: The Election of Failure." *Comparative Literature Studies* 16 (1979): 332–43.

Davis, Thadious M. "Expanding the Limits: The Intersection of Race and Region." *Southern Literary Journal* 20, no. 2 (Spring 1988): 3–11.

DeGrandis, Rita. "La problemática del conocimiento histórico en: *Historia de Mayta* de M. Vargas Llosa." *Revista de crítica literaria latinoamericana* 19, no. 38 (1993): 375–82.

DeMouy, Jane Krause. *Katherine Anne Porter's Women: The Eye of Her Fiction.* Austin: University of Texas Press, 1983.

D'haen, Theo. "Magical Realism and Postmodernism: Decentering Privileged Centers." In *Magical Realism: Theory, History, Community,* edited by Lois Parkinson Zamora and Wendy Faris, 191–208. Durham: Duke University Press, 1995.

Dimic, Milan V., and Juan Ferraté, eds. *Proceedings of the 7th Congress of the International Comparative Literature Association. Vol. I: Literatures of America.* Stuttgart: Kunst und Wissen, 1979.

Donaldson, Susan. "Subverting History: Women, Narrative, and Patriarchy in *Absalom, Absalom!*" *Southern Quarterly* 26, no. 4 (Summer 1988): 19–32.

Donnelly, Colleen E. "Compelled to Believe: Historiography and Truth in *Absalom, Absalom!*" *Style* 25, no. 1 (Spring 1991): 104–22.

Ermarth, Elizabeth D. *Sequel to History: Postmodernism and the Crisis of Representational Time.* Princeton: Princeton University Press, 1992.

Faris, Wendy. "Marking Space, Charting Time: Text and Territory in Faulkner's 'The Bear' and Carpentier's *Los pasos perdidos.*" In *Do the Americas Have a Common Literature?* edited by Gustavo Pérez Firmat, 243–65. Durham: Duke University Press, 1990.

———. "Scheherazade's Children: Magical Realism and Postmodern Fiction." In *Magical Realism: Theory, History, Community,* edited by Lois Parkinson Zamora and Wendy Faris, 163–90. Durham: Duke University Press, 1995.

Fayen, Tanya T. *In Search of the Latin American Faulkner.* Lanham, Md: University Press of America, 1995.

Ferguson, Russell, Martha Gever, Trinh T. Minh-ha, and Cornel West, eds. *Out There: Marginalization and Contemporary Cultures.* New York: New Museum of Contemporary Art, 1990.

Fernández, Pablo Armando. "Dreams of Two Americas." In *Reinventing the Americas: Comparative Studies of the Literature of the United States and Spanish America,* edited by Bell Gale Chevigny and Gari Laguardia, 122–36. Cambridge: Cambridge University Press, 1986.

Fields, Wayne. "*One Hundred Years of Solitude* and New World Storytelling." *Latin American Literary Review* 15, no. 29 (1987): 73–88.

Fischer, Russell. "*Invisible Man* as History." *CLA Journal* 17, no. 3 (March 1974): 338–67.

Fitz, Earl E. *Rediscovering the Americas: Inter-American Literature in a Comparative Context.* Iowa City: University of Iowa Press, 1991.

Flanders, Jane. "Katherine Anne Porter and the Ordeal of Southern Womanhood." *Southern Literary Journal* 9, no. 1 (Fall 1976): 47–60.

Foreman, P. Gabrielle. "Past-On Stories: History and the Magically Real, Morrison and Allende on Call." *Feminist Studies* 18, no. 2 (Summer 1992): 369–88.

Fowler, Doreen. *Faulkner's Changing Vision: From Outrage to Affirmation.* Ann Arbor: UMI Research, 1983.

Fowler, Doreen, and Ann Abadie, eds. *Faulkner: International Perspectives. Faulkner and Yoknapatawpha, 1982.* Jackson: University Press of Mississippi, 1984.

Fox-Genovese, Elizabeth. "Between Individualism and Community: Autobiographies of Southern Women." In *Located Lives: Place and Idea in Southern Autobiography*, edited by J. Bill Berry, 20–38. Athens: University of Georgia Press, 1990.

Franco, Jean. "El viaje al país de los muertos." In *Juan Rulfo: Toda la obra*, edited by Claude Fell, 763–74. Paris: UNESCO Colección Archivos, 1992.

Frank, Joseph. "Ralph Ellison and a Literary 'Ancestor': Dostoevski." In *Speaking for You: The Vision of Ralph Ellison*, edited by Kimberly Benston, 231–44. Washington, D.C.: Howard University Press, 1987.

Frisch, Mark. "Self-Definition and Redefinition in New World Literature: William Faulkner and the Hispanic American Novel." *Crítica Hispánica* 12, nos. 1 and 2 (1990): 115–31.

Gates, Henry Louis, Jr. "The Blackness Of Blackness: A Critique of the Sign and the Signifying Monkey." In *Black Literature and Literary Theory*, edited by Henry Louis Gates, Jr., 285–321. New York: Routledge, 1984.

Genette, Gérard. *Narrative Discourse: An Essay in Method.* Translated by Jane E. Lewin. Foreword by Jonathan Culler. Ithaca: Cornell University Press, 1980.

Giacoman, Helmy F., ed. *Homenaje a Juan Rulfo: Variaciones interpretativas en torno a su obra.* Madrid: Las Américas, 1974.

Gilbert, Sandra M., and Susan Gubar. "Introduction: The female imagination and the modernist aesthetic." *Women's Studies* 13, nos 1 and 2 (1986): 1–10.

Gilroy, Paul. *The Black Atlantic: Modernity and Double Consciousness.* Cambridge: Harvard University Press, 1993.

Givner, Joan. *Katherine Anne Porter: A Life.* New York: Simon & Schuster, 1982.

Glickman, Nora. "Los personajes femeninos en *La casa de los espíritus.*" In *Los libros tienen sus propios espíritus,* edited by Marcelo Coddou, 54–60. Xalapa, México: Universidad Veracruzana, 1986.

González Echevarría, Roberto. *Alejo Carpentier: The Pilgrim at Home.* Ithaca: Cornell University Press, 1977.

Gray, Richard. *The Literature of Memory.* Baltimore: Johns Hopkins University Press, 1977.

Harper, Phillip B. *Framing the Margins: The Social Logic of Postmodern Culture.* Oxford: Oxford University Press, 1994.

Harrington, Evans, and Ann J. Abadie, eds. *The South and Faulkner's Yoknapatawpha: The Actual and the Apocryphal.* Jackson: University Press of Mississippi, 1977.

Hennessy, Rosemary. "Katherine Anne Porter's Model for Heroines." *Colorado Quarterly* 25, no. 3 (Winter 1977): 301–15.

Hernández de López, A. M., ed. *En el punto de mira: Gabriel García Márquez.* Madrid: Editorial Pliegos, 1985.

Hoffman, Frederick J. "The Sense of Place." In *South: Modern Southern Literature in Its Cultural Setting,* edited by Louis D. Rubin, Jr., and Robert D. Jacobs, 60–75. Garden City, N.Y.: Doubleday, 1961.

hooks, bell. "Marginality as Site of Resistance." In *Out There: Marginalization and Contemporary Cultures,* edited by Russell Ferguson et al., 341–43. New York: New Museum of Contemporary Art, 1990.

Huston, Hollis. "Revolutionary Change in *One Hundred Years of Solitude* and *The Real Life of Alejandro Mayta.*" *Latin American Literary Review* 15, no. 29 (Jan.–June 1987): 105–120.

Hutcheon, Linda. *A Poetics of Postmodernism.* New York: Routledge, 1988.

Irby, James East. "La influencia de William Faulkner en cuatro narradores hispano–americanos." M.A. thesis. Universidad Nacional Autónoma de México, 1956.

Iser, Wolfgang. *The Act of Reading.* Baltimore: The Johns Hopkins University Press, 1978.

Jameson, Fredric. *The Political Unconscious: Narrative as Socially Symbolic Act.* Ithaca: Cornell University Press, 1981.

Jara, René. *Los límites de la representación.* Madrid: Fundación Instituto Shakespeare–Instituto de Cine y Radio-Televisión, 1985.

Jones, Anne Goodwyn. "Gender and the Great War: The Case of Faulkner and Porter." *Women's Studies* 13, nos. 1 and 2 (1986): 135–48.

———. *Tomorrow is Another Day: The Woman Writer in the South, 1859–1936.* Baton Rouge: Louisiana State University Press, 1981.

Jones, Suzanne W. "Reading the Endings in Katherine Anne Porter's 'Old Mortality.'" *Southern Quarterly* 31, no. 3 (Spring 1993): 29–44.

Kazin, Alfred. Review of *Leaf Storm and Other Stories*, by Gabriel García Márquez. *New York Times Book Review*, 20 February 1972, 1:14–16. Reprinted in *Critical Essays on Gabriel García Márquez*, edited by George McMurray, 26–29. Boston: G. K. Hall, 1987.

King, John. "Jorge Luis Borges: A View from the Periphery." In *On Modern Latin American Fiction*, edited by John King, 101–16. New York: Noonday Press, 1987.

Kirkpatrick, Susan. *Las Románticas: Women Writers and Subjectivity in Spain, 1835–1850*. Berkeley: University of California Press, 1989.

Kulin, Katalin. "Razones y características de la influencia de Faulkner en la ficción latinoamericana moderna." Translated by Aída Fajardo and Nilita Vientós Gastón. *Sin Nombre* 6, no. 1 (July–September 1975): 20–36.

———. "Reasons and Characteristics of Faulkner's Influence on Juan Carlos Onetti, Juan Rulfo and Gabriel García Márquez." In *Proceedings of the 7th Congress of the International Comparative Literature Association. Vol. I: Literatures of America*, edited by Milan V. Dimic and Juan Ferraté, 277–80. Stuttgart: Kunst und Wissen, 1979.

Ladd, Barbara. "'The Direction of the Howling': Nationalism and the Color Line in *Absalom, Absalom!*" In *Subjects and Citizens: Nation, Race, and Gender from* Oroonoko *to* Anita Hill, edited by Michael Moon and Cathy Davidson, 345–72. Durham: Duke University Press, 1995.

Lerner, Gerda. *The Majority Finds Its Past: Placing Women in History*. New York: Oxford University Press, 1979.

Levine, Suzanne Jill. *El espejo hablado: Un estudio de "Cien años de soledad."* Caracas: Monte Avila Editores, 1975.

Levins, Lynn. "The Four Narrative Perspectives in *Absalom, Absalom!*" *PMLA* 85 (1970): 35–47.

Lowe, Elizabeth. "Visions of Violence: From Faulkner to the Contemporary City Fiction of Brazil and Colombia." In *Proceedings of the Xth Congress of the International Comparative Literature Association, New York, 1982,* edited by Anna Balakian and James J. Wilhelm. *Vol. III: Inter-American Literary Relations*, edited by Mario J. Valdés, 13–19. New York: Garland, 1985.

Ludmer, Josefina. "Onetti: 'La novia (carta) robada (a Faulkner).'" *Hispamérica* 9 (1975): 3–19.

MacAdam, Alfred. "Carlos Fuentes: The Burden of History." *World Literature Today* 57, no. 4 (1983): 558–63.

———. Personal communication. 11 May 1998.

Machann, Clinton, and William Bedford Clark, eds. *Katherine Anne Porter and Texas: An Uneasy Relationship*. College Station: Texas A&M University Press, 1990.

Magnarelli, Sharon. "Framing Power in Luisa Valenzuela's *Cola de lagartija* and

Isabel Allende's *Casa de los espíritus*." In *Splintering Darkness: Latin American Women Writers in Search of Themselves*, edited by Lucía Guerra Cunningham, 43–62. Pittsburgh: Latin American Literary Review Press, 1990.

Manning, Carol S., ed. *The Female Tradition in Southern Literature*. Urbana: University of Illinois Press, 1993.

Marcos, Juan Manuel. "*La casa de los espíritus* (Review)." *Revista Iberoamericana* 51, nos. 130–32 (January–June 1985): 401–6.

Martin, Gerald. *Journeys through the Labyrinth: Latin American Literature in the Twentieth Century*. London: Verso, 1989.

Masiello, Francine. "Discurso de mujeres, lenguaje del poder: Reflexiones sobre la crítica feminista a mediados de la década del 80." *Hispania* 15, no. 45 (1986): 53–60.

Matthews, John. "Faulkner's Narrative Frames." In *Faulkner and the Craft of Fiction*, edited by Doreen Fowler and Ann Abadie, 71–91. Jackson: University Press of Mississippi, 1989.

Meyer, Doris. "'Parenting the Text': Female Creativity and Dialogic Relationships in Isabel Allende's *La casa de los espíritus*." *Hispania* 73 (May 1990): 360–65.

Meyer, Doris, ed. *Lives on the Line: The Testimony of Contemporary Latin American Authors*. Berkeley: University of California Press, 1988.

Mignolo, Walter D. *Literatura fantástica y realismo maravilloso*. Literatura hispanoamericana en imágenes. Madrid: Editorial La Muralla, 1983.

Mink, Louis. "Narrative Form as a Cognitive Instrument." In *The Writing of History: Literary Form and Historical Understanding*, edited by Robert Canary and Henry Kozicki, 129–49. Madison: University of Wisconsin Press, 1978.

Mintz, Sidney. "The Caribbean as a Socio-Cultural Area." *Cahiers d'Histoire Mondiale* 9, no. 4 (1966): 911–37.

Millgate, Michael. "Faulkner and History." In *The South and Faulkner's Yoknapatawpha: The Actual and the Apocryphal*, edited by Evans Harrington and Ann J. Abadie, 22–39. Jackson: University Press of Mississippi, 1977.

———. "Faulkner and The South: Some Reflections." In *The South and Faulkner's Yoknapatawpha: The Actual and the Apocryphal*, edited by Evans Harrington and Ann J. Abadie, 195–210. Jackson: University Press of Mississippi, 1977.

Monsiváis, Carlos. "Sí, tampoco los muertos retoñan, desgraciadamente." In *Inframundo: El México de Juan Rulfo*, 2d edition, edited by Fernando Benítez, 35–44. New York: Ediciones del Norte, 1983. Reprinted in *Juan Rulfo: Toda la obra*, edited by Claude Fell, 833–42. Paris: UNESCO Colección Archivos, 1992.

Monteiro, George. "Faulkner in Brazil." *Southern Literary Journal* 15, no. 3 (1983): 96–104.

Moon, Michael, and Cathy Davidson, eds. *Subjects and Citizens: Nation, Race, and Gender from* Oroonoko *to Anita Hill*. Durham: Duke University Press, 1995.

———. Introduction. In *Subjects and Citizens: Nation, Race, and Gender from* Oroonoko *to Anita Hill*, edited by Michael Moon and Cathy Davidson, 1–6. Durham: Duke University Press, 1995.

Mora, Gabriela. "Las novelas de Isabel Allende y el papel de la mujer como ciudadana." *Ideologies and Literature* 2.1 (Spring 1987): 53–61.

———. "Ruptura y perseverancia de estereotipos en *La casa de los espíritus*." In *Los libros tienen sus propios espíritus*, edited by Marcelo Coddou, 71–78. Xalapa, México: Universidad Veracruzana, 1986.

Morello-Frosch, Marta. "Discurso erótico y escritura femenina." *Coloquio internacional: Escritura y sexualidad en la literatura Hispanoamericana.* Madrid: Centre de Recherche Lat.Am./Fundamentos, 1990. 21–30.

Muñoz, Willy. "La Historia de la Ficción de Mayta." *Symposium* 44 (1990): 102–13.

Newman, Kathleen. "Historical Knowledge in the Post-Boom Novel." In *The Historical Novel in Latin America: A Symposium*, edited by Daniel Balderston, 209–20. Gaithersburg, Md: Ediciones Hispamérica, 1986.

Oberhelman, Harley. "Faulknerian Techniques in Gabriel García Márquez's Portrait of a Dictator." In *Proceedings of the Comparative Literature Symposium, Vol. X: Ibero-American Letters in a Comparative Perspective*, edited by Wolodymyr T. Zyla and Wendell M. Aycock, 171–81. Lubbock: Texas Tech University, 1978.

———. "García Márquez and the American South." *Chasqui* 5, no. 1 (November 1975): 29–38.

———. *The Presence of Faulkner in the Writings of García Márquez*. Graduate Studies No. 22. Lubbock: Texas Tech University Press, 1980.

———. "William Faulkner and Gabriel García Márquez: Two Nobel Laureates." In *Critical Essays on Gabriel García Márquez*, edited by George McMurray, 67–79. Boston: G. K. Hall, 1987.

———. "William Faulkner's Reception in Spanish America." *The American Hispanist* 3, no. 26 (1978): 13–17.

Oliveira, Celso de. *Faulkner and Graciliano Ramos*. Tubingen: Francke, 1993.

O'Meally, Robert. *The Craft of Ralph Ellison*. Cambridge: Harvard University Press, 1980.

O'Meally, Robert, ed. *New Essays on "Invisible Man."* Cambridge: Cambridge University Press, 1988.

Ortega, Julio. "La novela de Juan Rulfo: *Summa* de arquetipos." In *La contemplación y la fiesta*. Caracas: Monte Avila, 1969. 17–30. Reprinted in

Juan Rulfo: Toda la obra, edited by Claude Fell, 723–28. Paris: UNESCO Colección Archivos, 1992.

Ostendorf, Berndt. *Black Literature in White America*. Sussex, U.K.: Harvester, 1982.

Oviedo, José Miguel. "Terrorismo y novela." *Vuelta* 9, no. 105 (August 1985): 21–27.

Panjabi, Kavita. "*The House of the Spirits*, Tránsito Soto: From Periphery to Power." In *Critical Approaches to Isabel Allende's Novels*, edited by Sonia Riquelme Rojas and Edna Aguirre Rehbein. Series 22, Latin American Literature, 14: 11–20. New York: Peter Lang, 1991.

Parker, Robert D. Absalom, Absalom!: *The Questioning of Fictions*. Boston: Twayne, 1991.

———. "The Chronology and Genealogy of *Absalom, Absalom!*: The Authority of Fiction and the Fiction of Authority." *Studies in American Fiction* 14 (1986): 191–98.

Parr, Susan Resneck, and Pancho Savery, eds. *Approaches to Teaching Ellison's Invisible Man*. New York: MLA of America, 1989.

Pérez Firmat, Gustavo, ed. *Do the Americas Have a Common Literature?* Durham: Duke University Press, 1990.

Pilkington, John. "The Memory of the War." In *The History of Southern Literature*, edited by Louis D. Rubin, Jr., Blyden Jackson, Rayburn S. Moore, et al., 356–62. Baton Rouge: Louisiana State University Press, 1985.

Poniatowska, Elena. "¡Ay vida, no me mereces! Juan Rulfo, tu pon la cara de disimulo." In *Inframundo: El México de Juan Rulfo*, edited by Fernando Benítez, 41–52. New York: Ediciones del Norte, 1980.

Pratt, Mary Louise. "Margin Release: Canadian and Latin American Literature in the Context of Dependency." In *Proceedings of the Xth Congress of the International Comparative Literature Association, New York, 1982,* edited by Anna Balakian and James J. Wilhelm. *Vol. III: Inter-American Literary Relations*, edited by Mario J. Valdés, 247–56. New York: Garland, 1985.

Ramos Escobar, J. L. "Desde Yoknapatawpha a Macondo." In *En el punto de mira: Gabriel García Márquez*, edited by A. M. Hernández de López, 287–311. Madrid: Editorial Pliegos, 1985.

Reed, Joseph, Jr. *Faulkner's Narrative*. New Haven: Yale University Press, 1973.

Reisz de Rivarola, Susana. "La historia como ficción y la ficción como historia. Vargas Llosa y Mayta." *Nueva revista de filología hispanoamericana* 35.2 (1987). 835–53.

Rodríguez Fernández, Mario. "García Márquez/Isabel Allende: Relación textual." In *Los libros tienen sus propios espíritus*, edited by Marcelo Coddou, 79–82. Xalapa, México: Universidad Veracruzana, 1986.

Rodríguez Monegal, Emir. "A Game of Shifting Mirrors: The New Latin American Narrative and the North American Novel." In *Proceedings of the 7th Congress of the International Comparative Literature Association. Vol. 1: Literatures of America*, edited by Milan V. Dimic and Juan Ferraté, 269–75. Stuttgart: Kunst und Wissen, 1979.

Rojas, Mario. "*La casa de los espíritus*, de Isabel Allende: Un caleidoscopio de espejos desordenados." *Revista Iberoamericana* 51, nos. 132–33 (July–December 1985): 917–25.

Rollyson, Carl Jr. *Uses of the Past in the Novels of William Faulkner.* Studies in Modern Literature 37. Ann Arbor: UMI Research, 1984.

Rukas, Nijole Marija. "A Comparison of Faulkner's and Rulfo's Treatment of the Interplay Between Reality and Illusion in *Absalom, Absalom!* and *Pedro Páramo.*" Ph.D. diss. University of Arizona, 1982. Ann Arbor: UMI, 1982. 8217469.

Saldívar, José. *The Dialectics of Our America.* Durham: Duke University Press, 1991.

Schaub, Thomas. *American Fiction in the Cold War.* Madison: The University of Wisconsin Press, 1991.

———. "Ellison's Masks and the Novel of Reality." In *New Essays on "Invisible Man,"* edited by Robert O'Meally, 123-56. Cambridge: Cambridge University Press, 1988.

Schulz, Joan. "Orphaning as Resistance." In *The Female Tradition in Southern Literature*, edited by Carol S. Manning, 89–109. Urbana: University of Illinois Press, 1993.

Shapiro, J. P. "'Une histoire contée par un idiot . . .' (W. Faulkner et J. Rulfo)." *Revue de Litterature Comparée* 53 (1979): 338–47.

Shaw, Donald. *Nueva narrativa hispanoamericana.* Madrid: Ediciones Cátedra, 1981.

———. "Towards a Description of the Post-Boom." *Bulletin of Hispanic Studies* 66 (1989): 87–94.

Sherry, Charles. "Being Otherwise: Nature, History, and Tragedy in *Absalom, Absalom!*" *Arizona Quarterly* 45, no. 3 (Autumn 1989): 47–76.

Simas, Rosa. "'Ripples,' a 'Gyrating Wheel,' and a 'Spiral on a Square': Circularity in Three Twentieth Century Novels of the Americas." Ph.D. diss. University of California, Davis, 1990.

———. "'Ripples,' 'Una rueda giratoria,' and 'A Espiral e o quadrado': Circularity in Three Twentieth-Century Novels of the Americas." *Translation Perspectives* 6 (1991): 87–98.

Simpson, Lewis P. "Southern Fiction." In *Harvard Guide to Contemporary American Writing*, edited by Daniel Hoffman, 153–90. Cambridge: Bellknap Press of Harvard University Press, 1979.

Singal, Daniel J. *The War Within: From Victorian to Modernist Thought in the*

South, 1919–1945. Chapel Hill: University of North Carolina Press, 1982.

Slemon, Stephen. "Magic Realism as Postcolonial Discourse." In *Magical Realism: Theory, History, Community*, edited by Lois Parkinson Zamora and Wendy Faris, 407–26. Durham: Duke University Press, 1995.

Smith, Barbara. "Toward a Black Feminist Criticism." In *But Some of Us Are Brave*, edited by Gloria Hull, Patricia Bell Scott, and Barbara Smith. Old Westbury, N.Y.: Feminist Press, 1982. Reprinted in *Within the Circle: An Anthology of African American Literary Criticism from the Harlem Renaissance to the Present*, edited by Angelyn Mitchell, 410–27. Durham, N.C.: Duke University Press, 1994.

Snead, James A. *Figures of Division: William Faulkner's Major Novels*. New York: Methuen, 1986.

———. "The 'Joint' of Racism: Withholding the Black in *Absalom, Absalom!*" In *William Faulkner's* Absalom, Absalom! Edited by Harold Bloom. New York: Chelsea House, 1987. 129–41.

Snell, Susan. "William Faulkner, un guía sureño a la ficción de García Márquez." In *En el punto de mira: Gabriel García Márquez*, edited by A. M. Hernández de López, 315–26. Madrid: Editorial Pliegos, 1985.

Sommers, Joseph. *After the Storm: Landmarks of the Modern Mexican Novel*. Albuquerque: University of New Mexico Press, 1968.

———. "A través de la ventana de la sepultura: Juan Rulfo." In *Homenaje a Juan Rulfo: Variaciones interpretativas en torno a su obra*, edited by Helmy F. Giacoman, 39–60. Madrid: Las Américas, 1974.

———. "Los muertos no tienen tiempo ni espacio: Diálogo con Juan Rulfo." *Siempre!* 1051 (15 August 1973): vi-vii (cultural supplement). Reprinted in *La narrativa de Juan Rulfo: Interpretaciones críticas*, edited by Joseph Sommers, 17–22. Mexico City: Sep/Setentas, 1974.

Sommers, Joseph, ed. *La narrativa de Juan Rulfo: Interpretaciones críticas*. Mexico City: Sep/Setentas, 1974.

Standley, Arline. "Here and There: Now and Then." *Luso-Brazilian Review* 23.1 (Summer 1986): 61–75.

Stanton, Anthony. "Estructuras antropológicas en *Pedro Páramo*." *Nueva revista de filología hispanoamericana* 36.1 (1988): 567–606.

Stepto, Robert. *From Behind the Veil: A Study of Afro-American Narrative*. Urbana: University of Illinois Press, 1979.

Stout, Janis. "Estranging Texas: Porter and the Distance from Home." In *Katherine Anne Porter and Texas: An Uneasy Relationship*, edited by Clinton Machann and William Bedford Clark, 86–101. College Station: Texas A&M University Press, 1990.

———. "Miranda's Guarded Speech: Porter and the Problem of Truth-Telling." *Philological Quarterly* 66, no. 2 (Spring 1987): 259–78.

———. *Strategies of Reticence: Silence and Meaning in the Works of Jane Austen,*

Willa Cather, Katherine Anne Porter, and Joan Didion. Charlottesville: University Press of Virginia, 1990.

Strout, Cushing. *"Invisible Man* and the Politics of Culture." In *Approaches to Teaching Ellison's* Invisible Man, edited by Susan Resneck Parr and Pancho Savery, 79–85. New York: MLA of America, 1989.

Swanson, Philip. "Conclusion: After the Boom." In *Landmarks in Latin American Fiction*, edited by Philip Swanson, 222–45. London: Routledge, 1990.

Tiffin, Helen. "Commonwealth Literature: Comparison and Judgment." In *The History and Historiography of Commonwealth Literature*, edited by Dieter Riemenschneider, 19–35. Tübingen: Gunter Narr, 1983.

Titus, Mary. "Katherine Anne Porter's Miranda: The Agrarian Myth and Southern Womanhood." In *Redefining Autobiography in Twentieth-Century Women's Fiction*, edited by Janice Morgan and Colette Hall, 193–208. New York: Garland, 1991.

Tobin, Patricia Drechsel. *Time and the Novel: The Genealogical Imperative.* Princeton: Princeton University Press, 1978.

Valdés, Mario J., ed. *Proceedings of the Xth Congress of the International Comparative Literature Association, New York, 1982. Vol. III: Inter-American Literary Relations.* Edited by Anna Balakian and James J. Wilhelm. New York: Garland, 1985.

Valente, Luiz. "Marriages of Speaking and Hearing: Mediation and Response in *Absalom, Absalom!* and *Grande Sertão: Veredas." The Faulkner Journal* 11, nos. 1 and 2 (Fall 1995/Spring 996): 149–63.

———. "The Reader in the Work: Fabulation and Affective Response in João Guimarães Rosa and William Faulkner." Ph.D. diss. Brown University, 1983.

Vargas Saavedra, Luis. "La afinidad de Onetti a Faulkner." *Cuadernos hispanoamericanos* 98. nos. 292–294 (1974): 257–65.

Vickery, Olga W. *The Novels of William Faulkner.* Baton Rouge: Louisiana State University Press, 1964.

Vizzioli, Paulo. "Guimarães Rosa e William Faulkner." *O Estado de São Paulo, Suplemento Literario,* 11 April 1970, 1.

Wallace, Michele. "Modernism, Postmodernism and the Problem of the Visual in Afro-American Culture." In *Out There: Marginalization and Contemporary Cultures*, edited by Russell Ferguson et al., 39–50. New York: New Museum of Contemporary Art, 1990.

Weinstein, Philip, ed. *The Cambridge Companion to William Faulkner.* Cambridge: Cambridge University Press, 1995.

West, Cornel. "The New Cultural Politics of Difference." In *Out There: Marginalization and Contemporary Cultures*, edited by Russell Ferguson et al., 19–36. New York: New Museum of Contemporary Art, 1990.

White, Hayden. "The Historical Text as Literary Artifact." In *The Writing of History: Literary Form and Historical Understanding*, edited by Robert Canary and Henry Kozicki, 41–62. Madison: University of Wisconsin Press, 1978.

———. *Metahistory: The Historical Imagination in Nineteenth-Century Europe.* Baltimore: Johns Hopkins University Press, 1973.

Woodward, C. Vann. *The Burden of Southern History.* 1960. 3rd ed. Baton Rouge: Louisiana State University Press, 1993.

Woolf, Virginia. "Modern Fiction." [1925]. In *The Norton Anthology of English Literature Volume II*, 4th ed., edited by M. H. Abrams, E. Talbot Donaldson, Hallett Smith, et al., 2031–37. New York: W. W. Norton, 1979.

Zamora, Lois Parkinson. "The Animate Earth: American Books of the Dead by William Goyen, Elena Garro, and Juan Rulfo." *Mid-American Review* 13, no. 1 (1992): 62–86.

———. "The End of Innocence: Myth and Narrative Structure in Faulkner's *Absalom, Absalom!* and García Márquez's *Cien años de soledad.*" *Hispanic Journal* 4, no. 1 (Fall, 1982): 23–40.

———. "Magical Romance/Magical Realism: Ghosts in U.S. and Latin American Fiction." In *Magical Realism: Theory, History, Community*, edited by Lois Parkinson Zamora and Wendy Faris, 497–550. Durham: Duke University Press, 1995.

———. *Writing the Apocalypse: Historical Vision in Contemporary U.S. and Latin American Fiction.* Cambridge: Cambridge University Press, 1989.

Zamora, Lois Parkinson, and Wendy Faris, eds. *Magical Realism: Theory, History, Community.* Durham: Duke University Press, 1995.

Zapata, Roger. "Las trampas de la ficción en la *Historia de Mayta.*" In *La historia en la literatura iberoamericana: Memorias del XXVI Congreso del Instituto Internacional de Literatura Iberoamericana*, edited by Raquel Chang-Rodríguez and Gabriella de Beer, 189–97. New York: Ediciones del Norte, 1989.

3. Related Titles in Inter-American Literary Criticism

Chevigny, Bell Gale. "'Insatiable Unease': Melville and Carpentier and the Search for an American Hermeneutic." In *Reinventing the Americas: Comparative Studies of the Literature of the United States and Spanish America*, edited by Bell Gale Chevigny and Gari Laguardia, 34–59. Cambridge: Cambridge University Press, 1986.

Díaz-Diocaretz, Myriam. "Faulkner's Spanish Voices." In *Faulkner: International Perspectives. Faulkner and Yoknapatawpha, 1982*, edited by Doreen Fowler and Ann Abadie, 30–59. Jackson: University Press of Mississippi, 1984.

————. "Appendix A: Faulkner in Spanish." In *Faulkner: International Perspectives. Faulkner and Yoknapatawpha, 1982*, edited by Doreen Fowler and Ann Abadie, 320–24. Jackson: University Press of Mississippi, 1984.

Laguardia, Gari. "Marvelous Realism/Marvelous Criticism." In *Reinventing the Americas: Comparative Studies of the Literature of the United States and Spanish America*, edited by Bell Gale Chevigny and Gari Laguardia, 298–313. Cambridge: Cambridge University Press, 1986.

MacAdam, Alfred. *Textual Confrontations: Comparative Readings in Latin American Literature*. Chicago: University of Chicago Press, 1987.

Saldívar, Ramón. "Looking for a Master Plan: Faulkner, Paredes, and the Colonial and Postcolonial Subject." In *The Cambridge Companion to William Faulkner*, edited by Philip Weinstein, 96–120. Cambridge: Cambridge University Press, 1995.

Zamora, Lois Parkinson. "The Usable Past: The Idea of History in Modern U.S. and Latin American Fiction." In *Do the Americas Have a Common Literature?* edited by Gustavo Pérez Firmat, 7–40. Durham: Duke University Press, 1990.

————. *The Usable Past: The Imagination of History in Recent Fiction of the Americas*. Cambridge: Cambridge University Press, 1997.

Zavaleta, C. E. *Estudios sobre Joyce & Faulkner*. Lima: Universidad Nacional Mayor de San Marcos, 1993.

I N D E X

Agrarians, 17, 22, 24, 139, 140, 168
Allende, Isabel, 94, 125, 128, 129,
    130; and magic realism,
    101–102, 109, 111, 122, 200n.1,
    202–203nn.10, 12; and social-
    ism, 129; characters of (select-
    ed): Alba, 112, 113, 114, 123,
    125, 131, 132, 190–191,
    203nn.15, 16, Clara, 109,
    110–111, 113, 114, 125,
    203nn.13, 16, Esteban García,
    114, 124, 128, 190, 203nn.15, 16,
    Esteban Trueba, 110, 111, 112,
    123–126, 128, 133, 153,
    190–191, 203nn.15, 16. Work:
    The House of the Spirits, 39, 94,
    100, 109–115, 120, 122–127,
    128–129, 133, 190–191, and
    Alba's testimony, 111, 125–127,
    131, and the characters'
    activism, 110, 113, and Clara's
    magic, 110, 111, 112–113,
    202–203nn.12–13, and Clara's
    notebooks, 110, 111, 115, 125,
    202n.10, 203n.13, competing
    perspectives in, 123–127, and
    the dictatorship, 111–112, 114,
    124, 126, 128, 203–204n.18, and
    patriarchal society, 39, 109, 110,
    112, 113, 122, 124, 126, 203n.13,
    and resistance to the patriarchy,
    110, 112, 114, 122–123, 124–
    126, and rewriting official histo-
    ry, 39, 94–95, 96, 115, 129, 132,
    190–191, and the spirits, 111,
    113, 114
Antoni, Robert, 202nn.10, 12

Arguedas, José María, 96
Ayers, Edward, 208n.2

Bassnett, Susan, 97
Blake, Susan, 201n.6
Boom in the Spanish American
    novel (see also Donoso, José),
    15, 16, 17, 25, 33, 207n.19; defi-
    nition of, 21–22
Borges, Jorge Luis, 22, 25, 28, 29, 33,
    43
Brazil, 6, 44, 138, 195n.2
Brinkmeyer, Robert, 171
Brooks, Cleanth, 197nn.9, 12

Carpentier, Alejo (see also *real ma-
    ravilloso*), 20–21, 26, 31, 101,
    115, 12; and race, 188
Chapman, Arnold, 196n.7
Chevigny, Bell Gale, 13
Christie, John, 196n.8
Coddou, Marcelo, 113
Cooke, Michael, 14, 130, 200n.1
Cortázar, Julio, 22, 196n.7
Corvalán, Octavio, 11
Cuba (see also Guillén, Nicolás;
    Martí, José; Ortiz, Fernando;
    Spanish-American War), 46,
    183–184, 187, 189, 190; inde-
    pendence of, 185–186, 208n.1;
    and the South, 185–186
Cuban Revolution (see also Boom
    in Spanish American literature;
    Vargas Llosa, Mario: and criti-
    cism of the Spanish American
    Left), 15, 21, 40, 45, 90, 187; and
    political legacy, 46